BUSHDOCTORS

Annabelle Brayley trained as a registered nurse. When she married her husband, Ian, she went on to live on an isolated sheep and cattle station in south-west Queensland. Relocating in 2001 to the small rural community where they now live, Annabelle resumed employment in rural and remote health before retiring to pursue her passion for storytelling.

As a regular contributor to *R.M. Williams OUTBACK* magazine, Annabelle frequently tells the stories of people who live and work in the bush. She has developed a reputation for accuracy, honesty and sensitivity that enables people to tell their stories without fear of prejudice or sensationalism.

Facebook: Annabelle Brayley – Australian Outback Storyteller
Twitter: @AnnabellBrayley

ALSO BY ANNABELLE BRAYLEY

Bush Nurses
Nurses of the Outback
Outback Vets
Our Vietnam Nurses

BUSH DOCTORS

ANNABELLE BRAYLEY

MICHAEL JOSEPH
an imprint of
PENGUIN BOOKS

MICHAEL JOSEPH

UK | USA | Canada | Ireland | Australia
India | New Zealand | South Africa | China

Penguin Books is part of the Penguin Random House group of companies
whose addresses can be found at global.penguinrandomhouse.com.

Penguin
Random House
Australia

First published by Penguin Random House Australia Pty Ltd, 2017

1 3 5 7 9 10 8 6 4 2

Cover design by Louisa Maggio © Penguin Random House Australia Pty Ltd
Text design by Louisa Maggio © Penguin Random House Australia Pty
Cover photograph by Katrina Lehmann, Image of plane © Royal Flying Doctor Service
Photographs in this book are courtesy of the author unless otherwise stated
Typeset in Sabon by Louisa Maggio, Penguin Random House Australia Pty Ltd
Colour separation by Splitting Image Colour Studio, Clayton, Victoria
Printed and bound in Australia by Griffin Press, an accredited ISO AS/NZS 14001
Environmental Management Systems printer.

National Library of Australia
Cataloguing-in-Publication data:

Brayley, Annabelle, author.
Bush Doctors / Annabelle Brayley
9780143799696 (paperback)
Physicians–Queensland–Biography.
Rural health services–Queensland
Physicians–Anecdotes.

penguin.com.au

Contents

*Dedicated to the doctors past, present and future
who care for those of us who live in rural and remote
areas of Australia.*

Foreword

Dr Ewen McPhee

President, Rural Doctors Association of Australia

It was thirty-one years ago that I drove into Charleville, a small country town in South West Queensland. I had completed six years of medical school, and twelve months as an intern in the largest hospital in the state at that time. While I was a country boy, having grown up in Longreach the son of a policeman and an enrolled nurse, I was ill-prepared for the life of a country doctor.

In Charleville I was the second doctor in a two-doctor hospital with larrikin GP Dr Chester Wilson and the legendary Dr Louis Ariotti as visiting surgeon. I learnt the meaning of resilience and self-confidence in those busy days and nights, facing challenges alone with few resources.

Innovation occurred by necessity, learning happened by the bedside, supported by the mentorship of honoured peers, and confidence was built by experience – circumstances not enjoyed by students of medicine anymore. I entered rural medicine at the end of an era, at the time of the rise of technology that is now taken for granted as a conduit for medical expertise for country folk. Retrieval medicine was still in its infancy and people travelled for hundreds of kilometres to see a doctor.

I had many challenging experiences meeting the needs of rural people, some of whom remain my patients and my friends three decades later. I recall manning the Royal Flying Doctor Service radio and doing a clinic every Saturday to give the RFDS doctor a day off. Those clinics were unique, for in the days of the party-line telephone, everyone truly knew everyone else's business!

I have sat up the front of a Beechcraft King Air, landing by car lights and flare to retrieve an injured youth. I have seen uncommon illnesses borne by proud and stoic people grateful for any care that could be provided. I have seen TB, leprosy, measles, severe whooping cough, and diphtheria – conditions that are much rarer now than they were, but have the potential to return if we drop our guard on immunisation. I have been a jack-of-all-trades general practitioner, obstetrician, anaesthetist, surgeon and psychiatrist, often all in one day.

Altruism, dedication, and commitment to patients above self were all part of the rural ethos. Rural medicine was, and still is, a job for life. You grow with your patients; your life is intertwined with the twists and turns of country life; you learn when rain is good and when it isn't. I have had the delight of delivering the babies of babies I delivered a generation earlier, and the sad honour of being at the deathbed of people I have grown to love.

Rural medicine is no bed of roses. It has been tough, frightening at times, and can bring the most resilient person to their knees. There is, however, a brotherhood and sisterhood of rural doctors who care and will always lend an ear. The Rural Doctors Association has been a dominant force in supporting these doctors so that they can better look after their patients, and is held in the highest regard in Canberra for its honest, forthright and respected opinion on rural health care.

In recent years we have lost something vitally important, the presence of multi-skilled general practitioners in remote areas, to the belief that bigger is better, that the city is where the best care happens, that good care needs a super specialist.

This book tells the stories of the inspiring doctors who challenge these beliefs every day with their altruism, enthusiasm and refreshing approach to the complexities of delivering quality and expert care in resource-poor environments. Rural doctors know there is no better care than that provided to people in their own homes and towns, and it is their collective story that is driving the renaissance of interest in rural medicine as a viable, interesting and rewarding career for young students of medicine.

Introduction

One of the reasons I chose to write about rural and remote doctors was the fact that we don't have many, especially compared to when I first arrived at the Charleville Base Hospital in South West Queensland to finish my nursing training nearly forty years ago.

In 1978, Charleville had a population of roughly 3000 people and boasted several doctors. The remarkable Dr Louis Ariotti, world-renowned for his clever and often innovative solutions to complicated and potentially life-changing conditions or traumatic injuries, shared his private surgical practice with two highly respected general practitioners, Dr Dorothy Herbert and Dr Ron Parker.

Dr Ariotti started his practice in Charleville in 1947 and, over the course of his forty-year career in South West Queensland, performed everything from appendectomies to major orthopaedic procedures, caesarean sections to surgery for traumatic brain injury.

In May 1978, Dr Herbert had a serious accident prompt-
ing the early engagement of another of South West Queensland's
legends, Dr Chester Wilson. As his story, *The BFGGP*, reveals,
Chester not only holds a special place in the hearts of my own
family, but also in the hearts of the Charleville district as a whole
because of his enormous contribution to the medical, social,
musical and technological enhancement of the community.

These doctors ensured the health outcomes of everyone
who chose to use private health, while those who chose the
public system appreciated the excellent care provided by the
doctors at the hospital. In those days, Dr Greg Wuth was the
medical superintendent and there were always at least one registrar and one resident doctor on the hospital staff at any given
time. Dr Ariotti provided his surgical skills to both public and
private patients alike.

Dr Tim O'Leary was the fabled flying doctor of the era and
the Royal Flying Doctor Service (RFDS) base at Charleville
serviced the southern half of western Queensland with regular
clinic runs, bringing anyone who needed more comprehensive
care into Charleville for treatment. It was a rare patient who
was flown out to Brisbane and, even then, probably only if Dr
Ariotti was out of town.

Between them, there was nothing these doctors couldn't
handle and it was an excellent training ground for the endless
parade of student and newly qualified doctors who rotated
through Charleville as part of their training. Although I didn't
know it when I asked him to write the foreword to this book,
the president of the Rural Doctors Association of Australia,
Dr Ewen McPhee, was one of those young doctors who, as

he says, 'learnt the meaning of resilience and self-confidence' in the busy days and nights at Charleville Hospital. Being exposed to the gamut of medical and surgical experience in this way prepared these students, residents and registrars, well, not just for rural or remote practice but, indeed, for general practice anywhere.

I began this project all fired up with some very specific opinions about the centralisation of services and speciality streaming that I believe has contributed to the demise of the multi-skilled GP who not only provided excellent medical leadership in rural and remote communities, but also social leadership. As I write this in May 2017, I'm dismayed that, since the retirement of Dr Colin Case from his practice in Augathella three months ago, we no longer have any private GPs west of Roma; none in Charleville where once we had legends. We do, of course, have doctors who rotate through the hospitals of the south west on a Queensland Health roster but retention is challenging and continuity of care an elusive concept.

Happily, I discovered that we do have some cracking doctors working in rural and remote Australia and some excellent organisations that support them and promote the inland as a viable and desirable location for doctors to live and work.

In selecting the people who feature in these stories I was, as always, trying to represent a cross-section of the doctors who fit the rural and remote category. Some of them, like Paul Duff and Brad Murphy, live and work in less isolated country towns, while others, like Anne Richards and Janelle Trees, are definitely remote.

And then there's Kate Kloza, who removed the ruptured appendix of one of her friends on Casey Station in the Antarctic three and a half thousand kilometres south-west of Hobart.

In the words of RFDS doctor Claire Schmidt, 'It's a big challenge for a doctor to be in a tiny remote location, at least two hours by plane from any kind of comprehensive medical facility and facing something you may not have experienced before.'

What do you do? As Claire says, 'You have to step up . . .'

That's the underpinning feature I encountered with all these people; they all step up. They are clearly well-qualified, experienced doctors, but they weren't always. They had to commit and dedicate years to learn to do what they do just so they can care for others. They're vibrant, generous, enthusiastic, often exhausted but always resilient, and they love what they do. God knows they'd have to.

This book is intended as a tribute and celebration of all those people in Australia who fit that very special selection criteria – Bush Doctor.

1

Flying for Love

Dr Claire Schmidt, RFDS, Charleville, Queensland

Claire Eely-Sedding was still undergoing her orientation with the Royal Flying Doctor Service in Charleville when the locum doctor acting as one of her initiation buddies answered his phone in the middle of the night and was advised that a man at a remote oil field on a Channel Country station in far South West Queensland had had his arm traumatically amputated. Alerting the flight crew to their imminent departure, the locum also called Claire in as part of her introduction to the hands-on, day-to-day business of the RFDS.

As they barrelled down the runway at the Charleville airport a short time later, Claire – who had been given the thrill of sitting up front beside the pilot for her first retrieval – saw the strip lights flash by then disappear as the Pilatus PC-12 lifted gently into the pitch dark of the icy cold winter's night. Leaving the lights of town behind them, the pilot banked and headed west.

Claire had always chosen her own pathway, revelling in taking the road less travelled. Even so, flying quietly through the night, with only the pilot's occasional communication to break the silence, she acknowledged a buzz of shivery exhilaration despite the gravity of the situation. She'd worked in military hospitals as well as an emergency department in a civilian hospital so she was not unused to traumatic injury, but nothing in her previous life had prepared her for the dramatic reality of her first flare landing, in a remote location, during the witching hours of the night.

Approaching the station airstrip, the pilot directed Claire's eager gaze with a brief 'Look!' As they descended, the two distant rows of pinprick light she could see in the surrounding darkness steadily evolved into the extraordinary spectacle of flaming drums of diesel lit to mark the length of the landing strip.

As they rolled down the runway, decelerating past the burning flares, she could see nothing beyond the parameters of the lights. Slowing to a standstill, the pilot began the process of shutting down the engine while Claire, the locum and the flight nurse gathered up the gear they would need to stabilise and support the patient.

Once the last reverberations of the turboprop had stopped and the door dropped open, Claire garnered her composure and followed the locum and the flight nurse down the stairs into a pool of flickering light in the deeply shadowed landscape. As the night quiet drifted in, she looked up, momentarily mesmerised by the swathe of brilliantly sparkling stars splashed across the midnight sky.

Her attention was recaptured by the sound and sight of a handful of men in battered akubras and dusty work clothes slowly emerging out of the shadows and into the glowing light of the flares. Greeting the flight crew, they helped carry the medical gear over to one of the 4WD traybacks that would transport them all to the oil field where the patient awaited them.

As they rumbled along a dirt track, Claire recalled another night, eight months before, when she'd been sitting up reading the *British Medical Journal* while on call in a GP practice in Frimley Park in the UK, and the RFDS logo on a job advertisement had caught her eye. Even in her wildest dreams, she could never have imagined that reading that one little ad might lead to her being driven into the unknown Australian outback, in a vehicle she'd never heard of, with a bunch of men she'd never met, in the middle of a desert-cold night . . .

Born in Plymouth on the south-west coast of Devon, Claire, along with her mother, Denise, and her older brother, Nick, moved around a lot as they followed her career army father to wherever he was posted in the UK, Germany and various other locations across Europe. Claire believes it was all that moving around that has enabled her to relocate easily and generally fearlessly throughout her adult life.

After Claire's father died when she was eleven, Denise moved them to south Cornwall. 'It's *Doc Martin* country,' Claire explains, 'and it was a beautiful, beautiful place to live.' Living on a coastline dotted by one quaint fishing village after another, she gravitated to the beaches, sailing and various water sports until she followed Nick to secondary school in Bath. When she didn't quite get the grades she needed to get into her primary choice, psychology, Claire entered the University of

Manchester to do a degree in neuroscience because someone suggested it was quite close to psych. With hindsight she says, 'Foolishly I believed them and started the course but quickly realised it was not for me. It was awful!' She sidestepped into physiology, which she quite enjoyed, but soon found herself thinking, *This is all very well but what happens when it all goes wrong, when the body doesn't work the way it's meant to?* Unfortunately that flip side wasn't part of the course, but she continued to ask the question . . .

Purely by chance, in her third year of physiology she and a friend were attending a lecture at the medical school at Manchester, when her friend told her she thinking of doing medicine after she graduated. Claire was surprised, asking, 'Can you do that?' The thought had never crossed her mind, mainly because she'd never imagined she might have the intelligence to do it but, as a result of that brief conversation, she looked into it, applied and, after she graduated, entered the medical school at the University of Sheffield.

A couple of years into her medical degree, Claire decided it would be a good idea to join the army. It seemed like a nice link to her father and she knew the army would sponsor some of her degree. Accordingly, she signed up for six years and the army underwrote the last two years of her course. While she continued to live and attend uni as usual, Claire donned uniform regularly and joined various military exercises around the country as required.

After her graduation from Sheffield, reality kicked in as she spent her pre-registration house officer year, and then a second year after her registration, working full-time in military hospitals. In her fourth year in uniform, she finally admitted to herself that the reality of army life was quite different to the expectation she'd developed as a family member of an officer, and decided she wasn't cut out for defence force life. Clarifying her decision, she says with a fleeting smile, 'My personality really just didn't suit the army. We had quite different hopes and dreams.' Claire got out of the army with some difficulty, aided by a superior who pointed out that there was not much point keeping someone who so badly didn't want to be there.

Because Claire registered back when doctors were not required to choose a specialist stream upon registration, she was able to try a bit of this and that. In six-month blocks, she rotated through general medicine, general surgery, obstetrics and emergency medicine, before opting to try paediatrics simply because she was frightened by the idea of it.

Surprised to find she loved it, Claire got into a training program which terrified her all over again to begin with, as she was thrown straight into the deep end in the paediatric intensive care unit (ICU) at Southampton Hospital. She wasn't quite ready for that level of intense medicine but survived it, and then a rotation through neonatal ICU, one day at a time.

Content to continue in a paediatric stream, Claire worked as a paediatric registrar for a year in Salisbury, which she loved until changes to the training system ordained she could be sent anywhere in the UK at very short notice. Not wishing to be a roving registrar, Claire resolved to find a different pathway and opted for general practice at Frimley Park, near Blackwater. It was a perfect choice and she has only happy memories of her time there, saying, 'It was they who shaped my ability to be the GP I am now.'

Even so, she was feeling just a bit fiddle-footed. Although

she loved her job, she was living nearby in Ascot, about five seconds from the racetrack, and trying to keep up in a very trendy social circle whose members appeared to be focused on getting married, having children, buying very large beautiful houses and even smarter cars. Although Claire could party with the best of them, at times she found it all a bit over the top.

Consequently, when she was on call one night perusing the international job section of the *British Medical Journal* and she saw an advertisement emblazoned with the distinctive RFDS logo, which she says is very well known in the UK, her interest was instantly piqued.

The RFDS was advertising a job for a permanent doctor in Charleville. As she read, Claire was thinking, *No, no, I don't have the skills to do that . . .* but she looked it up on the internet anyway and found they were also looking for a doctor to work for the rural women's GP service, a job for which she felt she was qualified. Opportunely, it was daytime on a weekday in Australia so she rang Rachel, the contact named in the Brisbane office, explained her location and qualifications, and asked her if she thought she (Claire) could do that job.

Apparently they were deadly keen to have someone apply for the Charleville job, which had been undertaken by locums for some months, because Claire remembers Rachel saying, 'No, no, no, you don't want to do that, you want the job at Charleville,' persuading her over the phone that she should apply for it.

Rachel proceeded very quickly to organise an interview, which Claire did over the phone with a panel of senior RFDS staff. Waving her arms around and laughing at herself quite unselfconsciously nearly a decade later, she describes having every scrap of her paperwork spread out all over the kitchen bench and dining room table in her small Ascot apartment so that she could answer anything they might possibly ask her . . .

Having done the interview, Claire didn't really think she'd get the position because of her lack of experience in retrieval medicine, so pushed it to the back of her mind and got on with doing her job, still occasionally reading the ads and dreaming of faraway places.

A few weeks later she was sitting in the departure lounge in Heathrow Airport with her mother, waiting to fly to Spain to have Christmas with her grandparents, when she got a call from Rachel, who asked, 'Can you come to Australia? You've got the job in Charleville. We want you to start as soon as possible.'

Excitedly whispering, 'I got the job!' to Denise – who burst into tears – Claire replied, 'Okay great. Thanks. I feel sick. I'll be in touch. Thank you. Goodbye!' And promptly burst into tears herself. Relocating to the nearest champagne bar, they ordered a glass each while Claire tried to get her head around moving to Australia, muttering between gulps, 'Oh my God, oh my God, Australia, this is too much . . .'

Laughing again at the memory, Claire says her mother looked at her squarely and declared, 'This is just typical, Claire! You aim for something completely impossible and then when it happens, hope for the best.'

Claire arrived in Spain still feeling slightly sick as she wondered, a bit apprehensively, just exactly what she'd committed herself to. She had absolutely no idea where Charleville was, never having thought she might actually be offered the job, and wasn't quite ready to find out when her brother Nick turned up the day before Christmas with a handful of satellite maps of the land down under. There was one of Australia, one of Queensland, one of South West Queensland and a street map of Charleville.

By the end of two hours of her whole family poring over the maps, getting their heads around the size of Charleville –

'Look there's a bike track.'

'No, no it's a race track.'

'Look at that Waree-ga [Warrego] Highway. It looks like just one long straight road with only one bend.'

'It's even further to Brisbane than London to Edinburgh.'

– Claire says she begged them to stop.

'Can you all just put them away? This is my life and now I feel really, really sick! Please can we just do Christmas?'

Theatrics aside, Claire's never been one to turn down an opportunity for adventure and she decided to give it a go. She returned to Britain and continued to work in Frimley Park for the few months it took to get all her qualifications officially recognised in Australia and to organise her work visa, provider number and assorted other details.

Finally flying into Sydney in June 2008, Claire connected onto a flight into Brisbane, where she spent several weeks upskilling in anaesthetics at Queen Elizabeth II Hospital and undertook orientation at the RFDS base at Eagle Farm Airport. Advised during orientation that Charleville had no senior medical officer (SMO) at the time and that she was going to be 'it', Claire agreed to a six-month trial with an option to extend to twelve if she liked it. Finally as ready as she was going to be, she moved to Charleville in August, while vestiges of winter remained to ease her into the coming summer.

Claire says she had no idea what to expect in Charleville, choosing rather to keep an open mind about the possibilities and hoping it would be a little bit quirky. 'The quirkier a place is, the more I like it.' Seeing the western landscape from the air, what struck her most was the very real similarity it all had to the television series *The Flying Doctors*, which her family had watched when she was young. With a laugh she says, 'It was very popular in the UK and I could even hear the music in my head.'

And she definitely got 'quirky' when she saw the funny little arrival and departure shed that passed for a terminal. Until very recently, said terminal was a small, rectangular, unsecured timber box that sat on the edge of the tarmac, structurally incorporated into the very high, barb-topped fencing that secures the runway from terrorists and kangaroos alike.

Kate McGowan, the base manager in Charleville, met Claire at the airport and took her straight to see the RFDS plane sitting in its huge World War II hangar at the airport. Claire's very first sight of her new winged workplace, with its red and navy stripe-winged logo emblazoned on the side, was thrilling. After a recce around town, Kate delivered Claire to her new home with the promise that she'd collect her first thing Monday morning.

Eternally positive by nature, Claire was more than ready to jump into her new role when Kate collected her two days later. With the first of two buddy doctors on hand to guide her through orientation, she spent her introductory day in the office getting to know everyone and the run of the place, then devoted the rest of the week to clinic runs.

The first time she flew with the RFDS she was blown away.

'I kept having these "movie moments" seeing flashbacks of the *Flying Doctors* series; I'd have them all the time. We were flying around hopping on and off the plane like we owned it, with our own pilot and looking out at this stunning outback landscape that was like something out of David Attenborough. It was amazing!'

Claire was completing her orientation with her second locum buddy when he got the call requesting assistance for the man with the amputated arm. After the flare landing – which had all the ingredients for another 'movie moment' – they were driven about twenty minutes up the road to the oil field, where an ambulance from a town about a hundred kilometres away was already in attendance.

The ambos were assisting the first responders, who'd applied pressure bandages and given the man some pain relief – as instructed by the locum over the phone – from the RFDS kit they stored on site. They were all relieved to see the doctors and have them assume responsibility. While the locum and the flight nurse continued to prepare the patient for transfer, Claire was tasked with the job of retrieving and packing his arm in an esky to go with them, even though they knew it was too damaged to be reattached.

Once he was stabilised, they loaded him into the ambulance and drove in convoy back to the plane. A couple of hours later as they flew east to Brisbane and into the dawning day, Claire watched the first slivers of sunlight streak the sky and tried to get her head around the whole completely surreal experience.

Within a couple of weeks she was working solo. The pilots and flight nurses were all old hands and helped her assimilate into the role. When she wasn't flying, Claire was familiarising herself with the practicalities of managing all the medical aspects of the base. She alternated her roster with Dr Jon Outridge, who has, Claire says, 'been the most incredible mentor and friend every step of the way'. Jon flew into Charleville for his scheduled rotations and Claire quickly got into the habit of meeting him at the airport and giving him a running handover as she delivered him to the base. He'd give her his running handover as she delivered him back to the airport when her rotation began again.

The eight-day 24-hour shifts meant Claire did clinic runs most days of the week and oversaw all the retrievals at any hour of the day or night. Even if she didn't go out on a retrieval herself (75–80 per cent of retrievals are undertaken by a flight nurse unless it's a critical case or the doctor is specifically requested), she would take the call, arrange the response and stay on standby in case the first responder or flight crew needed her advice.

There were some days when the enormity of her task was a bit overwhelming, although Claire endeavoured not to show it. At those times she greatly appreciated the support of Dr Dean Taylor, the SMO who'd originally interviewed her, who was (and still is) something of a telephone mentor and sounding-board.

When the director of medical services asked her at the end of her first week what she thought she could do for the place, she told him she had a seven-point plan for moving forward. At the end of her first month she revised it to seventeen.

As it turned out, her first year was bumpy while some of the staff got used to having an SMO who had no hesitation in voicing her dismay when she discovered that there were few standard medical processes or systems in place and some very obvious things were not being followed up. Claire was equally appalled with the eight-day rosters for the doctors, which she considered an unwieldy, unsustainable model that clearly explained why they were unable to keep any of them. Finally, she was horrified to find they were still using paper records, especially since they'd already experienced one devastating flood that decimated all their documentation.

Claire acknowledges she ruffled a lot of feathers in her first year or two and confides that, had she then the knowledge that she has now, she'd have sallied forth with a little more diplomacy. As it is, she admits she pretty much crashed in like a bull in a china shop. This particular 'china shop bull' is the very elegant doctor on the front cover of this book and when that gorgeous smile lights up her face, as it frequently does, it live-streams all the positivity and joie de vivre of her happy disposition. Professionally, however, she is inclined to be composed (at least on the outside), very direct and uncompromising. She readily concedes that some of the staff were just not ready for her kind of management and especially not from someone so new to the RFDS, with no knowledge or experience of the outback and with a very posh, preppy British accent to boot.

With a shadow of regret, Claire says, 'I had the best intentions but no prior experience managing staff and there are certainly things I would do differently now. *I* knew my intentions were good but I was focused squarely on patient care and the overall function of the base. It was challenging,' she admits, adding, as the shadow lifts and her smile returns, 'but I do love a challenge!'

And the challenges weren't just political. Even though she always had a flight nurse with her, in those early days, Claire sometimes found working in isolation quite confronting. Her first really difficult retrieval was out of Quilpie, where a man had been punched in the pub. The RFDS got the call to say he'd hit the ground, hit his head on the concrete and the local doctor was unable to intubate him.

Flying in with her flight nurse at three o'clock in the morning, Claire was role-playing a confidence she didn't feel as she'd never done anaesthetics out in the field before, but she knew she had to get it done. Contemplating the alternative, she says, 'There is none. That's all there is to it. You have to step up and do what you've got to do.'

As it turned out, encouraged every step of the way by her flight nurse and the Quilpie hospital nurses, Claire successfully tubed the patient and they flew him out to Brisbane, but it's a memory that lingers and reiterates the challenges that face doctors when they're on their own, in a tiny remote location, at least two hours by plane from any kind of comprehensive medical facility and facing something they may not have experienced before.

While her professional life had some prickles on it, the highlight for Claire was the clinic runs; not just the flights across the outback, which she did find pretty awe-inspiring, but the people. 'The people at the clinics are amazing. The work that they do out in all those small isolated communities and on the sheep and cattle stations is incredible. I've never met harder working people than those I've met since I've been here. Understanding how stoic people are in the outback was such a big thing. You know, you'd ask someone who came in with half their leg dropping off how much pain they're in on a scale of one to ten and they'd say, "Two?" You'd know damn well it had to be at least eight on anyone else's scale. These people work all hours of the day and they only come to you when they're half dead; it was fantastic to be a part of that journey and to be able to help them to get well. It still is.'

Meanwhile, her social life gained traction fairly quickly thanks to a chance meeting at the Charleville racetrack with Karen Brook, whose family has a long association with the RFDS going back generations. Karen immediately pulled Claire under her wing and introduced her to her very large group of friends. For Claire, it made all the difference to have instant entree into a life outside work. And out in Birdsville, which was still serviced under the mantle of the Charleville RFDS base back then, Karen's family also extended their legendary warm hospitality to the new flying doctor. Having come to the outback from another country herself, Karen's mother, Nell, helped Claire find her feet in South West Queensland.

Claire was impressed by the authenticity of the people she was meeting and found them very refreshing in comparison to the scene she'd left behind where, she remarks, 'everything felt very status driven'. Being embraced by a large crowd of laidback, fun-loving young professionals and tradies alike in the Queensland outback was just about as far from her reality as she could get and still be in a first-world environment. It wasn't that they weren't getting married and having children and buying houses and cars, it was just that they were doing it in an environment of old-fashioned family values that seemed to be missing back home.

While the challenges she faced in her role as SMO did

prompt Claire to consider pulling the pin several times in the first twelve months, this new group of friends gave her life balance and prevented her from imploding. They were one reason why she stayed for the full year and then committed to a second; the other was the very intense satisfaction she got from her clinical work as the flying doctor.

Due for a good long holiday at the end of her first year, Claire planned to go to the Whitsundays for a week in early June then fly home to the UK for a few weeks. She was down at the pub one Friday night in mid May, when one of her friends sidled up to her and said, 'My friend Stevo fancies you.'

Just a tad taken aback, Claire replied, 'What are we? Fifteen?'

'Well,' said her friend, 'if I don't tell you no one will.'

Checking him out, standing off to one side in jeans, an unironed work shirt and dusty boots, Claire's first very British, eye-rolling thought was, *Oh my God. He's a cowboy!*

A week later, on 23 May, a date that's seared in her memory, she and Karen went to Roma Picnic Races, about three hours east of Charleville. Off duty and a long way from home, Claire settled in for some serious partying. Admitting only much later to being a little flattered by the attention and well primed by champagne by the time the post-race party started, Claire danced all night with Stevo and only remembered on the long, weary journey home with Karen next day that he was the same 'cowboy' she wasn't at all interested in just a week before.

Despite her reluctance to get involved with him and despite the fact that she was on call and allergic to horses, Claire couldn't resist Stevo's invitation to go to the afterparty planned for the polocrosse carnival that was being held in Charleville the next weekend, her last before she flew out. When he rocked up to collect her, all scrubbed up and just as nervous she was, Claire was shocked to realise that she'd completely changed her mind about him; he was not only totally handsome but, much more to the point, a really lovely man. They stayed at the polocrosse party until she had to leave because she was sneezing her socks off and the rest, as they say, is history.

Claire flew to the Whitsundays as planned and then home to her mother in Berkshire. Stevo rang her every second day and they talked for hours, building the deep and abiding friendship that underpins their continuing relationship. Suddenly Charleville had a whole new drawcard.

When Claire flew back in six weeks after she'd departed, Stevo met her at Brisbane Airport and whisked her off to the Sunshine Coast for a few days before taking her home to Charleville and moving in to her rental house with her while his place was being renovated.

As soon as they both had a free weekend, he took her to meet his parents and brother James on their home property in the Cunnamulla district, where she was welcomed incredibly warmly into the family. Being so far from the UK, Claire misses her own mother enormously, but says Stevo's mother, Kathy, has become a very dear friend, and she adores his father, Bean.

Ruefully remembering the 'cowboy' tag, Claire admits she couldn't believe how wrong she was about Stevo who, she discovered, was a successful businessman and grazier in his own right. Completely committed and blissfully happy together, Stevo and Claire moved into their new home at the end of 2009.

Meanwhile, at work, Claire slotted back into her usual

roster and her role as SMO after her trip to the UK. The clinic runs continued to captivate her and she accumulated plenty of experience overseeing retrievals, some with her on board, others not. In 2011, she took maternity leave to deliver her and Stevo's daughter, Amelie, into the world and then again in 2014, when she delivered Toby. In between, she was back at work when the RFDS opened a new base out at the airport and transferred the whole box and dice out to the new building just next door to their hangar.

Delighted with her life, Claire didn't think it could get any better until one weekend, when they were out at one of their cattle properties, Stevo sprang a surprise on her. Appreciating the significance of hills in her Cornish childhood, he took Claire and a bottle of champagne to the foot of the only remotely hill-like rise he could lay claim to and, just on sundown, asked her to marry him, a deal they sealed in October 2014.

Nearly a decade after she answered that ad in the *British Medical Journal*, and happily employed as part-time SMO now that she has Amelie and Toby to care for, Claire says, 'Working for RFDS has given me such a wide variety of professional experience and working here in Charleville in recent years has been just fantastic.'

While she recognises she may have been the catalyst, she is emphatic when she states that the excellence that distinguishes the current Charleville RFDS base is the result of a cohesive team effort. 'Everyone pulled together and made it happen. We now have really good recruitment and retention of staff, first-rate processes in place and we've got a fully computerised medical records system. Most importantly of all, we're providing top quality patient care, easily as good as you'd expect in an urban setting.'

Mission accomplished, Claire says the best part is still the clinical work she doesn't get to do as often as she did, but relishes all the more when she does. 'Having the capacity to help people who are so far from any other help is very, very satisfying. It's about so much more than just the excitement and drama that people often associate with the RFDS; when you see how hard most people live and work in the outback you just want to support them. It's incredibly rewarding to know that I've been helping to keep these people well.'

2

Choosing Country

Dr Rick Newton, Tullamore, New South Wales

It's 12.23 a.m. Rick Newton rolls over and grabs the ringing phone, answering quietly, 'Dr Rick Newton, RMCS,' as he swings his legs over the edge of the bed.

He's into the second half of his 24-hour shift and it's the first call since he went to bed a bit before 11 p.m. Chances are it won't be the last. Rick and two other doctors provide the Remote Medical Consultation Service to a number of small hospitals in the Central West region of New South Wales, and those that have no resident doctor or have GPs who choose not to do call are all well used to accessing the service.

The registered nurse on night duty in one of these hospitals tells Rick that a 22-year-old man has presented in some distress with sharp, right-sided chest pain. She says he was playing touch earlier in the evening and had to retire early gasping for breath, but he thought it was because he hadn't played for a long time and he was just knocked up. He'd gone home and gone to bed but woke around midnight with chest pain and shortness of breath. On arrival at the hospital he was pale, slightly clammy and short of breath but not panicking.

The nurse reels off the patient's observations for Rick, including temperature, pulse, respirations, blood pressure, blood sugars, oxygen saturation levels and his reading on the Glasgow Coma Scale and adds that he has no history of smoking, no family history of ischaemic heart disease or aneurisms, and he has said he doesn't use drugs. She knows him and believes him.

After some further discussion, and suspecting pneumonia, Rick asks her to take some blood and sputum cultures then insert a cannula in the young man's arm and administer some IV fluids before his blood pressure starts to drop. He orders a broad-spectrum antibiotic, to be administered via the IV tubing. Meanwhile, because of the patient's clamminess and shortness of breath, Rick arranges for him to be transferred to the nearest base hospital by ambulance rather than wait until his GP is available several hours later.

Once the case is sorted, Rick falls back into bed . . .

This is the kind of telehealth Rick has been practising since he retired from his private practice in Tullamore, 130 kilometres south-west of Dubbo in Central West NSW, in July 2016. He's on call with RMCS every third day from 8 a.m. to 8 a.m., which was problematic when he was still working full-time but now sits perfectly with his other passion in life, farming.

Growing up in Dundas in the western suburbs of Sydney, Rick went to Telopea Public primary school and then to Macquarie

Boys High which, he says, 'didn't have the best name. There were more fights than anything else.' Rick avoided the fights by playing a lot of sport, including rugby and water polo, which he claims gave him a kind of immunity because the fighters considered him their peer on the sports fields.

Born the youngest of four Rick decided when he was still quite young that he wanted to leave school and go to the country so he could learn to be a farmer. A taste of the dairy industry on school holidays convinced him that farming was the life for him. His father, who worked in middle management, and mother, who was a talented but untrained draughtswoman, convinced him pretty quickly that it wasn't, at least not without his Higher School Certificate.

His was a very happy childhood living with loving parents and older siblings in a devout Methodist home and he followed their advice. He shelved the farming idea, knuckled down and got his certificate. HSC safely in hand, Rick didn't quite get the results he needed to get into vet science which was, by then, his first choice. Disappointed but not deterred, he enrolled in a science degree at the University of Sydney, majoring in biology and human physiology, the latter of which he undertook with the medical students. He started thinking about the human body from the med students' perspective and got just a little bit hooked on the idea of doing medicine.

However, love and the Vietnam War got in the way. In his first year at uni, he met his future wife, Barbara, when she auditioned for a major role in a musical in which he was a chorus member. Rick was instantly captivated by the sixteen-year-old singer and in between studying science, wooing her and marching to protest Australia's involvement in Vietnam, he had little time for pursuing a change of pathway.

Complicating matters was the fact that Barbara was going out with Rick against her father's express wishes. Apart from believing they were way too young, Barbara's father considered Rick to be a long-haired, wildly rebellious uni student who, he was convinced, had thrown tomatoes at the NSW governor during a protest march. Rick denies any involvement and says he's never thrown tomatoes at anyone, much less Sir Roden Cutler, for whom he had the utmost respect, but Barbara's father wouldn't tolerate the idea of them having a relationship. He directed Barbara to give Rick up or leave home. When she wouldn't, he ordered her from the house, never to return.

Shattered, but determined nevertheless, Barbara moved in with Rick's older, married sister until she began her nursing training at Sutherland Hospital near Cronulla, a career choice partly ordained by the offer of accommodation in nurses' quarters that still accompanied hospital training in the early '70s.

As soon as Rick graduated, he and Barbara were married, by an unordained minister because Barbara couldn't get the required parental consent. Rick was twenty-one and Barbara nineteen. It was 2 December 1972, the day that Gough Whitlam was elected prime minister. Somewhere along the way they did formalise their marriage in a registry office but, as far as they're concerned, December the 2nd is the day they celebrate their anniversary. Barbara still had a year of her general nursing training to complete, so Rick got a job teaching at Holy Cross College at Ryde.

They were blissfully content in spite of the cost of their courtship, and by the time Barbara graduated she was pregnant and Rick was looking for a job for the following year. The two happy years that followed dictated the eventual direction of their lives.

Moving to teach at St Clement's at Galong, in the South West Slopes region of NSW, convinced Rick that he was better suited to living in the country. The establishment was owned and run by the Redemptorists congregation, who had built the beautiful old monastery in 1918 on land left to them by an Irish family. 'It was,' Rick says, 'a truly idyllic location.' He and Barbara both loved their life at Galong, living in a little worker's cottage just across the road from the monastery, and dreamt of a permanent life in the inland.

Contrarily, although Rick enjoyed his role 'teaching young men from the ages of fourteen to twenty-seven who thought they ultimately wanted to study theology and become priests', he was feeling a little disillusioned with teaching as a long-term profession and an unresolved desire to study medicine niggled. He actually thought about nursing as a possible alternative but Barbara, by then a registered nurse, knew it would drive him nuts and encouraged him to take a shot at medicine if that's what he really wanted to do.

When the school at St Clement's was closed at the end of his second year, Rick and Barbara and their small son returned to Sydney, where Rick took the plunge and enrolled to repeat his HSC with a view to gaining entry to the medical school at Sydney Uni. Ironically, Rick taught secondary science at St Pius X College at Chatswood during the day and studied for his HSC at night. When he resat the exams at the end of 1976, he successfully gained entrance into medicine. Meanwhile, Barbara safely delivered their daughter.

By the time Rick rocked up for orientation, the Newtons had just enough money saved for him to begin but, with two small dependent children, to make ends meet Barbara worked as a family day-care mum and part-time as a nurse while Rick drove taxis on weekends. After second year, he took twelve months off and returned to teaching at St Pius for a year to replenish their coffers, then returned to medicine and weekend taxi driving until he graduated in 1983.

Looking back, he says, 'It was really, really tough but at the time you don't actually realise how tough it is. We wanted to do it so we made it happen, but on reflection, I don't think we could ever do it again. We lived very frugally and we were probably the fittest we've ever been because we practically lived on tuna and rice. On Sundays we went to my parents for a big roast lunch or, when we knew her father was busy else-where, we went to Barbara's parents' house for Sunday lunch so that she could see her mother and sister. It wasn't easy, but we did what we had to do.'

After completing his first-year internship at Concord Hospital, Rick began a two-year program in family medicine at Hornsby Hospital up on the upper north shore of Sydney. His schedule included a GP attachment in Scone in the Upper Hunter, which gave him a taste of life as a country GP and renewed his interest in one day going bush. The family lived in a worker's cottage owned by the doctor who was super-vising Rick, and their children, by then ten and eight, went to school there. Rick says both kids enjoyed the experience. Coming from a big city to a small country town, his son sud-denly became something of a soccer star, and his daughter learnt to play 500, 'because that's what the kids used to do in

Scone'. For the three months they were there they had no tele-vision, read the newspaper every day and the kids roamed free with their new friends.

Storing the memories away like precious diamonds, they returned to Hornsby, where Rick completed the family-medi-cine program and then went into private practice in Gladesville, an inner western suburb where they bought their first house. Being back in Sydney enabled Barbara to sing with the Australian Opera, a position she very much enjoyed for four years and until she was offered a principal role. After heartfelt consideration, she decided it was a commitment she was unwill-ing to make and chose instead to return to nursing. By then, Rick was immersed in general practice, the kids were settled into high school, and before long Barbara was the health ser-vices manager for several large nursing homes. Life rolled on.

At the end of a decade in private practice, Rick was once again looking for something different and applied for a job as a medical adviser with the Health Insurance Commission, which was attached to Medicare. His role involved speaking with doctors whose practice behaviours looked unusual; for instance, they might be suspected of overprescribing or over-servicing patients.

Because rural GPs are always so busy compared to city doctors, Rick explains, their behaviour patterns can look abnormal in comparison. 'They might be working fourteen-hour days and they might be seeing five or six patients in an hour so their numbers are different.' Rick would drive out to meet them and get an understanding of the reasons for the var-iation in the numbers. It gave him the opportunity to see what he was missing out on and what rural general practice was like compared to city practice.

Three and a half years later, he was ready to move back into general practice, the kids had left school and Barbara was feeling burnt out in her managerial role. The country called them loudly.

Every week, Rick would read the job ads in the classified section in *The Sydney Morning Herald*, not exactly sure what he was looking for, but looking nevertheless. One day he saw an ad for a doctor in a tiny little town he'd never heard of called Cudal, near Orange, so he and Barbara decided to drive out and have a look. As people do in rural communities, the residents of Cudal welcomed them with open arms and drove them around, telling them that they were going to build a new house for the doctor who was appointed, which sounded amazing.

However, there hadn't been a full-time doctor in Cudal for some time. The lovely old doctor who had been practising there had lost his wife the year before and, although he still saw a few patients at the hospital, he'd lost heart for general practice. As he'd retreated from private patient consultation, most of his client list had started driving to Orange to see a doctor. Having the same debts a couple in their forties usually have, Rick and Barbara felt they couldn't afford to wait for that practice to build up again, so they drove home promising to think about it but quite unconvinced of the practicalities.

They were no sooner home than someone in the Greater Western Area Health Service rang Rick and said, 'Listen, I believe you've been somewhere out in the central west today looking at a practice, why don't you think about Tullamore?'

They'd never heard of it either, but told the guy they were interested and would drive out the following weekend and have a look.

Like Cudal, they found Tullamore to be a tiny little country town with a warm, welcoming feel to it. This one, though, came with a dinky little hospital that had registered nurses (RNs) on duty twenty-four hours a day and an active emergency department even though they hadn't had a doctor for eighteen months. The hospital, which had four beds for inpatients and twelve in the aged care wing, was operating on a shoe-string staff, with the RNs seeing any patients who turned up in outpatients and sending them off to doctors in other towns. It looked like a bit of a challenge but Rick and Barbara were both instantly attracted to the idea of it. They chatted about the possibilities all the way home to Gladesville and reckoned they'd like to give it a go. They committed for two years and never left.

Although the population of Tullamore was less than 300, the surrounding farms boosted the count considerably, so that when Rick reopened the practice he had a patient list of about 800. And once it became known that he was in the community, people started coming from other towns like Parkes where, he says, it could take three weeks to get an appointment with a GP. Over time the practice built up to about 1400, with some of Rick's patients travelling over 100 kilometres to see him.

The practice had a house next to it that was owned by the Parkes Shire Council, who offered to let the Newtons live there rent-free for the first year. While they appreciated the offer and accepted, Rick and Barbara missed the beautiful Gladesville views of the Parramatta River they'd left behind, and from the outset kept an eye out for something more aesthetically appealing.

When Barbara noticed a little house on a hill for sale with 20 hectares of land around it, the price compared so favourably to Sydney prices, it seemed like a giveaway. They bought it three months after they arrived in Tullamore and the farmer in Rick revelled in it every day. In good time, and with the shire's permission, they converted the house in town to a much bigger and more appropriate surgery.

Rick's experience in a 'walk-in' practice in Sydney had taught him that there will always be people who come in just as you are closing and, with no consideration for any inconvenience they might be causing, declare, 'I've had this pain in the belly for three weeks, Doc . . .' In Tullamore, however, he discovered that most country people don't do that, and on the rare occasion someone has bailed him up face-to-face about a medical problem out of hours, his response has always been, 'If you want me to talk to you about something just head up to the hospital and I can see you there.'

In Tullamore, he says, 'people actually respect you for the person you are and they treat you as a friend,' adding, 'in this community everyone has respected our privacy. No one's ever come to the house to consult us medically or even called after hours unless it was something they felt was really significant.'

The difficult aspect for him with seeing people socially and becoming close friends is then being a witness to losing them. 'I've lost three close friends, one with rapidly terminating cancer, one in a car accident and one when the truck cabin he was working under came down on him and suffocated him; that's really hard when you're in a small community like this. It's

hard on all the emergency responders because everyone invariably knows the person or people.'

One of those three was his closest friend and going to the
accident scene and pronouncing him dead was one of the hardest things Rick has ever had to do. 'You don't think about that
at the time, I guess, you just think you've got to get there. He
was dead and I was the one who went and told his wife and
children and mother.' With a slight fatalistic shrug, he says,
'You've got to get through those hard bits before you can even
think about yourself.'

Another challenge is debriefing. 'Confidentiality,' he
remarks, 'is obviously paramount and you don't really get a
chance in a one-doctor town to download. Apart from my
wife, there're no close colleagues that you can talk these things
over with so I don't think you ever really deal with them properly. You just get on.'

Treating the women's health issues of women he knows
very well socially also rates a mention as a challenge. 'But,' he
says, 'it's a lot easier to do than you think it might be. It's like
both members of a negotiation who see each other totally differently in a different environment. You walk into the surgery
and suddenly there's a total change of relationship, as if you
don't know them [socially] and they don't know you. It's actually quite interesting how it works.'

Coming to Tullamore on the heels of his three and a half
years with the Health Insurance Commission, Rick was well
prepared for some of the other tricky areas country doctors
have to negotiate. He knew exactly what constituted overprescribing and would never prescribe anything to anyone
he didn't know well medically, and especially not painkillers.

Likewise he was never a soft touch for a doctor's certificate just to enable someone to take time off.

On the few occasions he was asked, Rick made it clear he was not going to cross any lines. He says, 'There's just no way in the world you can do that. You explain to them that it would be fraud and you could go to jail. Doctors have a very real responsibility and if you start blurring the boundaries, people don't really know where they stand.' That way, he says, 'Not only did they know about it but in a small town it gets around very quickly and people get to know the type of person you are; you won't be taken advantage of. It's easier for them and for you.'

As far as Rick's concerned, the upsides of being a rural doctor far outweigh any downsides. He says there's never a dull moment. When he was still working in his practice, although he knew nearly everyone who walked in the door, he never knew what he'd be dealing with next because he was the only doctor and saw the whole gamut of medical and surgical possibilities.

When he was working full-time in Sydney, especially in public health, he was always looking for other things to fill his hours off duty because there seemed to be an emptiness in his life. He wasn't exactly bored, just unfulfilled. He studied English, undertook an MBA and, inspired by Barbara's musical talent, he learnt to play the cello.

Since they've been living in a rural community, however, he's hardly picked up the cello and hasn't been looking for anything new to do because, he confides, 'My life has been full, with a variety of things I can do. I think the advice I'd give anyone coming to the bush is that they've got to be enthusiastic about taking part in the community.'

Of course, in Tullamore, Rick has also been able to indulge his lifelong ambition to be a farmer which, in a district full of farmers, gave him an unplanned entree into the community because he engaged every farmer he came across in conversation about what he should, would or could do. It broke down barriers and enabled him to build relationships that have given him an insight into the wellbeing of the group of people who are, traditionally, the most reticent and stoic of all Australians when it comes to their health. They, in turn, have taught him what he needed to know to be a successful farmer.

Over time, Rick and Barbara have enlarged and enhanced the little house on the hill and bought more land as it became available to them. Although Barbara was never given the opportunity to reconcile with her father, who died in 1981, twenty-five years after his death her mother and sister moved to Tullamore to live on one of their neighbouring blocks.

They now own 1200 hectares, on which Rick runs beef cattle. He started out with Hereford-Santa cross cows, but when drought tightened its grip a couple of years ago he chose to sell them. As he has begun to restock, he's succumbed to the local enthusiasm for black cattle and is switching to Black Angus. Recently he has also started share farming a paddock with a neighbour for the first time. Happy as the proverbial pig, Rick continues to find farming just as fascinating as he thought it would be when he was dreaming about it as a kid.

Ask Rick which he prefers, farming or medicine, and he says, 'It's fantastic to have a balance.' And yet he was thinking of giving up medicine completely when he retired in mid-2016. He was on call with the Remote Medical Consultation Service by then, which was a bit frantic on the days when he worked in his practice because dealing with another patient in another place would interrupt his focus on the patient in front of him. If it was a particularly busy day, it was really very difficult, and sometimes he might be called three or four times after midnight as well. He was ready to give up the lot when Barbara convinced him that talking to cows all day would atrophy his brain. Twelve months later he's pleased he took her advice and maintained his position with the RMCS, saying, 'It keeps the cogs moving.'

When the RMCS was established in Bathurst about a decade ago, all the local doctors volunteered a few nights a month, which worked really well for a time, but eventually it unravelled and was taken over by Central Western Area Health. In the last couple of years the service has been looked after by fewer doctors. Now it is down to just three. Initially Rick was working three-day blocks alternating with the other two docs, until they worked out the current system of one day in three, which is much easier to manage. The roster is made out at the beginning of the month by one of the other doctors and if it clashes with weddings or anything else that any of them wishes to do, they cover each other.

The RMCS doctors diagnose and manage a wide variety of cases using phone and fax machines (because emails are not considered secure) and will later call back to check how the patient's going. As Rick says, 'It's a model that works and needs to work in rural areas because it's so difficult to get doctors to come and work out here. It's a model that also enables those doctors who do work out there to have some time off call.'

There are about twenty-four hospitals who use the 24/7 service, depending on their 'current doctor status'. Where there's no doctor in town, patients can go to the hospital or clinic any time of the day or night and the RN will triage them, note all their observations, then ring RMCS and give the on-call doctor the lowdown on how the patient presented. Sometimes the doctor will talk to the patient or the mother of a child to get the history directly.

The doctor will then direct the RN to do any appropriate tests, such as urine analysis or an ECG, and they might ask them to palpate the stomach if the patient has abdominal pain, or listen to the chest. Once the doctor has all the relevant data he or she will give a diagnosis and manage the patient remotely. According to Rick it works really well.

Australian medical personnel triage patients on a scale of 1 to 5, in which 1 is critical, requiring immediate assistance, and 5 is non-urgent. The RMCS calls are mostly for people triaged 5 or 4. If a patient is triaged 3, the doctor on call will usually talk to a doctor in a base hospital, who will take over if there's acute cardiac chest pain or similar; more often than not those patients will be transferred to the base hospital. No one triaged 1 or 2 is ever referred to RMCS. They're transferred, sirens blaring, to the nearest base hospital.

Patients triaged 4 or 5 might be admitted to the local hospital if, for instance, it's a child with a very high temperature, someone with an uncomplicated pain from kidney or gall stones, or, as in the earlier case, a fit young adult with pneumonia. As in that case, when there isn't going to be a doctor available for several hours, the patient will very likely be

transferred to the nearest base hospital rather than risk his or
her condition deteriorating while waiting to be seen by a GP.
Conversely, there are times when base hospitals transfer back
to local hospitals under RMCS care for post-operative conva-
lescence if the local GP is away.

Rick can do his job anywhere, provided he has a phone
and fax, and now works from home or, occasionally, from
the holiday house he and Barbara own over on the coast,
which also has a fax machine installed for just that purpose. The surgery in town has been taken over by a doctor
from a town 50 kilometres away whose wife is also a doctor.
When Rick decided he was going to retire, his new colleague
offered to work in Tullamore part-time. Six months before he
actually retired, Rick started to get the town used to the idea
by working three days a week, while the new doctor worked
one. As the patients got to know him they increased it to two
and ultimately Rick hopes he will go to three; that plus the
local hospital (which now engages a health services manager,
a senior RN and two other RNs as well as two enrolled nurses
and a couple of assistant nurses) and the RMCS is what the
Tullamore medical service looks like in 2017.

Getting involved in their community – and of course the
farm – is what has kept Rick and Barbara in Tullamore for
the last eighteen and a half years and chances are they'll never
leave. Rick has clearly transformed into the farmer he always
wanted to be and Barbara has turned into a bit of a political
animal and is currently the deputy mayor of the Parkes Shire,
a role she is relishing.

Reflecting on the years since they chose to pursue rural practice, Rick says it's been a wonderful experience. 'Immersing

yourself in a community like this is so worthwhile and we've just enjoyed it so much; the Tullamore community has given us much more than we've given them.'

Unlike city practice, rural medicine has given him the opportunity to enjoy real balance in his life. For sure, on the days when he's not on call, you'll find Rick Newton somewhere up the paddock . . .

3

Out on a Limb

Dr Sara Renwick-Lau, Mallacoota, Victoria

It's difficult to imagine that anywhere in Victoria is actually six hours from Melbourne and incredibly remote but the town of Mallacoota is exactly that. To get there, you turn off the Princes Highway in the tiny village of Genoa, just 15 kilometres from the New South Wales border on the far eastern edge of the state, and head east towards the Wilderness Coast. You drive for another 25 kilometres along a winding road through thousands of hectares of national park until you come out of the trees and there is Mallacoota. It's a bustling but relaxed little town resting on the mouth of the Mallacoota Inlet, which sparkles away to the north-west. To the south, there's a hundred kilometres of clean white beach stretching as far as the eye can see and the ocean is straight ahead. The tourism and abalone industries underpin the local economy and the community is as close-knit as small rural communities typically are.

When Dr Sara Renwick-Lau bought into the Mallacoota

Medical Centre at the end of 2007, there were two other doctors already in the practice to share the overheads, the workload and, in particular, the on-call component. Between them, they were able to offer a full suite of services to the community, which numbers about 1000 permanent residents and an expanded holiday crowd of 5000–8000 depending on the season.

Sara's life was cruising along beautifully. Working full-time and being on call a third of the time, she and her family were attaining exactly the work-life balance they'd imagined when they moved to Mallacoota. They all learnt to surf and joined the local pony club; they went out with friends and participated in school activities.

Then, as she'd known they eventually must, Sara's partners retired. Their departure left her with a vacuum, but she never imagined it wouldn't be easy to fill. Living in paradise, she assumed other doctors would want to live there too.

Apparently not.

Unable to find permanent replacements for her partners, Sara's hard-won balance slipped away as her forty-hour week doubled, and her one-in-three on-call commitment became 24/7. Although Sara was working longer hours, she was generating less money on her own and before long she was struggling to pay the rent.

When the ABC television series Back Roads visited Mallacoota at the end of 2016, it was obvious that despite it being an absolute gem of a place to live, the doctor shortage was definitely biting and, despite tremendous community support, Sara Renwick-Lau was stuck well out on a limb.

One way or another, Sara was used to remoteness long before

she set foot in a geographically remote community. Being half Chinese in the all-white, blue-collar manufacturing town of Geelong in Victoria ensured she felt a certain sense of isolation growing up, and although she was born in Australia, had some lovely friends and joined in a plethora of extracurricular activities at school, she never really felt as though she belonged.

Sara's father, Ngan Hua, who is known as Danny, was the son of a Chinese merchant, Lau Beuh Ching, who lived with his second wife, Chau Moh Cheng, at Sandakan in the remote north-eastern reaches of Malaysia, across the South China Sea from the Philippines. Her family is proud of the fact that her grandfather was officially recognised in a booklet at the Sandakan Memorial Park for the role he played in the local underground during World War II, helping Australian prisoners of war being forced to build an airstrip by the Japanese. Lau Beuh Ching was imprisoned in Kuching for two and a half years for his efforts.

Sara's family also admire the fact that her grandmother Chau Moh Cheng later insisted that all of their six children leave Sandakan and go to a western country to be educated. As Sara says, 'It can't have been an easy decision and must have cost them dearly.' Her father came to Sydney to complete his secondary education and then moved to Victoria to get his science degree at the University of Melbourne. Despite his mother's strict instruction to '*do* medicine and *do not* marry a white girl', Danny chose teaching as a career and married Jo, a blonde-haired, blue-eyed 'ten pound Pom' he'd met when she was doing her nursing training in Melbourne.

Commuting from the small community of Inverleigh, about twenty minutes west of Geelong, both Sara's parents worked in the port city, Danny as a teacher and Jo as a school nurse, which allowed her to juggle work and her children's secondary school commitments.

The early 1990s was a particularly difficult period of time in Geelong following the crash of the Farrow Group of building societies in Victoria. A lot of ordinary, everyday people had invested their life savings in the group and the state government instituted a 3-cent levy on fuel to try to recoup the 900 million dollars lost to the taxpayers of Victoria. Recovery took years and Sara remembers being well aware that both her parents were working full-time to pay the mortgage on their very small and modest house. She is particularly grateful that despite the recession they had a couple of acres of land around their house where her parents let her keep a pony.

Although Sara didn't know the story about her grandmother wanting her father to do medicine until she was a young adult, she grew up with the meme that education is everything and never considered for a moment not working as hard as she could. Sara knew she wanted to be a doctor from about the age of six and her determination never wavered.

Both she and her older brother, Adam, worked hard at school; like her, Adam was determined to go to university. Sara was the only kid in her graduating high school class in Geelong who wanted to be a doctor and Adam was already at uni in Melbourne when she moved there to start undergraduate medicine.

When she was in fifth year and doing her general practice rotation, Sara went to Wonthaggi in South Gippsland and worked for a GP who advised her, 'If you want to be a rural GP, you really need to do your residency in Darwin because the Royal Darwin Hospital will give you a really great all-round skill set. You'll do general medicine and general surgery and you won't end up in some narrow speciality somewhere.'

In her final year, Sara and her husband, Marcus – whom she'd met when they were both walking their dogs and married in 2000 when she was in fifth year – went to Orbost in East Gippsland, where she had a positive experience working with two wonderful country GPs who did everything from delivering babies to surgical procedures to holding the hands of people who were dying. Both doctors were also heavily involved in their community, which Sara really liked. They, and the GP at Wonthaggi, were the first of a long list of doctors who supported and mentored her as she progressed into rural and remote medicine.

While they were there, Sara and Marcus fell in love with East Gippsland. One of the GPs at Orbost had a tiny hut on 30 acres of land out at Combienbar, on the edge of the Errinundra National Park, which he urged them to visit for a weekend. They loved the natural pristine wilderness and could imagine being drawn back to the area – but that was as far as it went. Intent as she was on becoming a rural doctor, Sara followed the advice of her mentor from Wonthaggi and applied to do her internship in Darwin.

Even though her dark hair, creamy tanned skin and very beautiful dark eyes reflect a vestige of her Chinese heritage, as she gets older Sara looks more like her mother than her father. Inside, however, she has retained every scrap of the indomitable spirit she probably inherited from her Chinese grandmother and she's nothing if not clear about what she wants. From the outset she was determined to get a placement at Royal Darwin Hospital. Refusing to be deterred by the advice that RDH sourced most of its interns from the Flinders School of Medicine in South Australia, Sara rang the office of the chief medical officer at the hospital every two days until they agreed to take her.

Shortly afterwards, in 2002, Sara and Marcus moved to Darwin. Once she was settled in to her internship, Sara decided she'd learn an Aboriginal dialect. She figured if she had the intelligence to get a medical degree she ought to be able to learn a language other than her own. She enrolled in an Aboriginal language course at Charles Darwin University and chose to learn Gupapuyngu, one of the Yolngu Matha dialects of East Arnhem Land. While there are many different dialects, there is for the most part enough commonality to facilitate communication between them.

During the first couple of years of her internship, Sara did rotations outside RDH at Humpty Doo and at the Ngalkanbuy Health Centre in Galiwin'ku, a very large Yolngu community on Elcho Island, off the northern coast of East Arnhem Land. She enjoyed both but particularly the weeks on Elcho, which gave her a chance to try out some of her newly learnt vocabulary. Because she loved the remote aspect of the work there she decided to join the Northern Territory's GP training program.

In 2003, Sara and Marcus welcomed their daughter, Matilda, into their lives. Marcus had graduated in English Literature and completed his thesis on Jane Austen when Sara was in her final year of medicine. He planned to establish an online career, so happily opted to become Matilda's full-time carer, enabling Sara to continue her training as a rural GP. Consequently, in her fourth year post grad and second year as a registrar, Sara applied to return to Elcho Island to work as a GP registrar at Ngalkanbuy Health Centre for twelve months.

The Yolngu people of Elcho Island are believed to have one of the oldest cultures on earth, with evidence of their habitation all over the islands and coast of Arnhem Land dating back 40 000 years. The Galiwin'ku settlement was established in 1942 by Harold Shepherdson (known locally as Bapa Sheppy) from the Methodist Overseas Mission, as a refuge from possible bombing of the RAAF base on Milingimbi Island, about 100 kilometres to the west of Elcho.

In 1947, after World War II was over, the mission built a Methodist church in Galiwin'ku and established various industries there. In the 1950s there was a thriving market garden, a sawmill to cut local cypress pine and a flourishing fishing industry. The mission encouraged Aboriginal people to stay in their traditional homelands on the island and use Galiwin'ku as a service centre. After self-government was awarded to the Northern Territory in the late 1970s, the mission was closed and, while a market garden still exists, tourism, art and music have replaced timber and fishing as the main industries supporting a community of over 2000 people.

Unfortunately, just as Sara, Marcus and baby Matilda moved out to Elcho Island, Sara's supervising GP left and the clinic was unable to get a replacement. Thrown headfirst into the deep end, Sara found herself doing solo general practice in the second largest Aboriginal community in the Northern Territory, something she definitely hadn't planned on but embraced with gusto and a commitment to give it her very best shot.

It gave her great satisfaction to have enough vocabulary to be able to communicate with the Yolngu people on Elcho, especially about medical things. It broke down great barriers for her really quickly and she firmly believes that, without that capacity, 'you're asking people to take a giant leap of faith when they can't understand what you're telling them'. Although her social fluency was less well developed because she was mostly talking language at work, her medical vocab was quite good.

Sara's efforts to build viable working relationships within the local community were enhanced by the fact that she and Marcus had been adopted into a Yolngu family when she'd done her internship at the Ngalkanbuy Health Centre. As she explains, the Yolngu follow a traditional system of family hierarchy that dictates the flow of their interactions with each other and with other people. Anyone outside family is a bit of a mystery and difficult to accommodate in Yolngu relationships, but when an outsider 'belongs' it is easier for people to relate to and accept them.

Even so, most of the time Sara's workplace was so frenetic and so full of suffering it was terrifying, but she didn't really have time to think about it. She'd work twelve- to fourteen-hour days, go home to eat and crash, then get up next morning to spend some time with Matilda before she rushed out the door to do it all again. She readily admits that when she went back to Elcho years later, she realised just how completely in over her head she was. 'I didn't know what I didn't know and really I had no idea what I was doing a lot of the time. I just knew if I wasn't there, they had no doctor at all.'

There were two or three registered nurses who'd been at the clinic for years and knew exactly what they were doing, which was a great help but, Sara says, 'They were so under-staffed and under such enormous pressure all of the time, they were pretty stressed. Even though it is a dry community there was so much illness and trauma and disadvantage it felt like a war zone every day and you couldn't ever get on top of the chronic diseases.'

Of the many challenges Sara faced, one of the toughest things was addressing the mental health issues. People would present with acute psychosis and she'd be trying to respond appropriately but also in a way that was both respectful and safe for everyone concerned. She was also emotionally confronted by the number of people dying at a relatively young age.

One of Sara's abiding memories is the death of a man to whom many people looked for guidance and who had the potential to take on a leadership role in the community. He suffered from chronic ischaemic heart disease and had a cardiac arrest. Even though she worried that he might well suffer brain damage if he lived, Sara did everything she could to resuscitate him so he could be evacuated to Darwin. And all the time she was aware that half the community was standing outside the door waiting to see what happened. When he died, the grief was almost tangible and cloaked the community for a long time.

Thinking back to those long months in Galiwin'ku, Sara reflects that one of the unrecorded measures of the awful health statistics on Elcho while they were there was the fact that Marcus learnt to tell what was happening at the clinic by the resonance of the jet engines on the CareFlight plane.

Their house was right near the airport, and if the medivac plane landed and shut down the engines and didn't start them up again in a short time, Marcus knew that the medical team was up at the clinic helping Sara stabilise a patient and that she probably wouldn't be home for hours. On the other hand, if the engines started up again in a short space of time, he'd surmise that the patient was less critical and therefore more easily prepared for flight, which meant the ambulance had probably met the plane at the airport instead of the flight crew having to go into the clinic to collect the patient.

Because she was the only doctor on the island and because there was so much chronic illness and death, Sara was unable to distance herself from the end-stage sadness, the funeral arrangements and the grief that constitute sorry business. She credits the doctors who supported her through her GP training with teaching her to be mindful of her own mental health and with giving her strategies for managing the impacts of the stress and distress that surrounded her. They were all GPs who had personal experience working in remote communities, who really understood the issues, and she says their support was invaluable.

Still, on occasion, it all felt overwhelming . . .

A man who'd been diagnosed with chronic lung disease by Sara's predecessor was scheduled for evacuation to Darwin for more specialised treatment. The plane duly arrived and they had him on board ready for departure when he suddenly refused to go and walked off the plane. There was nothing the flight crew could do but let him go.

Two days later, one wing of a category 5 cyclone hit Elcho Island. Most of the buildings weren't cyclone rated so a huge crowd of people was jammed into the health clinic. Sara was sheltering at home with Marcus and Matilda when the storm hit. All the cyclone advice she'd heard warned people not to leave their shelter for any reason until the storm passed. Remembering a doctor who was killed trying to get to the hospital during Cyclone Tracy, Sara was terrified but pleased at least to be holed up with her family for the duration.

The worst of the cyclone eventually passed and they realised they'd survived. It was late at night and they'd not long gone to bed to try to get some sleep when there was a knock on the door from a woman summoning her to the health centre. As they hurried to the clinic she told Sara that when the storm passed and the crowd began to disperse, they had found the man with chronic lung disease collapsed on the floor. Sara examined him surrounded by the crowd, who were awaiting her verdict. She was aware of all her Yolngu family in the room as she diagnosed respiratory arrest and pronounced him dead. It was as though a switch had been thrown and, coming on the back of the raging storm, the ululation of grief left her momentarily breathless. The process of sorry business was only just beginning. And there was all the clean-up from the cyclone to deal with as well.

Although Sara has never for a second regretted the experience, working on Elcho Island was pretty shattering, and not just for her. Because they had no fence around their house, Marcus and Matilda couldn't go outside and play or go down the street; the camp dogs were everywhere and too much of a threat to Matilda. Likewise Marcus couldn't join the men in their traditional pastime of fishing because he had Matilda to care for. And because he was male, he couldn't spend time with the women either. As a result, he spent most of the year they were there with only Matilda for company and would be desperate for some adult conversation by the time Sara came home in the evening. But Sara was incapable of helping him; she'd walk in the door after a fourteen-hour day spent finding the correct Yolngu words to inform people they had terrible things wrong with them or that they were dying and tell Marcus she couldn't speak to him because she needed to eat and sleep.

Their situation was unsustainable and they were trying to work out strategies for getting through another year when they realised they couldn't; they needed to leave. In an attempt to temper some of their anguish with humour, Sara says they joked about flying out of Elcho with Marcus and Matilda sitting in straitjackets on opposite sides of the plane.

On reflection, she admits that while she loved the very intense kind of work she did in Galiwin'ku, she was probably depressed herself while she was there. She would wake, wide eyed, at 3 a.m., even though she'd always been a good sleeper. She was quite anxious about things that hadn't concerned her before and she'd sometimes find herself in a state of high alert with her heart racing.

Bidding a sad farewell to Elcho, they went to Kakadu, where Sara worked with another doctor who acted as her supervising GP in the Jabiru Health Clinic. Sara and Marcus both relaxed into their new life at Jabiru. Relieved of sole responsibility for the people around her, Sara wasn't working the same ridiculous hours she'd worked in Galiwin'ku, so Marcus could pursue other interests, and there was an active play group in the community, which meant he and Matilda had some meaningful interaction with other people. Sara found the work rewarding and the experience she accumulated very satisfying. The community had similar levels of chronic illness and traumatic injury and a comparable level of disadvantage, but it was smaller and there was more infrastructure and a larger workforce, which made it much easier.

Living through another tropical cyclone, however, had a big impact on Sara. As directed, she was sheltering at home with Marcus and Matilda when Cyclone Monica tracked in from Far North Queensland. They'd lost all power and communications very early on and the storm was raging and shrieking around them when Sara saw the clinic car come to collect her supervising GP from his house. Her anxiety, already high, ramped up. Terrified for the duration of the storm that something catastrophic must have happened to warrant him going out in such dangerous conditions, she was saddened to learn later that the person he'd gone to help had succumbed to respiratory arrest during the cyclone. Classified as a category 5, Monica was one of the most powerful cyclones on record and, for many years after, any very strong winds triggered a fear response in Sara.

Sara, Marcus and Matilda had spent eighteen months in the Jabiru community and nearly six years in the Territory when Sara and Marcus agreed that it was time to leave and head back south. Sara was pregnant with their second child, Hugo,

when they left Kakadu midway through 2007. They weren't
sure what was ahead of them but Sara already knew that she
couldn't work in an urban hospital or city practice and she
valued the experience she'd gained working remotely too
much to give it up. She told Marcus that they needed to find
somewhere very isolated but very beautiful to relocate to. He
agreed on the proviso it also had a play group and/or some
childcare!

After Hugo was born, Sara was searching for possibilities when she saw an ad for a locum at Mallacoota. Although
they'd been to Orbost and both of them remembered how
much they'd loved their weekend at Combienbar, they'd never
actually been out to the eastern edge of Victoria or into southern NSW. They had a look at a map and when Sara saw where
Mallacoota was, surrounded by wilderness country and the
Inlet and the ocean, she said to Marcus, 'Oh that looks remote.
We have to go there!'

Initially Sara took the locum position, but she knew there
was an option to buy into the practice and was keen to get
right into it. When she went back to Melbourne she talked
to her accountant, who urged caution and asked her to give
it three months before she committed herself. She did, but
barely, jumping straight in with her new medical partners,
Jenny Schlager and David Appleton.

Sara loved the new balanced lifestyle that allowed her to
spend quality time with Marcus and their kids doing all the
family-oriented activities the community boasted. She was in
her element and saw running the practice, learning the books
and taking on personal responsibility as a partner as just
another batch of new things to learn. David was semi-retired

by then and Jenny enjoyed taking some time off to do her own thing but, by arrangement with them, Sara was also able to take time off to go back to Elcho with Marcus and the kids to do a couple of locums. They all loved these trips because it meant they could spend some time with their Yolngu family, and Sara could practise Yolngu Matha for a few weeks.

Two years after they arrived in Mallacoota, Sara had their second son, Jimmy, and their lives were pretty much perfect . . . until, as they'd always known she would, Jenny decided to retire. Sara bought her out, and then David when he retired twelve months later. For the first couple of years Sara was able to manage by employing an overseas-trained doctor, but when he left she was on her own once again, practising solo.

With all of her accumulated experience, the medicine itself wasn't so much of a problem, although she felt her professional isolation in a way she hadn't until then. The big challenge was her inability to generate enough money to sustain the practice, and as the months rolled on her situation became untenable. 'The catch is,' she says, 'country people don't come in for a quick visit. They don't come at all until they have a serious issue and that all takes time. Many people in our community are retirees and older aged residents. In fact, over half our population is over sixty and many of their health complications are chronic. The overheads are the same whether there's one doctor or two or even three because you have to have the rooms and the resources and the ancillary staff. We run on very narrow financial margins at the best of times and, ultimately, we had to make some difficult choices about how to continue.'

When they got to the point of worrying about whether they actually had enough money each month to pay their bills, Sara went to the Gippsland Primary Health Network and told them she couldn't keep going as they were because she was running out of money and she wasn't prepared to redraw on her mortgage to keep the practice running.

Early in 2016, the Primary Health Network orchestrated the purchase of the practice by Orbost Regional Health, with the Victorian government coming on board to ensure the success of the deal. Sara would stay on to manage the practice. Unfortunately, the government pulled out at the last minute and the deal fell through, which, Sara says, highlights another important part of the problem with rural and remote health in Victoria. 'Unlike other states that are much larger and deal with the challenges of providing services (or not) to the outback, the Victorian government doesn't understand what our kind of remoteness actually means. They have no experience of it and we're a bit out of sight, out of mind.'

When the deal fell through, Sara realised she would have to close the practice and walk away. That felt wrong on so many levels because she had elderly patients who rarely, if ever, left the community and palliative patients who wanted to die at home. She had a whole community who would have no medical access at all.

Marcus had been working in IT and looking after their kids up until then, but with Jimmy starting school in 2016, his days were suddenly child-free. Knowing she could never just walk away, he suggested to Sara that they put off all her staff and he would take over managing the practice so that she could continue offering some kind of service to the community. So that's what they did.

Sara called a meeting in Mallacoota to explain the situation to the community. There were two important outcomes. A group of people in Mallacoota who have been raising money for twenty years so that they can eventually build a residential aged-care complex came forward and offered to buy the building that housed the practice and rent the premises back to Sara at a nominal fee, which relieved her immediate financial burden.

Another group was also formed – the Mallacoota Doctor Search Committee, who began actively advertising and lobbying for a second and, ideally, third doctor to relocate to the community. They started a Facebook page and set up a stall at the 2016 Rural Medicine Australia conference in Canberra to try to attract the attention of prospective applicants. Although they didn't get any immediate applications, they did garner an enormous amount of interest in their community approach to engaging doctors to a remote area.

Meantime, back in Mallacoota, with Marcus managing the office and a nurse coming in part-time when she's needed, Sara now works four very long days a week seeing patients. Technically she doesn't do call, but even working reduced hours, between seeing patients and dealing with their accompanying paperwork, she still works forty to fifty hours a week. But she says that's way better than the seventy to eighty hours she was working.

If people in the community need urgent out-of-hours medical attention they have to drive to the nearest emergency department a couple of hours away across the border in Bega, in NSW. The nearest teaching hospital is in Canberra, four and a half hours and two borders away. The politics involved in crossing one border is manageable; crossing two is a maze of paperwork only to be negotiated in dire circumstances. Fortunately 'dire' hasn't happened in the nine years of Sara's tenure but there's always a first time.

Sara does give her personal phone number to her palliative care patients. She knows when they're most likely to need her and considers it paramount that they know she is available to guide them through their final days. With a young family and no promise of another doctor coming to help her anytime soon, though, she must keep herself well and in good health so that she can continue to provide the best service she can. She goes surfing as often as possible, plays soccer with the local women's team and spends quality time with her family. She still has horses and they all enjoy pony club. And every now and then, they pack up and slip away to Melbourne for a weekend to enjoy some city treats.

While the future of the Mallacoota Medical Centre is still precarious and Sara is once again working out on a limb, she's out there in good company. There is nowhere else on earth that she and her family would rather live and work, so she stays, warmed by the knowledge that the community really wants them and is prepared to fight to keep them.

4

The Eye Angel

Dr Bill Glasson AO, Longreach, Queensland

The way Dr Bill Glasson explains it, looking into the eye of someone with a cataract is like looking in through a tiny milky window. 'Instead of seeing a nice clear, transparent lens, the lens is cloudy. I have trouble seeing in and the patient has trouble seeing out.'

Joyce Crombie says that's what her eyesight was like before Bill removed her cataracts. When she's not occupied in her job as a health worker, Joyce, a Wangkangurru woman, paints outback landscapes and wildlife. She's been painting for seventeen years but says she'd lost heart for it in the last year or so because she couldn't see well enough to be sure she was using the right colours. Bill removed the contents of the lens in her eye, leaving the lining behind. Then he inserted a tiny new intraocular lens into the lining and, voila, Joyce's vision cleared.

Some people have likened the process to shifting the focus ring on a camera lens so that everything that was a slightly blended blur is suddenly sharp and clear, in full-on glorious colour.

For Joyce it was life-restoring. Bill gave her back her eyesight and her faith in her ability. What's more, he did it in her local hospital in Longreach in central western Queensland.

Little wonder she calls him the 'eye angel'.

Bill Glasson was born in Winton Hospital and grew up on his family's sheep station, Kywong, about 70 kilometres north-east of Winton in north-west Queensland. He's the second of four children, and remembers a spectacularly adventurous childhood roaming free around the station when he and his siblings weren't confined to their school room with whichever long-suffering governess was teaching them at the time.

Typically, the Glasson kids weren't nearly as interested in school as they were in what was going on outside. They'd have much preferred to be out helping with sheep work or looking after the menagerie of 'pet' animals they'd accumulated; pigs, chooks, ducks, ponies and, of course, dogs, who inevitably produced puppies.

Mad about station life, Bill would be up at daylight every morning to help their old ringer, Artie, to milk the cows and then separate the milk and the cream. When they were finished, Bill would deliver the milk and cream to Artie's wife, Mrs Ben, who was the station cook.

Because Bill's father, Bill Snr, was very actively involved in the community and as often as not in town assisting with the local show or the rodeo or a race meeting or any other event in the district that attracted his help, Artie was something of a father figure to young Bill. It was Artie who taught him how to ride, how to shoot, how to crack a whip, how to do many of the things he needed to do in order to live and work on the land. Bill says Artie also taught him many of life's important lessons.

Artie's one shortcoming was the drinking benders he'd go on every few months when he and Mrs Ben went to town. With the possible exception of his wife, everyone loved old Artie and Bill pretty much worshipped the ground he walked on. Every morning while his family ate breakfast in the dining room, Bill sat out the back with Artie and Mrs Ben, rolling Artie's smokes for him. With his very first rollie of the morning Artie would take one truly magnificent drawback, turn slightly blue around the gills and then puff it all out with ever-decreasing gasps. Bill was so impressed he decided that's what he was going to do when he grew up; he was going to smoke cigarettes just the way Artie did.

When Bill's older brother, Doug, was ready to start school, Mrs Glasson tried her hardest to teach him, but he was a very reluctant participant and eventually she threw her hands in the air and admitted defeat. From then on, she employed governesses, who were an important part of the family's day-to-day lives, teaching throughout the day and pitching in to help wherever they might be needed. Every Sunday, the mail truck from Winton would deliver a package from the Brisbane Correspondence School. The school package included new papers for each student as well as their corrected papers from a couple of weeks before. It was the governess's job to deliver their lessons as dictated in the papers and supervise the written answers they all had to complete.

Each morning the kids would straggle into the school room somewhere between 9 and 9.30 a.m. depending on how long they could drag out the morning chores. Smoko and lunch couldn't come fast enough and while they were in the school room, even the merest whisper of a horse being saddled or a motor starting up was enough to have them hanging out the window to see what was going on without them. The minute school was done, they bolted.

Despite escaping the classroom as much as possible, they did learn enough reading, writing and arithmetic to make their transition to boarding school viable if not seamless. Following in Doug's footsteps, Bill went off to Brisbane in 1965 to board at the Anglican Church Grammar School, famously known as 'Churchie'.

Bill loved Churchie; he enjoyed boarding and while he was a little behind the eight ball having schooled by correspondence, it didn't take him long to catch up, or fit in. Discovering rowing launched a lifelong passion for the sport. Still a little fellow at the time, Bill coxed the Churchie First VIII to win Head of the River, the Great Public Schools' Association of Queensland's premier event, in 1969. The following year, while he was in his senior year, he coached the University of Queensland's girls' crew and later rowed himself for Union College and ultimately for UQ.

But before then he had to plan his future. After he matriculated at the end of his senior year, Bill went home for Christmas and to help his father with their January shearing. Unlike his childhood, when the seasons seemed to be all good, in the summer of 1969–70 they were in the middle of a blazing drought, things were tight and they couldn't afford to pay anyone they could manage without. They had six shearers, a wool classer and the wool rollers, but they did all the mustering and all the drafting, penning up, dipping and drenching themselves, as well as pressing all the wool into bales and getting the shorn sheep back out to their paddocks.

It was searingly hot, gut-busting work from before daylight until well after dark. One night, Bill was sound asleep in one of the wool bins when he was woken about 2 a.m. by the sound of his father coming back in with a mob of sheep. He went out into the moonlit night to greet him.

Bill Snr said to him, 'Well, son, what do you want to do?'

'I'm not sure, Dad, but, fuck, I'm not going to do this for the rest of my life!'

Although Bill thought about medicine, he decided to do optometry. His whole family is short-sighted so he figured he knew a bit about it. He lived with his grandmother in St Lucia in Brisbane and continued to coach the university girls' crew while he completed the three-year training for optometry, even though he realised, halfway through first year, that he'd really like to be an ophthalmologist. As soon as he finished he applied for a place at UQ to do medicine and for a place at Union College to live.

Because money was an issue, Bill accepted a bonded scholarship to go to medical school, which meant he was bound to work for the government for three years after he graduated. He loved medicine, finding every year of the course even better than the last. Best of all, he met his future wife, Claire Jackson, in among his peer group.

In his final year he and Claire both joined the Army Reserve. As an active reservist Bill was involved with an artillery unit in the army and later became a consultant to the Australian Defence Force in Canberra in relation to relevant medical policy making. He's still a consultant to the army although he will have to retire when he turns sixty-five.

Bill graduated from medicine in 1980 and spent his intern year at the Princess Alexandra and Mater hospitals in Brisbane rotating through medicine, surgery, obstetrics, paediatrics and anaesthetics. In his second year, he was sent to be the relieving doctor for the Western Darling Downs.

Travelling from town to town, Bill relieved the doctors in Dalby, Tara, Miles, Wandoan, Taroom and Jandowae for five-day blocks before heading back to Dalby for two days followed by his own five days off. Then he'd start the whole cycle again. The doctors he relieved were all GPs who acted as medical superintendents of their local hospitals with right to private practice, as is often the case in rural and remote towns. Bill would care for their private patients as well as covering their public duties at the hospital. All the doctors on the circuit supported him and because he'd been trained so well, medically Bill felt very safe. Socially, there were some surprises.

The first time he arrived to relieve one of the GPs, he was invited for dinner by the other GP in the town whom he'd not met and knew little of. Over dinner, the second GP regaled Bill with stories about his own particular talents, including his ability to insert breast implants. He'd buy six at a time then line up three women who'd requested the procedure and do them one after the other – in his surgery. Barely out of med school, Bill was a bit shocked, but not nearly as shocked as he was when the GP called his partner in and said, 'Hey, darl, take your clothes off and show Bill your breasts.' While the GP sat proudly admiring his work, Bill eyes skittered all over the room trying to focus on anything but.

Next morning, before Bill had even started the first of his five days, the same GP rang and told him he had to do an emergency laparotomy on a woman who was bleeding from a ruptured ovarian cyst and asked Bill if he'd come and give the anaesthetic. Bill told him he'd done anaesthetics but he wasn't very experienced. The GP said, 'Don't worry. I'll give you a hand to put her to sleep.'

Bill agreed and headed up to the hospital, where he found the woman was completely shocked with no blood pressure. Bill refused to administer an anaesthetic, telling the GP she needed to be resuscitated and given fluids and blood. He put the drip in and told the GP he needed fresh blood. The GP said, 'No worries. I'll get you fresh blood while you push her around to the theatre.' Bill duly wheeled her round to the theatre and next thing a second trolley pulled in beside him with another woman lying on it. It was 'Darl' from dinner the night before. Bill greeted her and asked, 'What are you doing here?'

'Oh hi, Bill,' she said, 'I've just come to give some blood.'

So the GP ran a litre and a half of blood out of Darl straight into the patient on the theatre bed, after which the patient was recovered enough to handle the anaesthetic Bill gave her. Shaking his head at the memory nearly forty years later, he says, 'It was the warmest, freshest blood I've ever transfused into anyone.' The GP found and dealt with the ruptured ovarian cyst and the patient survived. Bill too, just.

Once the operation was over and the woman was awake, Bill left her to the GP's ministrations, did his first hospital rounds with the matron and then headed down to the surgery of the doctor he was relieving.

When he was settled in the doctor's office, he called in the first patient. He was a big tall man and when he introduced himself Bill recognised him as the brother of someone he knew. The man said, 'That's right, Noel said I should come and see you.'

'Oh, okay, Mr V. Well what can I do for you?'

'I want you to castrate my horse.'

'What?' exclaimed Bill. 'I'm the doctor not the bloody vet!'

'That's alright,' Mr V said, 'I know you grew up in the bush so you'll know how to castrate a horse.'

'Well, that's all very well, Mr V, but you can do it. What do you need me for?'

Mr V replied, 'I want you to put him down with an anaesthetic.'

Stalling, Bill said, 'But I've never given a horse an anaesthetic in my life.' Mr V was insistent though and, since there was no vet in the town, Bill thought he'd better not let him down and agreed to come out to his farm on Saturday.

He rang a mate who was a vet in western Queensland and asked him how to anaesthetise a horse. His mate told him to use a drug called suxamethonium, which Bill was familiar with because it's used to relax muscles while anaesthetising humans.

'So I'll give it about four times the human dose then, shall I?' asked Bill.

'No!' the vet replied. 'Use about a fourth of a human dose and inject it into his jugular vein. He'll take about four steps then fall over and you can jump on him and castrate him and brand him and he'll be awake in about fifty seconds.'

'Righto, thanks,' said Bill.

Come Saturday, he packed up all the gear he thought he'd need and headed out to Mr V's farm, where he found not one but *five* unbroken horses awaiting his attention.

Mildly amused that he'd been so easily inveigled, he and Mr V ran the first one up the narrow crush and slid the gate behind it to keep it loosely trapped. Finding the jugular wasn't easy with the horse bouncing around, even with Mr V holding its head steady. Bill got the needle in, gave it the vet's recommended dose of suxamethonium and opened the gate. The horse side-stepped out, took another couple of steps and fell over. Quick as a flash, Bill was on him; he did a quick excision across the scrotum, pulled out and quickly snipped off the testicles and was done. Within a minute the horse was awake, rolling onto its knees prior to getting up, albeit a little unsteadily. By the time he'd finished the fifth horse, Bill was starting to wonder if he'd missed his calling.

Driving back to town feeling quite pleased with himself, he looked forward to relaxing for the rest of the day, even though he was on call, and maybe even the whole weekend.

On Sunday the ambulance rang him to tell him, 'Someone's been shot. We don't know any details.'

Oh my God, thought Bill in fear and trepidation as he wondered what awaited him and just what gear he should take. The ambos collected him and took him out to the farm where the incident had occurred. There was a woman lying out in the paddock with blood gushing everywhere out of her leg. She and her husband had been setting up a trap gun to shoot wild dogs coming in through their boundary fence.

She'd walked away and when she came back she forgot about the trip-wire and set the shotgun off. It blew away the front of her leg, taking most of her tibia and fibula; the bottom of her leg was just hanging on with skin and muscle.

While the ambos packed and applied pressure to the terrifying wound, Bill managed the woman's airway and breathing, then put a cannula into her arm and attached a drip line to get some replacement fluids into her. They got her loaded into the ambulance and he directed the ambos to drive straight through to Toowoomba with the siren on. Unfortunately, the cannula he'd put in wasn't very secure, so as they were driving into Chinchilla he asked the ambos to detour to the hospital to see if he could get a better one. When he explained his dilemma to the sister on duty, she said, 'I've got just what you need,' and ran and got the biggest cannula Bill's ever seen. It looked about the same size as his little finger, and he wondered how he'd ever get it into a vein. Fortunately he found just one viable one inside the woman's arm and managed to slide the cannula in and tape it down firmly. He reattached the drip line and the fluids poured into her like a running hose.

They handed her over to the emergency room staff at Toowoomba General Hospital and headed back west again. A couple of months later, the anaesthetist who managed her care in Toowoomba told Bill they hadn't been able to save her leg but they'd been able to save her life because that cannula allowed them to pour in all the fluids and blood she needed in the first few weeks, unimpeded. Knowing he was the one who'd managed to safely insert it gave Bill a certain sense of satisfaction.

Back on the road, he continued his circuit around the

Western Darling Downs, ducking back to Brisbane on his five days off to court his friend and now colleague Dr Claire Jackson. As their romance progressed, Bill worked out the year learning heaps about medicine, people and himself. 'I just loved the bush folk. They were wonderful and I felt very comfortable in that year.' To top it all off, he asked Claire to marry him and she said yes!

At the end of the twelve months, still bonded to the Health Department, Bill went to see the director-general of health to tell him he was getting married. He explained he'd done a year in Brisbane and a year on the circuit around the Downs and he wondered whether the DG might organise for him and Claire to go somewhere together. Several weeks went by without any news from the DG's office, then one morning Bill got a call from the lass who coordinated all staff movements to say they were going to Mt Isa.

'Oh that's great. Claire and I will both be in Mt Isa.'

'No,' she said, 'Dr Jackson will be at the hospital and you'll be on the relieving circuit going to Doomadgee, Cloncurry, Julia Creek . . .'

'How often will I be in Mt Isa?'

'Oh, about one day a month,' she replied.

Horrified, he said, 'I can't ask a city girl to marry me and go nearly two thousand kilometres away from all she knows and then only see her one day a month!'

Claire suggested postponing the wedding; however, after some timely intervention by the father of a colleague who explained to the DG just how impractical and ridiculous that plan was, they were both posted to Redcliffe Hospital, Bill as surgical registrar and Claire as medical registrar. They did one in three days on call and worked incredibly hard but loved it. Bill was studying for his primary eye exams and doing all his basic subjects for ophthalmology as well. The following year, he went onto an eye program and rotated through all the Brisbane hospitals doing eye work for three years, before relocating with Claire and their young daughter Gemma to the UK. Mainly focusing on eye tumours, eye socket reconstruction and surgery involving the lid and tear ducts, Bill completed his fellowship year at Moorfields Eye Hospital in London.

They were pretty poor but had a wonderful year, during which they made some lifelong friends and Bill soaked up all the skills and knowledge available to him.

Upon their return to Australia, Bill joined the Terrace Eye Centre in Brisbane with a satellite practice in Maroochydore and an occasional satellite clinic in Kingaroy in the South Burnett region.

A year or two later, Dr Tom Murphy, who was one of Longreach's most renowned GPs, rang to tell him that the ophthalmologist who'd been visiting Longreach was retiring and suggested Bill might consider replacing him. Bill said he'd love to.

Bill's now been going to central western Queensland to deliver ophthalmological services for nearly thirty years. It helps that a big piece of his heart is firmly entrenched in the bush and he still has grazing interests in the west. Bill owns Coopers Run, a property at Blackall that he jokingly calls 'my yacht'; they escape out there any chance they get. While they'll never relocate permanently – Claire is happy to visit the property but won't ever want to leave the city for good – they've had some grand holidays there as a family.

Bill's kids, Gemma, Nicola and William, have all learnt the skills he learnt while growing up at Winton. They can ride and shoot and brand a calf and they appreciate the challenges that go hand in hand with the rewards of living on the land. Better yet, Bill says, 'They've all learnt to handle stock. Animals teach you a lot about people.' The kids' schoolmates used to clamour for an invitation to visit in the holidays and Bill was in his element teaching them all the finer points of bush life. Even as young adults, Coopers Run still holds a special place in the Glasson siblings' hearts.

Three times a year, Bill flies into Longreach, picks up a hospital car and does the rounds of his outback practice. He's out there for seven days, four of which he uses to travel and consult with patients in Blackall, Barcaldine and Winton, followed by three days in Longreach consulting and operating. Once a year, Bill expands his western eye trip by three days to include Birdsville, Bedourie and Boulia; twice a year, he flies to Katherine in the Northern Territory to conduct clinics.

Wherever he overnights, he'll go to the pub for dinner and have a beer with the locals; he talks to everyone, therefore he knows people wherever he goes and they know him. Like his father before him, he's a gregarious man who makes an effort always to remember people because he's genuinely interested in them.

Back in Bill's student days, Bill Snr, a Country Party (now National Party) member, had entered politics as the state member for Gregory. Bill admits that his father's example, along with his own interest in people and the policies that affect the way they live, influenced his decision to enter into medico-politics. He got involved with the Australian Medical Association Queensland in 1995, eventually becoming president of AMAQ in 2001–02 and of the national body of the AMA from 2003–05.

Bill's commitment to helping people also underpinned his run in federal politics, when he was preselected by the Liberal National Party to be their candidate for Griffith, Kevin Rudd's seat in Brisbane. Bill loathed Kevin Rudd and everything he stood for, so he figured, instead of whingeing and complaining, he'd have a go at doing the job himself. In the 2013 election, he led Kevin Rudd on primary votes and caused the biggest swing against a Labor Party incumbent in Queensland, but when preferences kicked in, it wasn't quite enough to topple the prime minister. When, very much to Bill's surprise, Kevin Rudd resigned from politics at the end of that year, Griffith was forced into a by-election. Bill ran again but was defeated by the incoming Labor nominee. Having given it his very best shot, he says he has no regrets about trying but won't run again, believing that his strength now lies in other areas behind the political scenes.

Back in western Queensland, the very possibility of Bill winning Griffith sent waves of joyful support throughout the region, laced with very real regret at the prospect of losing their wonderful doctor. While Bill's many bush supporters were sorry he didn't win, they were delighted they got him back.

One of Bill's patients, 85-year-old Mrs Alison Milson, says, 'He's marvellous, you know, and he's made such a difference to how we live our lives out here.' Mrs Milson sees Bill in Longreach for her check-ups or consultations and, on the rare occasion she needs to, she chooses to go to Brisbane to see him for procedures. She could have them done in Longreach but opts for Brisbane because she's happy to go there and it frees up a space at the Longreach clinic for someone less able to travel.

Just before Christmas in 2016 Mrs Milson went down and had her cataracts done and a stent inserted in her eye to reduce the pressure that might otherwise herald glaucoma. Although she says she doesn't always understand exactly what Bill does to her eyes, she, like everyone else, has total faith in his ability. 'I never ask questions. I just accept whatever Bill does because I know he knows what he's doing.' She believes a lot of older people wouldn't go away to see an eye doctor, or anyone else, so if Bill didn't come to them; they'd just put up with whatever eye problems they have.

The maximum waiting time for surgery is the next time Bill visits. Unless it's urgent, he'll consult, diagnose and, where applicable, book surgery places for his next trip. He has total control over his list and absolute trust in the staff in Longreach, especially his scrub nurse, Karen McLelland, and the local GPs who administer his anaesthetics. With succession planning firmly in place, Bill's got a couple of young ophthalmologists working with him who are interested in taking over his satellite clinics when he eventually retires; Todd Goodwin is based in Townsville and Sunil Warrier works in Bill's practice in Brisbane.

When he first went to Longreach, Bill used to take all his own instruments and a little microscope. Now they have a fair bit of equipment and all the instruments he needs set up in the hospital out there. They have a brand-new phacoemulsification machine that enables Bill and his protégé Sunil to remove even more cataracts in a visit than they could previously, and they have the machine that enables them to measure eyes up for lens implants. They've even got a laser and an excellent up-to-date microscope, so these days Bill travels light.

And when he's not there, the hospital has a camera that photographs the front and back of the eye, enabling the GPs to share the images with Bill back in Brisbane, or wherever he is. Mobile phones have simplified that process even more in areas that have mobile access; the GPs can take a phone photo and message it through. That means most patients can be treated locally unless they have a penetrating eye injury or a retinal detachment, in which case they'd be immediately transferred to Bill in his rooms on Wickham Terrace in the city.

Bill goes out to run his outback clinics because in his heart he believes 'we should be bringing services to the people rather than people to the services'. The need is out there and he knows that travelling into Brisbane is a challenge that some people just don't have the capacity to manage. His way saves them the grief and ensures their eye health, which in turn contributes to their overall health and wellbeing.

As Bill says, 'One thing the droughts gave me was an opportunity to go and do something else and ophthalmology is a wonderful part of medicine in terms of what you can do for people's lives. It makes a significant difference when suddenly they can see.'

Joyce Crombie can attest to that. Joyce and her sister Jean Barr-Crombie are both elders of the Wangkangurru people. Their mother and grandfather were the last traditional Wangkangurru people to come in from the Simpson Desert to Birdsville. Their connection to the desert and the Channel Country is strong and vibrant and is reflected in a large painting they did some years ago called *Two Sisters Talking*. The painting tells the story of their family's transition into western ways.

Joyce first saw Bill when she was living and working in Bedourie as a health worker. He removed a cataract from one of her eyes and she enjoyed renewed sight for some time, but when she admitted to herself, in 2016, that she couldn't see well enough to be sure she was mixing the exact shades of colour that she wanted in her paintings, she lost confidence in her art.

She moved to Longreach during that year to work for North and West Remote Health and says, 'I could see to work okay but I was really squinting at the computer and I couldn't drive. My colleagues had to drive me everywhere.'

Joyce's second cataract removal was one of the last procedures Bill did in Longreach before they started using the new phacoemulsification machine in March 2017. She says she was lightly sedated but she could hear Bill talking to her as he worked. She wore a patch for a week, and her eye felt a bit gritty for a couple of days, but after the first twenty-four hours she was taking the patch off regularly to put drops in her eye, and every time was exciting. 'The colours came back. It took a few days but every time it seemed clearer. You know, it's good people can see him out here, especially people further out west. After they see him, they can see a lot better.'

When Joyce was finally able to look at some of the paintings she'd done prior to her surgery, she realised they really weren't the earthy outback colours she'd thought she was mixing. She just shook her head, but now she's on a roll again and she and Jean sit talking and laughing and painting whenever they can get together.

Joyce has great respect for Bill and was just as delighted as everyone else in the Queensland bush who knows him when, in May 2017, he was awarded the Australian Medical Association's prestigious Gold Medal, 'in recognition of his exceptional service to the AMA over many years, and for his long-term and ongoing commitment to the eye health of Indigenous people'. With a big happy smile lighting up her face, Joyce says, 'He's our Dr Glasson. He's the eye angel and absolutely a gentleman.'

5

Kimberley Calling

Dr Anne Richards, Kununurra, Western Australia

It was a hot, humid November morning in far northern Western Australia with the first storm clouds of the wet season promised for later in the afternoon. In the emergency department of the Kununurra District Hospital another busy Saturday was in full swing when, a little after 10.30 a.m., the phone rang. Dr Anne Richards ignored it, assuming a nurse would answer it. It rang on. Glancing around, she gave up, grabbed it and identified herself – only to be jolted into full alertness by a male voice calling from the Civil Aviation Safety Authority, requesting a medical retrieval team be sent to a remote location about 40 kilometres north of town where a helicopter had just crashed. Four men were on board; it was hoped there might be survivors.

Back then, in 2003, there were no paid paramedics in Kununurra and all the ambulance personnel were volunteers. The hospital provided all emergency medical care to the surrounding area. As the only anaesthesia-trained ED doctor on duty that day, it was Anne's responsibility to go and, because there were four potential patients involved, she arranged for an ED nurse to go with her. Slipping into theatre overalls, she grabbed the disaster backpack and shoved a few ampoules of various drugs she might need into her front pocket, while the nurse added a couple of units of 'universal' O negative blood and a cold brick to a small esky. Packed and ready for anything, they bolted out the door to meet the helicopter waiting for them at the airport.

Along with a police officer, Anne, the nurse and all their medical equipment were quickly whisked into the air. As they flew north, Anne quietly considered what might lie ahead. Before she'd relocated to Kununurra permanently a few months before, she had been a district medical officer at the Derby regional hospital, and prior to that, a registrar at Kalgoorlie Hospital. In the course of her career, much of which focused on emergency medicine and acutely unwell patients, she had attended several and varied accident scenes, and she knew she had the skills and knowledge she'd need to deal with whatever traumatic injuries they might encounter.

Descending into the accident zone, however, it was immediately very clear that her skills would not be needed; that there could be no survivors.

On the ground Anne officially confirmed the deaths and completed the formalities, then they reboarded the helicopter for the short flight back to town. The mood was very sombre, but Anne had seen death before and she was used to dealing with such tragedies. She had always had the ability to deal with it then move beyond the moment, and knew she would go home, as usual, at the end of the day and put it behind her.

What she hadn't expected, and had no time to prepare for, was what awaited her at the airport . . .

Until she left school, Anne Richards had barely set foot outside Perth, except for a couple of trips to local holiday spots. She grew up with two older brothers and a selection of pets in the house her parents built in the 1960s in Alfred Cove, a southern suburb of Perth beside the Swan River. When she was old enough to start school, and with her brothers to guide her, Anne walked every day to Booragoon Primary School and later rode her bike to nearby Applecross Senior High School. Her father, Barry, worked for the Fremantle Port Authority and her mother, Zigrida, was a nurse. Theirs was a more or less typical suburban life of the 1970s and '80s, the less typical bit being the somewhat exotic food Zigrida prepared.

Zigrida and her mother, Berta Zaho, had fled from Latvia during World War II and eventually came to Australia as refugees after spending several years in displaced persons camps in Europe. Berta was a pharmacist in Latvia, in itself a remarkable achievement for a woman in the 1920s. Anne can remember her grandmother telling them stories about rolling the pills she'd compounded and growing digitalis plants to make digoxin tablets for her customers.

However, when Berta, her second husband, Konstantin, and Zigrida stepped off the ship in Fremantle in 1949, neither Berta nor her fifteen-year-old daughter could speak English. Berta was sent to work as a domestic at Northam District Hospital and Zigrida got a job as 'house girl' working for a doctor and his family in Northam. As she learnt English,

Zigrida practised her language skills doing crosswords and perusing the medical journals that lay about the doctor's house, a habit that may have influenced her later decision to train as a nurse.

Even though she didn't plan to be a doctor, Anne credits her mother with unintentionally promoting her own interest in medicine, saying, 'As a kid I always enjoyed looking at Mum's nursing books. They had a lot of fantastic photographs of all sorts of diseases, and body parts. Some pictures were gruesome, but they were all in black and white, and so intriguing, with the occasional drop of old blood on the pages! Zigrida had been a midwife and also worked at Royal Perth Hospital. Then after children she worked in a general practice.'

Best of all, Anne loved playing with the discarded medical paraphernalia that her naturally frugal mother brought home from work, just in case it might prove useful. Anne spent many an hour playing with an old stethoscope or putting together and dismantling the old glass syringes and needles that her mother used each year to inject brandy into the Christmas cake.

Having grown up surrounded by pets, Anne initially wanted to be a vet, and as a teenager got a job working in a suburban veterinary clinic. Quickly disillusioned by the seemingly never-ending process of euthanising pets, she soon decided that all the vet did was spay cats and dogs, or put them down, and all too often for reasons that didn't sit well with her.

Even so, in the end, the decision to do medicine was more pragmatic than anything; Anne got a higher tertiary entrance score than she needed for vet science so she accepted an offer to do medicine at the University of Western Australia.

Her parents were incredibly proud of her achievement, but

her mother especially was concerned about her capacity to withstand the long hours she would be on her feet. As a child Anne had developed slipped upper femoral epiphysis, a condition in which the growth plate at the top of the thigh bone is weakened, causing the ball at the top of the bone to slip down and backwards. Anne had quite extensive surgery when she was thirteen to pin and plate the weakened bone, resulting, she says with a grin, in 'an epic scar on my hip and a very unattractive waddling gait that seemed to bother everyone else much more than it ever bothered me'.

By this time already inwardly protesting against the social and behavioural restraints of her Northern European mother, Anne admits with another twinkly eyed grin that she wasn't above doing medicine just because her mother said she shouldn't.

For all that, she wasn't outwardly rebellious and, inclined to academia, she never really got into the medical student social scene while she studied at the UWA School of Medicine from 1986 to 1991. Anne would attend lectures then go home and study and, although she had friends among her classmates, she mostly socialised with her childhood friend Catherine. They first sat next to each other in Grade 1. Catherine helped Anne with spelling; Anne helped Catherine with maths.

In fifth year, during the elective term, most of Anne's medical cohort chose to go overseas to Africa or India to study. Anne, however, didn't have the financial wherewithal for an overseas airfare and she didn't want to go to Sydney or Melbourne or Adelaide or any other city because she figured that would be just like doing an elective in a tertiary hospital in Perth.

Deciding that an experience in rural or remote medicine

would broaden her horizons, she got out a map, searched all over the state and picked Halls Creek simply because she'd heard of it. It had been in the news. Unfavourably, she admits, but that was never going to deter her. Without any comprehension of just how far it actually was from Perth, she naively thought she would drive her little old Holden Gemini there. Conceding her lack of mechanical knowledge, however, good sense prevailed and she travelled the 3000 kilometres on a bus, an enlightening experience in itself.

The two weeks Anne spent at Halls Creek and another four weeks at Derby Hospital were life-changing and she still has vivid memories of them. It was her first real chance to live away from the city and to leap into a whole new world where no one knew her and, other than the obvious professional ones, no one had any expectations of her.

The doctor in Halls Creek used to fly his own plane and Anne was able to go with him to do clinics at Balgo, a community on the southern edge of the Tanami Desert, and Turkey Creek, another community on the Great Northern Highway, halfway to Kununurra. For a city girl who'd never flown in a small plane before, it was an incredible opportunity to see something of the magnificent landscape that is the Kimberley, and Anne loved every bit of it.

'It was,' she declares, 'so inspiring, and so much fun! I learnt a lot about myself and about my capabilities and surprised myself in so many areas.' She also had a hell of a good time away from the restrictions of her life at home in Perth. 'It changed my life and was the defining factor that brought me back to the Kimberley as a proper doctor.'

Before then, however, she had to complete the course and

qualify, which she did after a year's internship at Royal Perth Hospital. Meanwhile, her good friend Catherine had completed her studies and been appointed as a school psychologist in Kalgoorlie. At that time, as part of their residency, junior doctors could go to Kalgoorlie Hospital for a three-month emergency medicine term. Anne applied to go, knowing that she would be able to hang out with Catherine when they weren't both working.

Building on her adventure in the Kimberley, Anne found working in the emergency department in Kalgoorlie a different medical experience to her usual urban environment, with more responsibility. It was also more fun socially as a single female in a mining town. She and Catherine and her new group of friends, many of them the doctors, nurses and allied health staff she was working with, would go out together and enjoy whatever was on offer in the gold city. She says, without a scrap of regret, 'We worked really hard, then at the end of shift we played really hard. We went out on camping trips, we drank too much in the pubs and we danced the night away.' She returned to Kalgoorlie as a medical registrar the following year.

Although she was thinking about an eventual speciality – maybe orthopaedics, maybe physician training – it was meeting doctors in Kalgoorlie who were practising rural medicine that nudged her career compass in a completely new direction. When she returned to Perth, Anne met a foundation trainee from the very new Western Australian Centre for Remote and Rural Medicine training program who inspired her to have a conversation about the possibilities with the director of WACRRM. Anne applied to join the program at the beginning of the following year, 1996, and consequently it wasn't long before she returned again to Kalgoorlie, this time as a GP registrar.

Third time round Anne yet again enjoyed the work and the great social life, but when she was advised to do some general practice work either in an alternative private practice in Kalgoorlie or in another town for the second half of the year, Anne couldn't resist the urge to return to the Derby regional hospital. In order to get a job there, however, she had to be able to offer them practical procedural skills. Accordingly, in the first six months of 1997 she completed her Diploma of Obstetrics and Gynaecology and then successfully applied for a job as district medical officer in Derby. Having ditched the Gemini in favour of a Toyota Hilux, she loaded up her trusty ute with all her worldly possessions and headed north . . .

When Anne rolled into Derby after three days on the road, she stopped at the roadhouse to wash and brush herself off before proceeding to the hospital. It was about 8 p.m. by the time she strolled into the ED, where she was greeted at the triage window by a poker-faced old nurse peering at her over a pair of narrow-framed spectacles. Weary but full of enthusiasm, Anne said cheerily, 'Hello, my name is Anne Richards and I'm the new doctor here at the hospital.' With a lift of one eyebrow and a twitch of her lips, the nurse looked Anne straight in the eye and said drily, 'Dr Richards, if you choose to turn around now and escape, no one will ever know you got here . . .'

Chuckling with laughter at the memory, Anne says, 'She looked me up and down that first night and smirked as though she thought I wouldn't last five minutes in a town like Derby.

Then she handed over the keys to my hospital quarters, gave me quick directions on how to get there, and said, "See you tomorrow morning then, Dr Richards." She was such a good old stick. She actually got on really well with all the staff and was always good for a laugh. She used to come camping up the Gibb River Road with some of us young doctors and nurses and she had this amazing ability to throw together a fantastic meal for whoever needed it, out of what seemed to be nothing!'

Much as Anne loved her new job, it was incredibly hard work; so hard, in fact, that she never got around to unpacking her suitcase. Ruefully she says, 'I left that suitcase on the floor of my bedroom for years. After washing my clothes, those that didn't need ironing got folded up and placed back in the suitcase.'

Being a regional hospital, more complicated patients came to Derby from smaller hospitals and clinics. When Anne was on call she invariably worked very long hours; she'd either be overseeing a labour and delivery, or running the ED, out on a medical retrieval, doing a remote clinic, or on the wards following up her admissions. On top of the local patient load, most transferred patients were generally pretty sick or badly injured so it was constantly busy. Anne found herself managing chronic illnesses she'd never really seen before and traumatic injuries inflicted by domestic violence on a level she'd never dealt with before. It was a full-on five years, broken only by a year back in Perth training in anaesthetics, a bit of time in Exmouth Hospital, and five months working in a private practice in an upmarket suburb of Perth.

After completing her anaesthetics training, Anne found her role in Derby just as challenging but a little less stressful. In fact, she says it made a huge difference. 'Before I did anaesthetics, I'd always feel as if there was more that I could, or should have known to do. Whereas with anaesthetics training, I was more confident with what I needed to do, and that, in the end, I'd have done all I could.'

As for her five months of metropolitan private practice, it was such a blazing contrast to Derby Anne vowed never to do it again. With a shrug she acknowledges, 'It just wasn't me. I hated the fact that I had to dress up every day and wear proper shoes. I mean the patients were fine, they were nice, but I just didn't like the lifestyle. And I found I didn't like the ten-minute consultations with people I didn't know, day in day out, Monday to Friday. You don't get time to really connect with anyone.'

The experience did confirm for her that she liked procedural medicine more than straight general practice, and the wide variety of medicine she practised every day in Derby gave her plenty of opportunity to perform procedures, especially in ED. 'I like doing things that show an immediate result. You know, if you stitch someone up, or put a drip in their arm and fluid resuscitate them, or put them to sleep for an operation, or to set a fracture, and then watch them wake up with their problem sorted, there's an immediate outcome.'

Even though she was still living out of her suitcase, Anne settled into the community very happily, and acquired a kitten, which she named Zigi after her mother. When she and her mates weren't working hard, they were out camping, or walking in the gorges, or having luxurious weekends in Broome to balance the pressures of their jobs. Zigi went eve-rywhere with her. Anne covered many miles in her Hilux with the short-haired, skinny-tailed, fat-bellied tabby cat riding beside her. 'She was such a cool cat,' laughs Anne. 'She stood her ground with any mangy dog that came her way and made a point of despising any gentleman callers that may have come my way!'

In early 2003, not quite single but wanting to be, Anne volunteered to go to Kununurra District Hospital. They were short on anaesthesia-trained doctors, and Derby had several doctors available. Zipping her suitcase closed, as it was still half packed, she loaded it and Zigi into the ute and set off very early one morning to drive the 900 kilometres east to Kununurra.

One of the things Anne loved about the remote towns she worked in is that she could always find her accommodation really easily. The blue hospital sign is always one of the first coming into any country town. Proving just how small a place the Kimberley is for those who live there, when she rocked up to Kununurra Hospital later that night, rang the doorbell, and introduced herself to the night nurse, she was welcomed cheerily with, 'Great to meet you, Dr Richards, my mum is your patient in Derby and she's told me all about you!'

Anne met a lot of friendly people in those first few days at Kununurra Hospital. She was invited out at sunrise one morning for a paddle on Lake Kununurra, a reservoir built in 1963 as part of the Ord River Irrigation Scheme, nine years before the massive Lake Argyle main dam was opened, and around which the town of Kununurra has grown.

Out on the water in a kayak, Anne thought it was absolutely fabulous and was immediately hooked, despite everyone apologising for the 'terrible' conditions. Remembering that day, she says, 'It was a little bit windy and choppy but it couldn't have got any better in my mind. Plus they brought freshly baked homemade muffins and coffee to share. I soon ordered my own kayak and learnt how to bake muffins!'

On her first weekend off call, a group of nurses invited her to join them for a sunset cruise on Lake Argyle, some 70 kilometres out of town. The nurses were good friends with the crew that lived at the 'Top Dam', as it is known by locals, and they planned to camp the night in the caravan park. Anne had learnt very early on in her training to always keep 'in' with the nurses who, she says, 'share an amazing sisterhood, particularly in country towns'. Committed to working hard and having fun when they could, these were her kind of girls, especially when she discovered they also shared her taste for sparkling white wine.

They had a wonderful afternoon on the lake and readily accepted an invitation from the guys driving their boat to get together for a barbeque with the other crews at their staff house. The boys dragged a huge hunk of meat out the freezer and lit a fire, while everyone grabbed a cold drink and mingled. Before long they were all munching on salty rib bones. That night Anne met several blokes who could drive a boat, who lived on a lake in a beautiful part of the world, but only one of them was special. She and Greg Smith just clicked straight up. By the end of the night, she knew she'd found her paradise.

Greg was the owner of Argyle Expeditions, now Lake Argyle Cruises. A man of few words – unless he's talking boats and Lake Argyle – he had a dog, named after his Willys jeep, who was his constant companion. Despite Willy, when Anne introduced Greg to Zigi, the cat clearly approved. Absolutely astounded, Anne knew their relationship was going to last.

From then on, when not on call in Kununurra, Anne took every opportunity to explore Lake Argyle. Greg's home was the perfect base for long kayaking trips, or gentle bush walks, but sometimes she'd go to his house at the lake just to sleep, in peace; with no mobile phone coverage, no one could find her.

At the end of her locum placement, Anne returned to Derby, handed in her resignation and worked out the remaining three months of her contract. The day she finished, she packed that suitcase for the very last time, loaded all her gear in the Hilux and headed east with Zigi happily sitting up on the seat beside her. She had no job to go to, but was prepared to wait. She was back on the roster within a week.

Anne had been back in Kununurra just a short while when Marian Furness made an appointment to see a doctor in outpatients for a diabetes check-up. Marian and her husband Ray had moved to Kununurra for twelve months in the late 1990s to see what work opportunities there were in the fruit industry and they never left. At the hospital, she was sent in to see Anne.

Marian liked Anne's relaxed manner and says, 'She never made you feel as though you were being rushed or anything and she was always really genuinely interested in whatever you were talking to her about.' Marian decided she'd make her next appointment with Anne as well.

Sadly, their next meeting was at the Kununurra airport after the helicopter crash.

Ray Furness and some mates had gone fishing up on the coast very early that November morning. They were due to return before lunch. Late in the morning, a family friend came around to tell Marian that there'd been an accident. The friend started by saying, 'I'm sorry, I'm so sorry . . .' Marian thought something must have happened to his wife. Then he said, 'The second helicopter went down and they think Ray's been killed.'

Shocked beyond real comprehension, Marian and her daughter and grandchildren all went to the airport to await news, hoping against hope that Ray was alive.

When Anne and the crew walked into the hangar, the waiting group surged forward, eager to know what news there was of their loved ones. Marian reached Anne first and, being much shorter than Anne, grabbed her hands to attract her attention. Anne clearly remembers that moment. She says quietly, 'Marian looked up into my eyes and asked me if her husband was alive. I hesitated, unable to speak for a second, then I told her, as gently as I could, that he wasn't; that none of them were alive. It was awful; just awful.'

Sharing bad news with patients and their families is part of the job for doctors and it's stressful but, Anne says, 'Most times when you're the treating doctor of someone who passes away, you have, at the very least, a moment or two to collect your own thoughts before delivering the bad news; a moment to just separate yourself from the grief that is about to unravel. You usually have a moment to formalise in your own head the answers to the questions that are about to be asked of you; to "be the doctor".'

That day, however, Anne had no time to prepare herself for this particular 'doctor' role. Fourteen years on, neither Anne nor Marian remember much about the rest of that day but,

Marian says, 'It must have been just awful for Anne to go out there; awful for all of them.'

The next time she saw Anne, Marian was in hospital with cellulitis. Anne hadn't been on duty when Marian presented to the ED, but when she realised Marian was there, she went to see her. It was one of those instant-bonding, reconnecting moments that accompany shared experience. Marian hugged Anne, who readily hugged her back, understanding better than most the extent of her loss.

Marian started making regular appointments to see Anne in outpatients to monitor her diabetes and became 'Anne's patient'. Noting that there is something very special about their relationship in the aftermath of Ray's death, Marian says she's always hugged Anne when she sees her, whether in the consulting room or down at the post office collecting the mail.

Marian had never really managed her diabetes well and especially not after she was widowed, she admits, acknowledging that it was Anne who urged her to look after herself and helped her to manage her condition. 'She asked me, on one of those early visits, what I'd eaten for dinner the night before. I told her it was a packet of Cheezels. She said, "Now, Marian, I want you to do this. When you go down that shopping aisle and you see the Cheezels and chips, I want you to imagine a hypodermic syringe on the shelf because, if you keep eating like this, that's where you'll be going. You're going to end up having to inject yourself every day with insulin."' Laughing, Marian adds, 'Even now, all these years later, I can't see chips without seeing a hypodermic syringe as well.'

Anne says of their relationship, 'Over the years I helped look after her medical issues, and often saw her in clinic, or at the post office, or in the supermarket. We'd chat about her health, but also about other stuff; we still do. And every year, when the dry season ends and clouds start to build up, and the weather is hot and humid, she'd make a special appointment with me. It was probably the most therapeutic doctor–patient relationship one could ever have, and I was not necessarily the doctor!'

Having built a strong and continuous relationship with Anne as her doctor and chronic care manager, Marian really missed Anne when she went on maternity leave to have her daughter Samantha in early 2007, and again at the end of 2008 to have her daughter Alison. Anne's decision to return to work part-time after the arrival of the girls also put a bit of a spanner in Marian's works because, as she says, 'appointments with her were as scarce as hen's teeth because everyone got in and made their appointments as soon as the schedule came out'.

And then, in 2016, the system at the hospital changed and GP outpatient appointments were discontinued in favour of private practice GP appointments. Marian now attends a private practice in Kununurra, but misses her appointments with Anne. 'I was so comfortable going to Anne because she knew my story so intimately. She was someone I felt I could really talk to because she understood my situation.' Fortunately, they still run into each other quite often on the post office steps and Marian is just as interested in Anne's general welfare as she knows Anne is in hers.

After each of her babies arrived, Anne took a full twelve months' maternity leave, a luxury she acknowledges a lot of female doctors don't have, especially if they are chief breadwinner. When she returned to work after Samantha's birth, she dropped her obstetric and anaesthetics credentials on the grounds that 'I think you need to be actively working full-time to be able to maintain those skills appropriately. Now I am employed part-time for only my GP and ED skills, which suits me just fine. My family is the most important thing in my life now, and I am always grateful that the hospital supported me through those early years of child rearing, and continues to be flexible when it comes to my commitment to family.'

In April 2017, at the Rural Health West conference in Perth, Anne was presented with a Doctors' Service Award acknowledging her twenty years of service to rural communities. It's a recognition of which she is justly proud and one she never for a second imagined when she was a young Perth teenager reading her mother's medical books.

Anne has, she says, the very best life. She lives on an amazing lake in the most beautiful part of the world. She works part-time in the hospital that has played such an integral part in the course of her life. She's a full-time mum with two gorgeous daughters, sharing her life with the man who caught her eye the first time she saw that spectacular lake.

Indeed, the way she tells it, the Kimberley called and now she has it all.

6

The Heart Truck

Dr Rolf Gomes, outback Queensland

Jeneve Barnicoat can't remember exactly where she first heard that a doctor by the name of Rolf Gomes had created something called the Heart of Australia truck to travel around inland Queensland providing comprehensive specialist cardiology consultations on a regular basis. However, when she and her husband, Barney, received an email from their local department of primary industries telling them that Dr Gomes's truck was coming to Charters Towers, Jeneve decided that Barney should get an appointment.

Barney's last major overhaul had been seven years before when the AgForce Healthy Farmers initiative provided the opportunity for him to have a full health risk assessment in Townsville. Other than slightly elevated cholesterol levels, the outcome was generally good, and since then he had been seeing his local GP in the Towers every two years or so. They asked him how he was, ran a few blood tests and checked his blood pressure, and then he went home and got on with it. But he was now in his mid-sixties and his father had had some heart problems, so Jeneve was keen to err on the side of caution and felt that he needed to have a really thorough check-up.

The Barnicoats were living on their cattle station 75 kilometres south-west of Charters Towers just off the Flinders Highway. Their son, Kim, was running the place but Barney was still very active, so much so that he didn't 'do' holidays; the very idea filled him with dread. Working physically hard every day was his idea of fun and if there was no work at home for him, he'd go and help their neighbours or anyone else who needed a hand. Consequently, he was pretty fit, although he felt a bit dull in the head and had noticed a touch of breath-lessness when walking back up the soft lawn slope from the vegie garden to their house.

Agreeing it wouldn't hurt to go to the heart truck, Barney found it took a bit of pushing to get a referral from his GP when he seemed so well, but get one he did. Jeneve rang Heart of Australia and took the first available appointment, three months hence. Their lives went on as usual, with Barney work-ing daylight to dark.

On the due date, they drove into Charters Towers, where Jeneve left Barney at the heart truck having his initial con-sultation with cardiologist Dr Yong Wee and went off to the business centre of town to do some jobs and post a parcel to her granddaughter. She'd barely walked through the post office door when Barney rang her and asked, 'Can you come straight back.' When she arrived she found Barney none the wiser but Dr Wee was clearly perturbed as he told her, 'We have to get him to Townsville *now*.'

While Dr Wee made some phone calls organising an immediate evacuation to the Mater hospital in Townsville, Barney explained to Jeneve that he'd been all wired up to the ECG machine when the technician, who was watching the computer screen, asked him not to move while she went and got the doc. Dr Wee looked at the screen for a minute then asked Barney to get on the treadmill and walk. Still wired up, Barney had done that for another minute until Dr Wee called stop, and told him to sit and not move.

When Dr Wee got off the phone, Jeneve suggested they go home and she'd drive Barney down next day. 'No, no,' said Dr Wee, 'he has to go to the hospital here immediately and then go to Townsville. He must go now! He must go in the ambulance. He cannot go there in your car.'

Barney and Jeneve still didn't understand what the problem was and he had no pain or discomfort so they assumed it wasn't too serious. In reality, though they didn't say so, they thought Dr Wee was overreacting a bit and making a fuss about nothing. Even so, Jeneve took Barney to the Charters Towers hospital, where he was admitted and told not to get out of bed for anything until the ambulance came. While he waited, Barney spent the afternoon on the phone cancelling all the work he'd planned to do for other people in the next couple of days. The ambulance arrived about 5 p.m. and he headed east to Townsville while Jeneve went home to gather up the gear they'd need for a day or two at the coast.

When Jeneve arrived at the Mater next morning, Barney was booked in and waiting to go for a coronary angiogram. After the procedure, during which dye was injected into the vessels of his heart via a catheter in his femoral artery, Barney returned to his room to recover, quite sure that he'd be home next day. He and Jeneve were both genuinely shocked when the cardiologist called in that afternoon to tell him that two of his coronary arteries were completely blocked and two were 80 per cent blocked and he needed immediate open-heart surgery.

Barney Barnicoat was pretty much a walking disaster waiting to happen. If Rolf Gomes's heart truck hadn't come to Charters Towers, chances are he'd be dead.

Rolf Gomes was born and lived his first ten years in the teaming, chaotic, kaleidoscopic streets of Calcutta. His parents were middle-class professionals who both had jobs. He doesn't remember ever feeling poor but, even so, they didn't have a car or a washing machine or a television. The power supply was intermittent and he can clearly remember trying to do his homework by the flickering flame of a kerosene lamp when the lights had blacked out yet again. It's an experience that gives Rolf a lot of perspective about how fortunate he is that his parents brought him and his siblings to Australia.

His maternal grandparents lived with their nine children in Krishnanagar, a small village near the border with Bangladesh. They lived a subsistence kind of lifestyle with a few ducks and chooks, a couple of dogs and several coconut trees. They sold everything they produced but it was still a very humble existence. His grandfather was trusted in the community as a policeman and homeopathic type of medicine man. Rolf recalls an area on the front verandah of his grandparents' tiny two-room house where people waited to consult his grandfather.

It was partitioned off with a curtain. His grandfather had a small wooden chest that held a stethoscope and some pills and some other bits and pieces of his trade. When he visited with his family, Rolf remembers being curious about what happened behind the curtain and what his grandfather did with all those things. He wondered what happened to the people; whether they got better or not. Although he had no vision back then of being a doctor, he accepts that his grandfather's healing profession may have influenced his feeling of appropriateness when he finally segued into medicine.

Rolf's mother, Sylvia, is the most academically qualified member of her family. Thanks to her dogged determination to gain a university education and various scholarships that were integral to her doing so, she graduated with a Bachelor of Arts, an almost impossible achievement given her origins, but one that served as a model to aspire to for her own children.

Rolf's father came from a family where there were lots of university-educated people, particularly teachers, so attaining his economics degree was less of a challenge. His father's father was exceptionally bright and successfully completed a law degree, a maths degree and an arts/science degree at Oxford University. The small minority Catholic community to which their family belonged had raised the money to send him, and when he returned to India as a practising lawyer, out of gratitude he did mostly pro bono work for members of his church. He was very well respected but clearly didn't make a lot of money. Rolf has a sense that his paternal grandfather's practice of giving back underpins his own desire to give back to the country that welcomed his family so warmly nearly forty years ago.

Both of Rolf's parents wished for a better standard of living and wanted their children to have opportunities they knew they were unlikely to have if they remained in India. They migrated to Melbourne in 1983 with four children, four suitcases, $200 and a bucketload of determination to succeed. Grateful for the chance to start again in a new country, they both worked hard and Mr Gomes worked two jobs for thirty years to ensure their independence. Consequently, all of his children are wired to work and work as hard as they can.

Rolf was a very good student with a talent for maths and science. After he finished school, he embarked on a degree course in electrical engineering at the University of Melbourne. It was a prerequisite that all the students in their final year undertake a subject completely unrelated to engineering. He's never really understood why, but Rolf chose physiology and was surprised to find he liked it. That year he also applied successfully for a summer research grant called the Wright Scholarship and spent six weeks looking at the calcium levels in two-day-old rat embryos through the lens of a confocal microscope. Once again, he really enjoyed it.

Nevertheless, he graduated as an engineer and got a good job with a petrochemical company. However, it didn't take Rolf long to realise that he'd rather work with people than computers. When he reflected on all the years of his schooling he began to appreciate that he'd loved being surrounded by people and that people generally seemed to like his company as much as he liked theirs. And he acknowledged that he seemed to gravitate into leadership roles.

Opportunely, at just about the same time as he was second-guessing his career pathway, three Australian universities introduced a four-year postgraduate medical degree. Rolf saw it as a sign and promptly applied for the GAMSAT (Graduate Australian Medical School Admissions Test), which he passed. Flinders University in Adelaide had a very small intake, which didn't appeal to him, and he didn't think he could afford to live in the Harbour City if he studied at the University of Sydney. When he was researching the University of Queensland, he noted that it had the largest intake and then saw a picture of South Bank and thought Brisbane must be right near a beach. That tipped the deal and he successfully applied to UQ. Roaring with laughter, he admits that when he arrived in Brisbane in 1998 his first question was, 'But where's the beach?'

Although he never entirely discounted going into general practice, Rolf was drawn to specialised medicine, and cardiology in particular, during his cardiac-surgery term as a junior house officer. 'Added to which,' he says, with a self-deprecating grin, 'the other specialties were too hard and obstetrics scared the hell out of me.' His first sight of a heart beating in an open chest was mesmerising; the doctor in him was fascinated by its utter magnificence while his engineering brain instantly recognised it as the quintessential pump.

He met his future wife, Kylie, in his final year of medicine and they moved in together, announced their engagement and then married all within a couple of years. In his second year of residency, he went out to work in a rural area for the first time and was struck by the warm hospitality, friendliness and stoicism of the country people he met. He'd lie in bed at night wondering why there weren't better services in the inland and why the people who lived there didn't have better access to specialists. Frame by frame the idea of the heart truck evolved.

The images stuck in his head and he began talking about the heart truck even before he completed his cardiology speciality training at the Royal Brisbane Hospital. In particular, his words resonated in the empathetic ears of another of his cohort, Dr Rob Perel. Rob's mother, Margaret, grew up on an isolated sheep station in the Charleville district and he had extended family in the area so he immediately got the remote-from-services factor. Rob was definitely interested in Rolf's ideas and happy to discuss the potential with him, although his own priorities lay elsewhere. After they completed their training he took off to Canada for a couple of years to specialise in cardiac electrophysiology.

Meanwhile, Rolf opted to set himself up as a sole cardiologist in a business that is generally dominated by group practices. Although he was warned it would be financial suicide to go out on his own, he went anyway. Kylie says, 'Once he's made his mind up, that's it. He's going to do it.' Fortunately, the naysayers turned out to be wrong, which just confirmed for Rolf that people often base their opinions on conjecture, not fact. The analytical side of his brain will always look for the supporting facts.

When he left Royal Brisbane, he received a call from the Queensland Cardiovascular Group. They'd heard Rolf was going out on his own and wanted to wish him luck and to ask if he would like to be a part of their on-call roster. Setting up practice is an expensive investment, as is paying off a home to house your growing family, so Rolf had a lot of debt. He said yes, knowing it would be regular helpful income. He's still on the roster and takes his turn accordingly.

Rolf opened his Medihearts practice in the Brisbane suburb of Taringa and never looked back. His rooms are situated
a floor above a 21-doctor GP practice, which is convenient
for them and him. As busy as he quickly became, though, he
never relinquished the dream of a heart truck and remained
preoccupied with the idea of taking his services to the inland.
'I'd look at the technology in our rooms and wonder why we
couldn't just load it all into a vehicle and take it out to people
who don't have the kind of access to it that city people take for
granted.'

There was a long list of things he'd need, not least a lot
of money to build the truck and cardiologists to travel with
it. He went to see Jim Cameron, one of the directors of the
Queensland Cardiovascular Group (QCG), and asked if they'd
be interested in being involved in the heart truck initiative.
Jim invited him to come and deliver a presentation to their
next directors meeting, which Rolf did. He believed they'd
either think he was completely nuts or they'd go for it; no in-
between. Three weeks later, Jim rang back and told Rolf if he
undertook all the other details and made the truck happen,
the QCG would support the roster of cardiologists. They gave
him a letter of support that he took with him every time he
pitched his presentation to prospective investors.

He wrote to 180-odd GPs in the inland and went and spoke
with some of them. Everyone agreed it was exactly what they
needed, but he still had to find a million dollars to build the
truck and another million to run the program.

For the next couple of years, when he wasn't consulting
in his rooms he was trying to drum up interest in his project – a difficult enough assignment in any circumstances, but

a gargantuan one in this case, requiring a total leap of faith by investors as never before had anything like it been tried. Many people were interested but not prepared to commit, or they just didn't get it at all. The latter group disheartened him but as long as there were people who could see what he could see he was determined to keep trying.

Finally he hit upon the idea of talking to all the councils in rural and remote Queensland, and organised to host a breakfast meeting at the local government authority conference in 2013. He confirmed the venue and arranged for the invitations to be distributed to the councillors. That evening, his wife, Kylie, went into labour.

With the baby safely delivered later that night, Rolf jumped in his car next morning and returned to the Sunshine Coast to meet with all his breakfast guests. Devastatingly, due to a communication breakdown on the part of the organisers, only one of the councillors got the invitation, but she was the perfect one.

Donna Stewart was the mayor of Balonne Shire at the time. She has a reputation for straight shooting, bold ideas and total passion for the bush. When she read what Rolf was envisaging, she was immediately engaged by the brilliance of the idea and decided she'd go and hear what he had to say.

As she entered the room, which was beautifully laid out for a breakfast Rolf had personally paid for, Donna was instantly struck by the sheer presence of the very tall, very good-looking man standing in the middle of the empty room. She introduced herself to him and as they waited for no one else to turn up, he told her about his dream truck. She was captivated. Even now, several years after they became firm friends, Donna says she couldn't believe there was this person so committed to helping people in the inland, adding, 'He is the most amazing and inspirational person I've ever met.'

So it was that Donna suggested Rolf approach the resource industry to look for sponsors. Several coal seam gas companies were rocketing along with their push into the Western Darling Downs and Surat Basin, but their image had taken a beating and she knew they were always looking for good PR opportunities.

Serendipitously, the very next person of significance that Rolf met was Andrew Harvey, CEO of the Medicare Local. Like Donna, Andrew immediately grasped the merits of the heart truck, and facilitated Rolf's attendance at an upcoming energy and mining forum in the Surat Basin. Rolf was given a five-minute time slot at the end of a session to present his case, and by the close of the evening Arrow Energy had shown interest, later coming on board as major financial sponsor. In fairly quick succession, PACCAR Australia donated the use of one of their Kenworth K200 trucks, Brown and Hurley pledged to maintain it and iOR Petroleum committed to keep the fuel up to it.

Ross Fraser, from Frasers Livestock Transport, heard about the Heart of Australia project on the *Queensland Country Hour* and offered to sponsor the drivers of the truck. Frasers operates all over rural and remote Australia and, dealing as he does every day with people on the land, Ross knew as well as any the reticence and resilience of bush people who are well versed in doing without services. He says, 'Bringing the doctor to their doorstep made perfect sense to me.'

Suddenly, after several years of struggle to get going, Rolf's vision of the heart truck had legs, but the state and federal governments seemed disinterested and Rolf was still a long way short of his target. He and Kylie had talked and talked and talked about it for months and in the end she backed him when he opted to remortgage their home and borrowed another $800 000. Finally, at the eleventh hour, just prior to the program launch and thanks to the persistence of Senator Barry O'Sullivan, the state and federal governments contributed $250 000 apiece.

Rolf informed the directors at QCG that he'd be needing their roster of cardiologists in the foreseeable future, then the engineer in him went to work overseeing the building of the mobile rooms he'd long since designed. Constrained only by the shape and size of the 25-metre trailer, the fully air-conditioned Heart of Australia truck has two clinic rooms, a testing room and a reception area. On one side of the truck, the back half of the side wall lifts out and up to cover the verandah that slides out hydraulically for use as a waiting room.

Rolf went next to St Andrew's War Memorial Hospital to discuss resourcing. He'd talked to them in the early days and they'd been supportive though doubtful that he'd get the kind of corporate sponsorship and government assistance he was originally hoping for. Delighted that Rolf had succeeded in securing investment to get his show on the road, St Andrew's undertook to provide all the diagnostic equipment and technology he'd need to fit out the vehicle.

The Heart of Australia truck was officially launched in October 2014. In the first two years, the circuit grew from five towns in southern Queensland to thirteen towns across the state. Their roster now includes five cardiologists, an endocrinologist, respiratory and sleep physicians and, soon, a gastroenterologist.

Rolf's old friend Rob Perel is one of the five cardiologists. Rob works for QCG, who free him up three days every month to join the truck in Charleville and Roma. Rolf also joins the truck for the Dalby, Goondiwindi, St George and Moranbah legs, although he has been on every leg of the journey at one time or another.

Patients require a referral from their GP to access the service. Just as they do in the city, they must ring and make an appointment and then they're sent a text message the working day prior to confirm.

On the designated day, patients turn up, check in at reception and then see the cardiologist, who takes their history. The patient hops up on the bed for a physical examination and then they're either cleared to go, prescribed medication or directed into the testing room if they need further non-invasive investigations like an ECG, an ultrasound, a stress test, a breathing test and so forth. They don't have to go elsewhere for the testing and they don't have to wait; it is done then and there. Test results will usually be followed up when the cardiologist returns, or as soon as possible in more urgent cases.

The service is accessible to all people in all communities in the inland. It's not free but Rolf relies upon GPs to use their discretion and, where fitting, refer patients as bulk billed. While there is an out-of-pocket cost for everyone else, it's well balanced by the savings in travel, accommodation and loss of income. If you have to go away for a specialist appointment and, as a result, get a referral for another test you may not be able to have for some weeks or even months, it impacts on every facet of your life; worst-case scenario, by the time you get a diagnosis and treatment you might well be dead.

Barney and Jeneve Barnicoat know that as well as any. When the cardiologist in Townsville told them Barney needed a quadruple bypass urgently, they were totally shocked. Jeneve admits, 'We had absolutely no idea he was that bad. We had no idea he even had a problem. If the heart truck had not been in Charters Towers we'd not have insisted on a referral and we might have lost him.'

As it was, the morning after he learnt that he needed surgery, Barney was trundled into theatre at the Mater Hospital and the blocked sections of his four dodgy arteries were bypassed with pieces of blood vessel taken from the underside of his ribcage and his left arm. He has no memory of leaving his room, much less rolling into theatre. When he woke properly in the intensive care unit twenty-four hours later, what he *does* remember most vividly is that his head was completely clear for the first time in a very long time. He concedes it wasn't until he felt really well again that he realised he hadn't felt crash hot for a while.

Barney and Jeneve were extremely pleased to meet Rolf in Charters Towers several months later. Rolf sorted out a couple of teething problems Barney had been having with his medications and Barney now feels as well as he has in years. In fact, his only problem is Jeneve insisting that he practise having holidays. He growls and mutters about having nothing to do, but they gave it a first shot in 2016 when their daughter, Kylie, took them to New Zealand, and apparently it wasn't as bad as he imagined!

That's not a problem Rolf Gomes has to deal with. Even

though he loves people, relishes a good party and agrees in principle with the concept of 'life balance', Rolf himself inclines towards 'work more'. His upbringing taught him to appreciate and value the rewards that accompany hard work and he worries about a society in which people are so obsessed with stuff, saying, 'We live in a country with such a high standard of living, with so much disposable income and yet the rates of depression and mental illness are very high. So many people are miserable.' He believes there's a lot of therapeutic value in useful endeavour and that people actually like to feel productive – and he should know.

All these years while he's been pushing and negotiating and talking and persuading people to come on board the Heart of Australia, back in Taringa he's been running his one-man Medihearts practice as well. In fact, that business has expanded and he now has rooms at Ipswich, which he visits once a week. Even though he's incredibly busy, he says it's because he's a sole practitioner that he's able to include the Heart of Australia in his workload. He doesn't have to run everything he does by a board of directors and, while he never takes any of his patients for granted, he says, 'Everyone has a heart therefore there will always be people seated in the waiting area of my urban rooms.' Having that business ticking along feeds his mortgage and enables him to drive the heart truck initiative.

Reflecting on their progress thus far, Rolf says, 'Being an engineer definitely helped. While a doctor's pledge is to prolong life and ease suffering, an engineer's is to make things happen. If you want to get something done, ask an engineer and they'll immediately start joining the dots.' While his doctor brain was imagining the lives they might save, his engineering brain was breaking down the big picture into categories of jobs to be done: raise the money, engage community support, design and build the truck, find the staff, et cetera.

Although he was occasionally disheartened along the way, he never really feared that he wouldn't make it happen because he knew the pain of not doing it would eat away at him just as insidiously as untreated heart disease in people who have no access to treatment.

When Rolf was doing his cardiology training, he lay awake some nights thinking about the heart truck and the people it could help in rural and remote areas.

After he opened Medihearts, he'd lie awake some nights wondering how he could convince people to invest in his dream.

Now he has the heart truck, he lies awake wondering how he's going to convince the government of its value and contribution to the wellbeing of so many Australians.

In fact, there are a whole lot of things he worries about, not least the fate of thousands of people living out in the bush who are dictated to by a handful of people sitting in offices in the city. 'Why,' he asks rhetorically, 'does anyone think it is reasonable for a few people to be making decisions for other people with whom they wouldn't trade circumstances?'

He worries about opportunities going past because institutions are so politically straitjacketed they can't embrace the obvious, much less the innovative and adventurous. He worries that politics is starting to shape people's ethics instead of people's ethics shaping politics.

He worries about the leadership vacuum, saying, 'We've lost the really inspirational thinkers. You know, when Kennedy thought about sending a man to the moon it wasn't about anyone's local electorate, it was just an inspirational plan to explore the frontiers and it drew the whole human race along with it. Now everyone's worried about local issues; they're lobbying for cheap quick fixes and politicians have their own agendas.'

Rolf is not looking for money to build a memorial or to buy a new piece of equipment for an urban hospital; he's raising money so he can continue to deliver basic services to a portion of the population who've been denied them thus far because of their geography.

In just the first twenty months of operation, Heart of Australia saw 2627 patients and saved eighty-two lives, thirty of them with referrals for open-heart surgery. The heart truck covers about 8000 kilometres a month around Queensland and as people become more aware of its existence, the referral lists get longer. The specialists who travel with the truck are delivering education sessions to local GPs and, where appropriate, information sessions for the general public.

In an ideal world both the state and federal governments would be ensuring the heart truck's continuation and building its capacity, but while Rolf awaits their interest, his determination and commitment have been rewarded with support from an unexpected quarter. As recorded on *Australian Story* in May 2017, a family who wish to remain anonymous came forward with a donation of a million dollars toward the cost of a second truck. The look of joy and relief on Rolf's face was priceless.

Rolf Gomes is a big man with big ideas and now he's on a roll. Chances are he'll be lying awake sometime through the night tonight, thinking about the other services they could take to the inland and the other people they could help across regional Australia if they could just round up a whole fleet of heart trucks.

7

Walking the Line

Dr Molly Shorthouse, Nhulunbuy, Northern Territory

Early in 2011, late in the wet season, three crows landed on the top branch of a starkly sculptured dead eucalypt on the edge of one of the most remote Aboriginal communities in East Arnhem Land. Most of the time there's nothing at all unusual about any number of crows sitting on a branch, but something about the way these three were behaving triggered alarm bells for the local Yolngu elders, who recognised a very bad sign of *galka*, or black magic.

Shortly after, two teenage girls took their own lives. Fear sliced through the community and the threat of others following was very real. An Aboriginal health worker and the resident remote area nurse identified one young woman who was so at risk that they contacted the district medical officer (DMO), Dr Molly Shorthouse, in Nhulunbuy and implored her to organise the girl's evacuation to Gove District Hospital. At the time, Molly had no knowledge of *galka*, but having great respect for her colleagues' knowledge and abilities she trusted their assessment and immediately arranged the girl's transfer.

Molly had completed some years of training in emergency medicine and with the Royal Australian and New Zealand College of Psychiatrists, as well as in cognitive behaviour therapy, and had also commenced working towards her advanced specialised training in mental health since accepting the DMO post at Nhulunbuy in 2009. But, even so, she felt less than well prepared for this particular retrieval.

As she waited for the ambulance to arrive, the terror-stricken face of a man who'd hung himself a few months previously seared through her peripheral memory; another two boys who'd suicided before that slid unbidden into her mind.

When the clearly distressed girl was rolled into the emergency room Molly knew, looking into the abyss of her terrified, darkly beautiful eyes, that the teenager had no mental illness that she'd been trained to treat. Standing on the precipice of the unknown, frighteningly aware of the two other girls lying in the morgue a mere hundred metres away, Molly was deeply grateful for the knowledge and expertise of her Yolngu co-workers.

Molly is a third-generation Northern Territorian whose grandparents moved to Darwin from Adelaide in the 1940s. Molly, her identical twin sister, Alice, and two younger brothers, Daniel and Josh, grew up in relative isolation as residents of the solar-powered village their parents, Pam and Peter Garton, established on the fringes of Humpty Doo, a small community about 40 kilometres east of Darwin. Thriving like untamed weeds, the Garton kids went to the little Humpty Doo Primary School with a mixture of white and Aboriginal kids. Once classes were over for the day, they were gone.

For their first dozen years, they had no television or electronic gizmos to anchor them to the house; instead, they ran wild in the surrounding bush, leading the kind of wide-roaming, adventurous lifestyle that only outback kids can know. The siblings and any available neighbouring kids spent long happy hours building cubby houses, searching the bush for elves and fairies and escaping outside the borders of the solar village, where they'd clamber up and down sand dunes and swim in any handy creek. Never bored for a second, when the surrounding countryside failed to amuse them, the twins convinced their brothers and friends to play high-stakes games of double dare. Alice once dared Molly to eat an earthworm. Without turning a hair, Molly fried it in a pan, doused it in tomato sauce and gobbled it down with the speed of a Paul Jennings character.

When there were no more games to play, there were always pets to care for. They raised orphaned wildlife, kept wallaby joeys instead of puppies and made friends with the 4-metre olive python that lived in their ceiling.

And in between play and chores, there were plenty of books to read. Both Molly and Alice read and read and kept on reading long after they finished primary school and transitioned to Darwin High School, which they accessed each day by bus. Molly loved the school's location, on a very beautiful piece of land overlooking the sea, but says her motivation to succeed had nothing to do with the scenery and everything to do with some wonderful teaching.

After achieving a suitable ATAR, tertiary admission rank, Molly was studying a Bachelor of Science majoring in neuro-anatomy, neurophysiology and psychology at the University of Adelaide when she became a devotee of the world-renowned physician and neurologist Oliver Sacks. She read everything he ever wrote about his particular fascination, the human brain. It was the catalyst for rerouting her career path into medicine and, ultimately, for her intense interest in mental health and the emotional wellbeing of her patients and the people around her.

Illustrating perfectly the theory that people who grow up in rural and remote areas are likely to have a preference for rural and remote practice, Molly took advantage of various rural scholarships and placements offered to her because of her background and obtained her medical degree from Flinders University in 2003.

Offered a residency in emergency medicine in Hobart, Molly worked in Tasmania for a couple of years before switching to psychiatry and relocating north to Melbourne to work as a psych resident at St Vincent's Hospital. While she was at St Vincent's, with absolutely flawless timing, she went up to Byron Bay for a few days and met her future husband, Aaron Shorthouse, aka Aari, who was staying there with his sister. Aari, a pilot, was flying between Townsville and Papua New Guinea for a mining company. Given the nature of his work and living as they were at opposite ends of the eastern seaboard, Molly and Aari's relationship developed by mail and telephone.

In 2008, Molly moved to PNG to be with Aari who was, by then, working with his missionary parents, Kevin and Gail Shorthouse, providing assistance to the villages in the north of the country. From their base at Vanimo, on the northern shore of PNG just near the Indonesian border, Aari and Kevin, also a pilot, would fly their little Cessna all over West Sepik Province. Winging each day through dangerous mountains, landing on almost inaccessible airstrips, they'd deliver basic supplies to remote villages. They provided vaccinations for babies, retrieved pregnant women at risk of complicated childbirths and cared for people who were ill and less able. They even carried the occasional pig to be sold to pay for supplies needed in the villages. Molly was terrified every time she waited with Gail, watching for the first tiny sign of the Cessna reappearing before the sun slipped below the horizon. After every close call, and there were several, she'd think, *I'm not letting him go again*, but Molly admired them all enormously and soon realised it wasn't her place to dictate what Aari should or should not do. As she reconnected with life lived in a remote community, she found she particularly enjoyed living in another culture and learning another language. It piqued her curiosity about Australia's Indigenous peoples.

At the end of twelve exhilarating and inspirational – albeit sometimes scary – months, Molly needed to return to practise medicine in Australia, but neither of them could conceive of living in a big city again. They knew Aari needed to be able to fly and they were both keen to live with and learn from Indigenous Australians, so an opportunity to return to the Northern Territory to work with the Yolngu people in Nhulunbuy, 650 kilometres east of Darwin and 1100 kilometres west of Cairns, sounded perfect. According to the Australian Bureau of Statistics, Nhulunbuy and all of the communities in East Arnhem Land fall into the category of 'very remote', a classification that includes 85 per cent of the country but only 8 per cent of the population.

Immediately after she and Aari moved to Nhulunbuy in early 2009, Molly enrolled with the Australian College of Rural and Remote Medicine (ACRRM) to acquire the extra knowledge and skills she needed to work as a remote GP and RG (rural generalist) in East Arnhem Land. Credentialed to work primarily in a hospital setting as well as community-based private practice, RGs need to have gained recognition for advanced specialised training in at least one of the appropriate disciplines: emergency medicine, internal medicine, Indigenous health, mental health, paediatrics, obstetrics, surgery or anaesthetics. Molly chose mental health.

While Molly was learning her way around her new role at Gove District Hospital, Aari slotted in to a job flying with a Northern Territory airline. Out in the community, Molly was practising the primary health care that is the core of all general practice, but at the hospital she was dealing with a lot of emergency medicine because of the very high incidence of chronic disease and traumatic injury, most of the latter the result of alcohol-related violence. Added to that, there are specific dangers in the area – crocodiles, poisonous snakes, cane toads, excessive heat and sometimes viciously damaging storms as the cyclone season evolves. In a community burdened with mental health issues, and with one of the highest suicide rates in the world, Molly was also frequently called upon to practise her psychiatric skills.

All of Molly and Aari's previous experience directed them to hasten very gently and respectfully into the community, but from the first day they felt welcomed and comfortable. Molly was incredibly busy but both of them were happy with their career choices and even more delighted, soon after their arrival, to realise that Molly was pregnant. There were only locum GP obstetricians coming and going from Gove District Hospital that year but Molly had a wonderful midwife who supported her all throughout her pregnancy and for the delivery.

Molly and Aari's first son, Noah, was born in late October 2009. Very early one morning, Molly had woken with a contraction, followed closely by her waters breaking. Calmly walking outside to watch the first rays of the sun streaking in over the trees, she felt an overwhelming urge to go to the beach.

When she woke Aari and told him, he was surprised – 'Aren't you meant to go to hospital?' – but agreed to take her to the beach, where she spent a couple of hours walking up and down on the sand, dropping to all fours to pant through the pain when it viced her.

There was no one else anywhere on the beach as the sun rose across the water. Molly was on her hands and knees, gripped by excruciating pain, in a zone of her own, when Aari nudged her and, pointing to the water, urged, 'Molly, Molly, quick look at this, look at this.'

As the contraction waned, she turned to see a huge hammerhead shark swimming back and forth along the shoreline. It stayed for five or ten minutes then swam back out to sea. When the midwives at the hospital helped Molly deliver Noah into Aari's hands a few hours later, the powerful river of energy that flowed through her felt as though it connected them all. In a way, Noah's birth strengthened their links to the Yolngu community and landscape.

There's a certain serenity reflected in Molly's stunning dark-ringed, green irises as she says, 'The Yolngu believe my totem is *Mana*, meaning shark, and Noah has always been absolutely obsessed with sharks – toys, drawings, dreams, stories.'

Like many doctors working in remote communities, Molly has the utmost respect and admiration for her Indigenous co-workers. She says, 'In the Gove hospital, we have an Aboriginal health liaison and an Aboriginal health worker who is the daughter of one of Arnhem's most important elders. Their cross-cultural knowledge is priceless.'

Molly acknowledges Aboriginal health workers as experts and is eternally grateful to the Yolngu staff who were by her side after the crows came and the two girls suicided. Their assistance was, she says, invaluable.

Even though she was the DMO by then, as the third girl lay gripped in the talons of sheer terror, Molly was starkly aware of her own inadequacy in the face of tens of thousands of years of Yolngu culture and beliefs. Fortunately, the Yolngu staff were able to guide Molly as she managed the teenager's initial care. After lengthy consultation with her family back in their remote community, Molly organised the girl's relocation to Cairns, where she had close family members to support her and access to appropriate psychiatric and psychological care. The girl's recovery and subsequent return to the community about six months later confirmed Molly's belief in the importance of working in local communities with local staff rather than dictating systems and solutions from afar.

Of course, as DMO, mental health care was only one

facet of Molly's myriad responsibilities. With Aari in the role of house husband looking after Noah, she recalls long days and sometimes even longer nights on call; nights when she'd be standing in the emergency department suturing someone's head while the RN held the phone to her ear so she could answer a call from one of the far-flung communities for which she was responsible. Once or twice she even directed a resuscitation over the phone while stitching.

Things got even more hectic during Molly's second pregnancy, which was nowhere near as tranquil or easy as her first. At around fourteen weeks she felt the first pain of a tear in one of the ligaments that connect the two halves of the pelvis. The pain intensified as her gestation progressed. Being one of those people who when they are stressed or distressed just get busier and busier, Molly says, with some incredulity, 'There were only a handful of doctors back then and we had way too many duties. I can remember being thirty weeks pregnant with Leo and answering phone calls all night from the remote area nurses in communities across Arnhem, plus we had to be on call for the hospital. There are triple the doctors now and we don't undertake the DMO role anymore. It's much safer.'

Back then, however, pregnant and ready to give birth, the ligament tear dictated that Molly have a caesarean section to deliver her second son, Leo. Molly says her experience was a positive one as the two GP obstetricians who performed her surgery and the GP anaesthetist were all close and trusted friends who'd been in Gove all year. And, as with her first baby, her midwife once again guided her right through to delivery date. Molly's admiration for both of the midwives who supported her through her pregnancies is so strong she actually questioned her career choice at one point, wondering if she should have been a midwife instead.

In fact, by then, she was questioning her whole career in medicine. As a woman, wife, mother and a doctor she was constantly overwhelmed by shared knowledge of the tragedies in other people's lives; of childhood sexual abuse so horrific it left her gasping for fresh air to try to stop the waves of nausea flowing over her; of people who appeared as community leaders but carried their own hidden suffering; of the cycle of intergenerational trauma and neglect that she knew people were trying, without opportunity, to break. And finally, by the realisation that if you ask the right questions, almost every patient will have mental health issues to share with you instead of their physical ones.

By the end of 2011, Molly and Aari came to the conclusion that it was time for a change.

Molly resigned her position and they relocated to Hobart, which she imagined would be everything that Nhulunbuy was not. While she was there, she commenced further training in emergency and child and adolescent psychiatry, learning quite a lot about herself and her responses to her experience in East Arnhem Land along the way. Even so, neither she nor the psychiatrists nor the GPs nor the mental health RNs she was working with recognised that Molly herself was in trouble.

The emotional cost of working among people who were so disadvantaged – who dealt with such extreme trauma – had fractured her own mental wellbeing. Add the hormonal rollercoaster of a new baby and she was paddling backwards flat out just to keep on top.

On reflection, she says, 'I didn't seek any help and I think that's a big issue because nurses, doctors, ambulance officers, in fact all emergency service workers, have this sense that we should be able to cope. But piece by piece by piece it adds up until you end up with your own episode of trauma often without quite realising it.'

It was Aari who recognised it. Acknowledging his 'extraordinary emotional intelligence', Molly says, 'It highlights that you don't need training in mental health to be able to recognise distress in another human. All of us can play a part in helping those with mental illness.'

Later, from the safe haven of elsewhere and with the clear eyes of hindsight, Molly was able to identify some pieces of her own hidden distress that weren't directly related to work. At the time, in the random reaches of her awareness, they had seemed interconnected and she had shoved the lot into the back recesses of her mind and soldiered on.

Molly realised that her reaction after the suicides had been more than just burnout – she was indeed suffering from postnatal depression (PND). Despite her surface positivity about Leo's delivery at the time, her earth-mother self had never really imagined not being able to deliver her second baby as naturally as her first. Although her logical doctor self knew that the only safe way to bring Leo into the world was by caesarean section, in her heart she felt a measure of guilt and even deprivation that it hadn't been the same lovely event she'd had with Noah. And then there was the guilt about feeling those feelings at all, surrounded as she was by people who know real deprivation and hardship. While she had smiled cheerfully at every passing face and set about nurturing Leo through his first months of life, those buds of negativity wrapped up in the raging hormones of childbirth had blossomed and nudged her stealthily and relentlessly into PND.

It was an incredibly difficult period in Molly's life that added another dimension to her understanding of mental health and mental ill health, and highlighted for her the absence of bias where mental illness is concerned. It can hit anyone at any time. Because of her experience in both Arnhem Land and Tasmania, Molly has also learnt that mental illness disproportionally impacts on people who are disadvantaged, regardless of where they live.

While she was in Hobart studying, Molly worked as a locum at an outer suburban GP practice to enhance her GP skills. It was a bulk-billing practice in a low socio-economic area. She was stunned to realise that many of people she was seeing faced similar trauma and sadness to those she'd seen in East Arnhem Land and that their mental health needs were just as neglected.

People would come in with simple straightforward requests for attention to some physical ailment and, because she asked the right questions, would end up baring the true, untreated trauma in their lives: abuse, bullying, suicide, learning difficulties, loneliness, depression . . .

Molly heard it all and understood for the first time that social, economic and cultural disadvantage is not confined to remote, out-of-sight communities, though it's certainly easier to ignore in them. She realised just how essential GPs are to the mental health and wellbeing of their patients and how integral good mental health is to good physical health.

One day, some months after they'd left Nhulunbuy, Molly was reading about *kintsukuroi*, the Japanese art of repairing broken pottery by bonding the pieces back together with lacquer mixed with powdered gold, silver or platinum. The guiding principle behind the practice is the understanding that the repair of the object is part of its story and not something to be hidden.

Molly was deeply moved by the article as it reminded her of all the people she had guided through mental illness who were changed but also stronger and wiser after the journey. Accepting that, like an object, a person can be more beautiful after they've fallen to pieces helped to repair some of the cracks in her own mental wellbeing and reminded her just how much she valued working in mental health.

Coincidentally, around the same time, Molly had a conversation about rural and remote health with Dr Lucie Walters, a rural obstetrician and then president of ACRRM, who inspired her so much she began to reconsider her future. Consequently, at the end of 2014, armed with the extra training she'd undertaken and a determination to highlight the incidence of mental ill health in rural and remote Australia and lobby for better support for both patients and professionals on the front line, Molly packed up and returned to East Arnham Land with Aari and the boys.

Shortly after they arrived back in Nhulunbuy, Molly met a female patient on the ward who had a whole range of the chronic diseases that plague people in remote locations. She'd been described during handover as 'particularly difficult' because she refused to go to Darwin where they could give her dialysis and scans and various treatments that might prolong

her life. She was only fifty-one and really sick but she refused
to have a drip and some of the intravenous medication that
would have helped to offload the excess fluid she was carrying.

After rounds, Molly went and spent a while reading her
file. She read that the woman had lung disease resulting from
bronchiectasis that had damaged her airways, which she'd
gotten from living in poverty in overcrowded housing as a
child. She had kidney disease as a result of poor management
of diabetes, which she had because she was unable to hunt or
live her traditional life and had instead been eating a western
diet. She'd also been the victim of family violence because of
alcohol abuse in a community where everyone suffered intergenerational trauma and collective grief as a result of past
events. And then, as Molly read on, she concluded that instead
of helping the woman, every time the 'white fella' health system intervened there seemed to be some adverse consequence
adding to her health morbidity. As far as Molly could see, she
had every right to be angry.

For the next couple of days, when Molly did her ward
round, she would just sit and talk quietly with the woman and
leave her room as soon as she was asked. She didn't try to
examine her or take bloods or force any medical intervention.
On day three, the woman let Molly put a drip in and administer medication to get rid of the excess fluid. She felt so much
better she went home the next day.

Over the next year she presented at the hospital three or
four more times, and each time Molly just waited until the
woman told her what she wanted. Then one night she came
in very sick. She had pneumonia on top of all her other
health problems and her organs were barely coping. Molly

went in and listened to her heart and did all the usual doctor things while the woman just looked at her as though she was humouring her. Finally, she took Molly's hand and held it tight, looked her straight in the eyes and said, 'I'm going to die tonight, Molly.'

Even as she said, 'No, we can do this and do that,' Molly knew she was probably right. She was aware that most of the woman's family were out of town at a funeral but she called in the two family members who were available and the three of them held the woman while she died.

After her last breath, when the feeling of energy had left her body and left the room, Molly put her stethoscope on the woman's chest, thinking it would be silent and knowing the family were waiting for her to make the 'official' announcement.

Molly heard the slightest and quietest of final heartbeats for what seemed like an eternity and stood quietly, not wanting to move until it stopped. She's not really sure what happened in that moment but something shifted in her and changed her. Now, as she moves around among her patients, Molly often thinks of that woman. She imagines her watching and hopes she does nothing the woman might disapprove of.

There were other, external, changes after Molly's return to Nhulunbuy, too. Restricted alcohol laws had really kicked in and they were seeing way less incidence of traumatic injury presenting at the hospital and less incidence of domestic violence. Community leaders were stepping up and leading the changes integral to closing the gap from their end but, then as now, all levels of government needed to facilitate that by providing appropriate support services to enhance what the leaders were already doing rather than going in and taking over. Constantly open to learning herself, Molly says, 'The Yolngu are one of the strongest cultures in Australia and their leaders are worth listening to.'

Molly, Aari and the boys resumed learning local language and culture and the boys in particular meshed right into the community. Noah and Leo went to the local school and outside school hours they went hunting and fishing with their mates, although apparently their spear throwing needed some work! Life was much simpler and quite uncluttered in Nhulunbuy and living there was a privilege Molly and Aari took seriously and treated with great respect; they knew it was a unique opportunity for all of them. They had more time together as a family with no commuting and no busy social schedule. They never thought about needing a babysitter; the boys went everywhere with them.

Reflecting on their life's journey thus far, Molly says, 'Our time in Arnhem Land has forever changed us – Aari, myself and the boys – and I can never express enough gratitude for what we have learnt from the Yolngu. We have moved on, as most *balanda* (white people) do, because it wasn't our land, our place and our family – that's part of accepting stages and transitions. But we know now we will always live rural remote.'

In 2017 Molly and her family returned to Tasmania which, she points out, 'has the second highest suicide rate in Australia (after the NT)'. Promisingly however, she continues, 'It's at the beginning of establishing a rural generalist–led medical service for its non-urban population, so I am excited about being part of leading that change.'

As she told a breakfast briefing for federal politicians in Canberra in 2016, she wants to see the mental health system in Australia 'turned around, and upside down and inside out'. She wants 'dirty laundry out on the line and for advantaged people to know what is happening to the disadvantaged in Australia because no one chooses disadvantage'.

With that in mind, Molly was delighted to contribute to the position paper on mental health released last year by the Rural Doctors Association of Australia (RDAA). A blueprint for developing long-term strategies to address the mental health needs of rural and remote Australians, it's about bringing the care to the people because, as she says, 'If you want to close the gap, you have to close the distance!'

She's also excited to have been asked to join the board of the General Practice Mental Health Standards Collaboration, a national group that monitors and makes decisions about mental health skills training, making sure that GPs are trained to an appropriate standard. 'It's the GPs,' she says, 'who must feel comfortable working in mental health because in rural and remote areas they're usually the only choice. Even in some urban areas they're often the first and only choice. Ultimately, they are in the position to make the greatest contribution to improving the mental health of Australians.'

Molly is frustrated by the age-old adage that people who go to rural and remote areas are either 'missionaries, mercenaries or misfits', and with the belief that professionals who choose to live and work in remote areas are not good enough to work in urban environments. It's a misconception that's steadily being corrected thanks in big part to the rural generalist pathway developed by ACRRM and the RDAA to address the medical skills shortage in rural and remote Australia.

In fact, apart from the much broader experience she has gained from working in a remote area, Molly has also had the opportunity to participate in and speak at conferences in a way that she'd never have had as an urban GP. Not to mention the boards and committees she's been invited to join . . .

Moving as she has been between remote and urban Australia, flanked by two completely different cultures, language groups and public health profiles, Molly is quickly becoming more proficient at walking the line between two worlds. She is balanced, compassionate, empathetic and articulate and she's steadily building a reputation for no bullshit, especially when she's addressing policy writers, politicians and bureaucrats in urban Australia who think they have a gilt-edged right to make decisions about people they've never met, who live in places they've never heard of, in circumstances they make no effort to understand.

As she contemplates the current status of rural and remote health, Molly Shorthouse clearly sees the shattered edges of 'the gap' and she's on a mission to fix it. If you were to compare this undertaking to the art of *kintsukuroi*, you would have to conclude that her particular brand of lacquer is laced with pure gold.

8

On a Wing and a Prayer

Dr Barry Kirby, Milne Bay Province, Papua New Guinea

Slogging along the last stretches of the incredibly awful, winding dirt road through the jungle and mountain ranges between Lae and Menyamya in Papua New Guinea's Morobe Province late one night in 1990, Barry Kirby had already driven past the sack lumped on the left-hand side of the road when he realised it was a body.

Mindful that he was pulling a heavy trailer loaded with building materials behind his equally heavily loaded Landcruiser, he carefully braked and backed up until the car lights exposed a woman lying wrapped in a traditional *malo*, or cape. As Barry got out of his vehicle, a large group of people surged up from a village hidden down below the edge of the mountain road. He walked over to the woman, asking the gathering group in pidgin English what was wrong with her. One of them told him she'd been sick with *pekpekwara* (diahorrea) for a few weeks and that they thought she was a witch so she'd been shunned; they said she was up on the side of the road to die. Her cheeks and eyes were very sunken and he could see she was very weak.

Barry knew he was only fifteen minutes from Menyamya, where he was project manager on the site of a high school his company was building. He said he'd take her to the hospital there, so a couple of the men picked the sick woman up and went to throw her on top of the load in the back but Barry told them to put her in the cab beside him.

As he began to drive off, he realised she was probably very uncomfortable so he tried to make conversation, but neither of them spoke the other's language and she clearly didn't speak pidgin. He asked her if she had any brothers or sisters and she just smiled at him. Even though she was so emaciated and dehydrated, he was very moved by that smile.

When they arrived at the hospital, Barry gently carried her featherweight in and laid her on a bed before going to the hospital orderly's house to rouse him to come and attend to her. It was about 10.30 p.m. by then and the orderly told Barry the volunteer doctor was six hours away in Lae, but that he would go down shortly and see to the woman.

Barry went back and found a blanket to cover the woman while she waited and, patting her shoulder and promising to return in the morning, he headed off to his quarters. When he called in to the hospital the next morning to see how she was, he found the bed empty and the room reeking of bleach. He asked where she was, and was shocked to be told that she'd died in the night.

It was a defining moment in Barry Kirby's life.

———

Going to school at St Laurence's College in Brisbane, Barry was never much of a student, being far more interested in sport and what was happening at home on the family farms in northern New South Wales and in the Blue Mountains than in academia. After he matriculated in 1968, he got a job as a trainee accountant at Milsons Point in Sydney.

Bored witless by mundane inactivity, he spent his weekdays thinking about the Megalong Valley farm in the Blue Mountains that he'd take off to at the end of the week. Up there, he spent his time chasing cattle, building fences and working in the stockyards. Enamoured of the wide-open spaces, the practical hard work, the clean, fresh air and the everlasting stars of the mountains, he dreaded returning to his dingy little office in the rushing, busy city every Monday morning.

Barry is nothing if not impulsive and one morning he decided he'd had enough. He threw in the towel then and there, without a plan, although he figured he might follow in his father's footsteps and become a carpenter.

As luck would have it, he went to mass that week and ran into a builder he knew who worshipped at the same church. After the service, Barry strolled up to him and asked him if he had a spot for an apprentice.

'For you?' the builder asked.

'Yep,' said Barry.

'Come and see me tomorrow,' the man replied.

And that was it. Barry had an apprenticeship and, four years later, a ticket as a chippy.

He worked in Sydney for a time before moving to Alice Springs to set up his own business. When that went belly up several years later, he took a sabbatical and moved to Cairns to live for a while. Even though he was now questioning the faith that had sustained him when he was younger, Barry recognised a yearning to do something good and useful with his life. Medicine did vaguely cross his radar but his dismal academic background discouraged him.

Instead, when he saw an advertisement for a project manager role with a construction company building a high school in the Morobe Highlands of Papua New Guinea, he considered his father's long-time wish that he should meet the wonderful people of PNG, and applied for the job. A World War II veteran, his father had been in an Australian artillery unit fighting against the Japanese on Shaggy Ridge in 1943 and although he rarely shared his personal memories of the war, he always spoke about the beautiful people and magnificent landscapes of PNG.

The construction company told Barry that, if he went, he'd be the third project manager they'd had up there, as the first two had bolted. Typically, Barry was inspired rather than daunted and went anyway.

When he arrived in Menyamya in 1986, few Papuans wore European clothes. Most still favoured traditional dress: grass skirts and a *malo* worn over the head for women; a small *tapa* covering made from grass and tied at the back with twine for men. There was a variety of decorative beading and/or bone embellishment and most of the women carried a *billum*, or sling pouch, with a baby in it or sometimes food from the markets.

Barry hadn't banked on it, but he fell in love – with the people, the country, the slower pace. It was a dramatic change from what he'd known in Australia. Even so, it took a little while for him to really comprehend the true level of disadvantage that surrounded him. He found himself vexed by the contradictions and wondered how people could have so much back in his homeland when there were so many people in PNG with so little. Barry felt compelled to help them.

He dabbled with the idea of medicine again, but mostly he considered it a pipe dream and, instead, appreciated that he could at least help in a practical way by building schools and facilities for the communities.

And then he drove to Lae to collect a load of supplies in 1990 and, on his return, came across the woman on the side of the road.

Devastated by the unknown woman's death, Barry found himself walking out of the hospital promising himself and God, 'Okay, that's it, I have to do this. Lord, I'll give this ten years and if I can't get into medicine in that time, I'll just keep doing what I'm doing . . .'

At the time, Barry had a good job, he was financially secure and the company was pressing him to stay; he knew he'd be giving all that up. He also knew he'd have to undertake an undergraduate degree before he could even get into medicine, and that being a student in his forties with his academic background was not going to be a walk in the park. He really had no idea how he was going to begin or how he would make it happen but, nevertheless, committed himself to train as a rural and remote doctor then return to PNG to assist in the one way he knew would make a tangible difference in communities like Menyamya.

Barry resigned and returned to Sydney, where he admits he

needed help just to fill out the application forms to enrol in a biomedical science degree at the University of Technology. He persevered and, with his particular version of tunnel vision, got through. His journey grew wheels when he transferred up to Brisbane to complete his degree with honours at Griffith University four years later.

Supervised by Dr Harry Gibbs, Barry was doing a project on ultrasound and carotid artery disease for his honours year. In the course of his research he visited the vascular and cardiology labs at Princess Alexandra Hospital, where he met the director of the clinical physiology department, Colin Case.

There's something a bit yin and yang about Barry and Colin. Forever dressed in tradie shorts and a short-sleeved drill shirt, both with plenty of pockets for carrying stuff, and thick-soled work boots, Barry is a sturdily built, medium-height force of nature with a big voice, a big heart and an endless supply of optimism. Col is quieter, more thoughtful, a scholarly look-ing man with a mind that computes data like code and a dry, quirky sense of humour that completely contradicts his mildly straitlaced manner. They were either going to be great mates or bored with each other in five minutes. A mutual love of boats, respect, strong faith, and lashings of genuine humanitarianism ensured they developed an immediate camaraderie.

The more he heard of Barry's story, the more Col admired his ambition. Realising how tough his mature-age student existence must be, Col helped Barry get a part-time job as a cardiac technician doing ECGs in the cardiology labs. Coincidentally, Col's marriage was breaking up, so when he discovered Barry was living down at Manly on a boat that he'd bought as a virtual wreck and had done up, Col started escaping down there on the weekends with his twin sons to help with a bit of spit and polishing followed by a feed of prawns on the back deck. They became good mates.

In due course, Barry completed his degree and started applying for a place in medicine in Australia. Reflecting on the age discrimination that allowed every university Barry applied at to turn him down, Col says, deadpan, 'He even dyed his hair. He had hair back then.' Barry just roars with laughter, but there is something in his sea-blue eyes that suggests the cut ran deep.

Back at the drawing board, Barry decided he'd try doing a PhD first, and Harry Gibbs and Col co-supervised his project. Barry found another part-time job working in the Aboriginal and Torres Strait Islander Commission office at Woolloongabba. Shaking his head, Col reminisces, 'Barry had some great ideas for sharing health information and education with the clients of ATSIC and a talent for engaging high-profile people to speak on behalf of them; Christine Anu and Neville Bonner are just two of the names that come to mind. He also had an uncanny capacity for setting little health projects to help people, for which he had no funding but somehow, someone would always come to the party and pay for them to happen.'

Meanwhile, by then in his mid forties, Barry's sense of urgency was escalating. Refusing to believe that he couldn't achieve his goal, in the second year of his PhD he began applying to universities in countries that might appreciate his very specific ambition to work in PNG: the University of Papua New Guinea in Port Moresby, the Vellore Medical College in southern India, the University of Nairobi in Kenya . . . so it went on.

Then he answered a phone call from a friend who was in Madang in PNG, who'd had dinner the previous evening with the dean of the School of Medicine at UPNG. He told Barry, 'Ring the dean on Monday. I've just spoken to him and he said he wants to have a yarn with you.'

The UPNG medicine faculty rarely takes expatriate students – their usual intake is restricted to Papuans and Pacific Islanders – but the dean invited Barry up for an interview during which, Barry says, 'He basically told me, "You've contributed already to this country so we'll give you a go."'

Finally in with a chance, Barry was over the moon. He sold his boat for $50 000, nearly enough money to pay for his whole course, and his parents helped him with the rest. He moved to Port Moresby at the beginning of the next academic year. Because he'd done four years of biomed, plus his honours and a year and a half of his PhD, the University of PNG credited him with a year of his medical degree and he went into second year. He recalls, 'We had some marvellous lecturers, and because the hospital was right next door to the uni, we practically lived over there after second year.'

Jumping straight in with his usual enthusiasm, he says he was a little shocked when reality set in. 'It was a bit of a war zone. It was all critical tropical medicine, and it was all very good training for me but I had some catching up to do and it *was* hard, it was tremendously hard and the conditions at the school were extremely difficult. Everyone boards at the school and the rooms were, without exaggeration, only about three metres by two and a half. Then there was the food, which consisted of tinned fish and rice every second day and lamb flaps in between. It was really tough and I didn't know whether

I'd survive it. I thought if I did, it might affect my health for the rest of my life but I was so concentrated, I kept going. I had this very clear focus on this poor community where people die very young and women especially have a very difficult life; the image of the woman who died at Menyamya was still there in my memory. It gave me constant energy to go on. I knew exactly what I was doing and why I was doing it.'

Although they hadn't sighted each other in a long while, Barry and Col kept in touch by occasional email, and in 2000, while Barry was in his final year, Col and his sons went to PNG to walk the Kokoda Track with Barry and several others. By the time they set off, the others had cancelled for various reasons but Barry, Col and the boys – now about twenty-one and in their final year of uni – went anyway.

As they walked, Barry told them stories of his experiences working in PNG thus far and started saying to Col, 'You could do this. You ought to get your medical degree and come up here and work.' Although it initially appeared to be a wild idea, Barry admits he actively encouraged Col to do medicine because he hoped he'd come up to PNG and help him.

About halfway up the track, Col says his sons got in on the act and started urging him to have a go. With a droll look, Col says, 'There's something about the tropics. Your brain gets half cooked and you start agreeing to stuff you wouldn't normally.' By the time they returned, having successfully completed the walk, Col had promised he'd sit the Graduate Australian Medical School Admissions Test. He aced it.

Consequently, at the age of fifty-one, thanks to a change in the attitude towards mature-age students just the year before, and with every intention of going to PNG and joining Barry,

Col applied successfully to do medicine at the University of Queensland.

After graduating, he did two years' residency at Princess Alexandra Hospital, still with a view to going to PNG, but then chance stepped in. In the September of the second year, Col was sent on a five-week rotation to Charleville and Augathella in South West Queensland. At the time, the incumbent GP in Augathella had announced his intended relocation to the coast at the end of the year, and he encouraged Col to buy his practice.

Knowing that he needed some practical bush experience before he went to PNG, Col decided to go ahead, enrolling at the same time in the Remote Vocational Training Scheme to acquire the skills he'd need to accompany that experience. He bought the practice and moved to Augathella at the beginning of 2007. By the time he finished his course and might have sold up and gone to PNG he'd fallen in love with Sue Lyons, a local grazier, and with the life of a country doctor.

Meanwhile, back in Port Moresby, while Col had been getting started in medicine, Barry was graduating from UPNG. He finished at the end of 2000, with just $50 in his pocket and his motivation completely undiminished. Because it was in a very rural community and near the water, he applied to Alotau General Hospital, in Milne Bay Province on the eastern tip of mainland PNG, to do his internship. Floating in the back of his consciousness was the possibility of owning another beautiful wooden boat. But first he had to gain some experience and save some money, no mean feat on his wage of $250 a week.

Barry had been working at the hospital in Alotau for about three years and was starting to think about where to next when both his parents became very ill at the same time. He came back to Australia to look after them and, for the duration, got a job in the emergency department at Redland Hospital in Brisbane. Taking advantage of the opportunity while he was in the country, he applied to the Australian Medical Council to do the course that would enable him to work as a fully accredited doctor at home as well as PNG.

He soon realised he didn't much like practising medicine in Australia as it was veering too far away from his original vision, but he stayed on well after his parents recovered and passed his qualifying exams. Then he hotfooted it back to PNG and a job as senior medical officer on Lihir Island. There were about 17 000 Papuans on the island and around 5000 expats.

While Barry was happy to be back working among the people he most wanted to help, he eventually concluded that he needed to have at least obstetric, probably gynaecology and maybe paediatric skills, because most of the people he saw were women and babies and although there were no real statistics he believed the maternal mortality rate was scandalously high.

To that end, in 2010, he enrolled in a Diploma of Obstetrics back in Alotau and practised obstetrics for a whole year at Alotau General Hospital. He was sixty years of age and once again working for nothing; he lived off the money he had saved while working on Lihir.

As well as all the clinical work required – including performing forty caesarean sections and several other procedures on his own throughout the year – Barry had to do a research project and submit his findings. Wanting it to be something really purposeful and meaningful, Barry chose to investigate thirty-one recent maternal deaths in the area. The reports that already existed told him nothing conclusive or even helpful about why the women had died. He organised to go out to the villages and into the very rooms where those women had spent their last hours and talk to the people who were there when they died; he wanted to ask them what actually happened. He knew it was the only way they would be able to begin addressing the maternal mortality rate.

Barry spent three very busy months going out to remote islands in Milne Bay Province in a little boat, visiting the beach villages then hiking up into the ranges to the even more remote mountain villages, talking to the people who were present for each of the thirty-one mothers' last moments. Despite their tidy woven bamboo huts, their apparently cheerful and relaxed lifestyle, their magnificent views of tropical splendour and, for some, pristine turquoise oceans, Barry found these people's lives to be incredibly challenging, at least from a health perspective. There was no trained help on the ground, no electricity, no reliable form of communication and usually, at the very least, a full day's walk, sometimes with an added boat trip, to get to the nearest health clinic, if they were even inclined to go. Barry's gut instinct was that isolation was the major factor in the women's deaths. As he completed his investigations, he came to believe that all of the women would have lived had they been in a health clinic with appropriate assistance.

It had as dramatic an impact on him as the death of the woman he'd found on the side of the road.

Barry called Col, who was by then happily practising in Augathella, and asked him if he would help translate all the information he'd gathered into reportable statistics for his project, which, of course, Col gladly did. In that same year, Col booked a locum to cover his practice, flew to Alotau and went out on several clinic visits with Barry. This has since become an annual pilgrimage, interspersed with visits to Tanzania where, for many years, Col's partner, Sue, has spent several weeks each year supporting an orphanage in Arusha.

Once Barry had submitted his project, passed his exams and gained his obstetrics and gynaecology qualification, he initially focused all his attention on reducing the number of women dying in childbirth in Milne Bay by training staff in the health centres to deal with emergencies at time of delivery. Noting that it's a two-way street, he says, 'Every situation and incident is an occasion to learn as well as teach.'

The next steps were even more elemental. Barry explains, 'We went and bought some baby baths, filled them up with nappies, pads and pants for the mothers, bed sheets, toilet paper, oil and powder, and singlets and pants for the babies.' As he travelled around holding clinics wherever there was a gathering of people, he gave each expectant mother one of the bundles and explained to them the advantages of going down to their nearest health clinic in good time for their delivery.

Additionally, dusting off his carpentry skills, Barry got the local men to help him build waiting houses next to the health clinics so that mothers would have somewhere to stay when they came in. He also gave long-distance mothers market money to buy food so that they could afford to come to the health centre and wait.

Since Barry has been working in the area, the maternal mortality rate has been reduced by 75 per cent. He aims to reduce it to nil but that's a goal that depends on educating men to look after their women and not beat them. At least two of the thirty-one deaths Barry originally investigated were suicides committed as a result of domestic violence. It will take a great deal of education and perseverance to turn around an entrenched culture of violence towards women, but he has an idea . . .

In 2014, Barry invested in an aircraft, an amphibious de Havilland Beaver with skis that enable it to land on water. He'd earned his pilot's licence in 1980 but hadn't really used it much other than putting in the minimum hours to maintain it. After watching the market for several years, he'd spotted the Beaver for sale in Minnesota in the USA. The exchange rate was favourable and the seller was prepared to keep it in his hangar and let him pay it off, so Barry paid the deposit, which he'd saved from a doing a locum. When he made the final payment twelve months later, he flew to Minnesota to collect the plane, then flew it to Alaska, where he did eighty hours training with an instructor before flying it back to San Francisco, dismantling it and shipping it home. He rebuilt the plane at Archerfield in Queensland and then flew it to Alotau, where he now uses it 'flying doctor' style.

When someone needs Barry's professional help in a remote village, they can radio him and he will fly straight in or, at the very least, support and advise the local health workers until he can get there. The Beaver has a long history of use in the remote areas of Canada and Alaska and its old technology means that it is easier and more practical to maintain in Alotau than a modern machine would be. Its particular attraction for Barry, however, is its distinctive sound, which he hopes will help him address domestic violence.

It's a leap that makes some sense when he explains, 'The guys up there are pretty stoic, warrior types with little education. They're subsistence farmers, practical men with age-old beliefs that no one's ever challenged before. It's a very male-dominated, chauvinistic society and domestic violence is an accepted part of their culture. They don't want to talk about women's business so I've had to think of a way to attract their attention and engage them so that I can teach them that they should be bringing their women down to the health clinics to have their babies. I want them to learn to cherish their women and to understand the pain the women go through to deliver their babies and maybe to not have so many babies.'

It's a tall order, but he has a plan. When he was a kid growing up on the family farm, radio serials were all the go. One of Barry's favourite characters was Hop Harrigan, an American comic-book aviation hero, and Barry can still clearly hear the sound of the Rolls-Royce Merlin engine starting up in Hop's aircraft, heralding the start of the program.

Barry's plan is to write and produce a series of plays to educate men about childbirth, danger signs in pregnancy, domestic violence and appropriate behaviour, using the Beaver to transport his hero around. He'll engage Papuan men to perform the plays while he's working at the health centres and record them so they can be played on the radio.

Working on the premise that sound brings on thought, the

introduction will be a recording of the Beaver's engines, which
Barry hopes will attract immediate attention among the men
and ensure a connection to the life lessons he's planning to
impart. He has no idea if it will work but says, 'Sometimes you
have to lash out with crazy ideas and just make them happen
and hope they'll work.'

His occasional sidekick Col says drily, 'Barry has a habit of
starting things without knowing how he's going to make them
happen and somewhere, someone in the world pops up and
provides the resources he needs. They inevitably work because
his enthusiasm is infectious.'

That said, initially Barry funded all his work in PNG himself by doing locums in places like Lihir Island, remote Western
Australia and Kazakhstan. Gradually, as word of his work
permeated the Alotau neighbourhood, some local businesses
began providing in-kind sponsorship, and then Canberra-
based organisation Send Hope Not Flowers heard about him
and came on board.

Send Hope Not Flowers aims to help women survive
childbirth in developing countries by encouraging people in
Australia to donate the staggering amount of money that is
thrown out of vases in maternity wards every time a mother
is discharged with her new baby. Since hearing about Barry's
work, the charity has undertaken to provide the funding for
the baby-bath bundles that he distributes. Even better, the contents of the bundles are purchased in Alotau so it's a win-win
initiative.

Early in 2017, Barry's work also received support in the
form of a $100 000 grant from the Australian Agency for
International Development, which he will use to expand his

program, and a visit from NSW Senator Concetta Fierravanti-Wells, who promised to support his application for recognition of his own charity, The Hands of Rescue. Barry was delighted when THOR was registered by the Australian Charities and Not-for-profits Commission and granted full tax-deductible status by the Australian Taxation Office on 20 April 2017. 'It means,' he says, 'people in Australia can now donate directly to THOR if they wish.'

Barry's patients are very poor. Unlike people in first-world countries, their expectations are very low, but he wants to give them the very best care because he doesn't believe they deserve anything less. A glimmer of tears sheens his eyes as he says, 'It breaks your heart to see how accepting of tragedy they are.' He wants to support the health centre staff so that they can support their people better; to not just fix stuff, but teach the Papuans to fix things themselves.

Barry won't live in Australia again, although he will always come home to see his parents, now in their nineties, and his sister, all of whom are very proud of him. He loves his homeland but he gets bored very quickly in the land of plenty; the whingeing grates on him and he can't find the same passion here where people have so much.

He's been used to spending time on his own and doesn't get lonely although there've been occasions when he's wished there was someone he could share some special moment with; a mountain panorama, a gloriously feathered bird, a night sky full of diamonds. In recent months, Barry and his Papuan emergency nurse, Kila Dobo, have been enjoying a developing relationship but it's early days and they're both taking it slowly.

Fred Hollows is one of his personal heroes and sets the bar

as far as Barry is concerned. 'He went out there and saw the need among the Aboriginal people and said, "I can do something about this" and he did.' Ultimately, Barry wants to set up a Fred Hollows–style foundation so that when he's gone the work can and will continue. He says that while medicine is not a highly desirable occupation in PNG, there are plenty of Papuans who have the capacity to take over running the program. He has a succession plan in mind and is hopeful that he can oversee it.

In the meantime, Barry's inner strength and faith give him the confidence and authority to go on. That's what sustains him – that and knowing that this is the right thing to do.

9

Dr Polarbird

Dr Kate Kloza, Casey Station, Antarctica

On 22 December 2010, the Australian Antarctic Division's icebreaker *Aurora Australis* was anchored in the harbour at Casey Station in Antarctica for the annual resupply. Various station crew were out in the polar morning lending a hand with the lengthy process of transferring fuel from the ship to the onshore fuel tanks via a pipe snaking across the harbour.

Taking on roles they'd not normally assume is one of the many attractions of going to the Antarctic, according to those who've been. Multitasking with the best of them, station medico Dr Kate Kloza was in an inflatable rescue boat helping to safeguard the floating fuel pipe from hunks of drifting ice that might damage it when she was called urgently to the *Aurora Australis*.

Kate had been at Casey for six weeks when the icebreaker arrived bringing supplies and a second summer doctor, John Cadden. Given no details over the open airwaves, she imagined that one of the ship's crew had a problem and that John wanted a second opinion. She'd not been on the icebreaker before and, after the driver nudged the boat up against the side of the ship, couldn't help a quiver of excitement as she climbed the swaying rope ladder up to the bunker door and scrambled on board.

Looking around with intense interest as one of the crew guided her to the ship's medical facility, it never occurred to Kate that the patient she assumed she was here to see would be someone she knew, let alone a good friend . . .

Kate Kloza grew up in inner suburban Brisbane, undertook her education at St Rita's school at Clayfield and spent her holidays at the beach. A city girl through and through, there was nothing even mildly rural about her upbringing.

She doesn't know why she wanted to be a doctor, only that she never considered any other career path. In Grade 8 or 9 her class participated in an event to raise money for the Hamlin Fistula Ethiopia organisation, but it was reading Dr Catherine Hamlin's book *The Hospital by the River* that really sparked the burn under her plan to do medicine.

Unfortunately, by the time she completed her secondary studies with an OP (tertiary entrance rank) of 2, the University of Queensland had changed their protocols for medicine, making it a postgraduate degree rather than undergraduate. With no time to waste, Kate searched around Australia for undergraduate courses and applied successfully to attend the University of Adelaide medical school. She moved to South Australia to begin just after she turned eighteen.

RFDS Senior Medical Officer Dr Claire Schmidt with her husband Stevo and children Amelie and Toby on their cattle station north west of Charleville, South West Queensland. *Photo: Stevo Schmidt.*

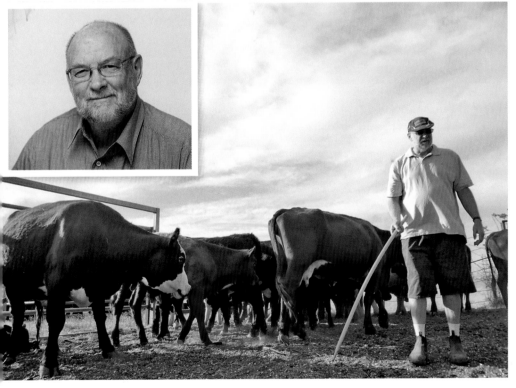

Once the local GP, Dr Rick Newton now balances telehealth and farming at Tullamore in Central Western NSW. *Main photo: Rick Newton. Photo inset provided courtesy of Rural Doctors Network NSW.*

ABOVE: When she's not in GP mode, Dr Sara Renwick-Lau enjoys all the benefits of living in her special kind of paradise in Mallacoota, Victoria. *Photo courtesy of Vanessa Janss.*

BELOW: Joyce Crombie enjoys renewed sight thanks to her 'Eye Angel', Brisbane-based ophthalmologist Dr Bill Glasson, who provides regular clinics to the people of central western Queensland. *Photo: Bill Glasson.*

LEFT: Dr Anne Richards lives her dream life with her family on Lake Argyle and working at the Kununurra Hospital.
Photo courtesy of Linda Hannig.

RIGHT: Dr Rolf Gomes was still a cardiology student when he first dreamed up the concept of a mobile cardiology unit. Now the Heart of Australia truck rolls through inland and outback Queensland on a regular rotation taking specialist services to the bush.
Photo courtesy of RACQ.

Pictured with her husband Aari and sons Noah and Leo, GP Dr Molly Shorthouse is vitally interested in the mental health and wellbeing of both her patients and her medical colleagues who work in rural and remote Australia.
Photos: Aari Shorthouse.

RIGHT: Dr Barry Kirby and his emergency nurse Kila Dobo in front of the de Havilland Beaver he recently bought to provide aero-medical services in the Milne Bay area of PNG. (LEFT) He is greeted enthusiastically wherever he goes . . . *Photos: Barry Kirby.*

When Dr Kate Kloza went to Antarctica for the first time it never occurred to her that she'd be performing an emergency appendectomy on one of her mates soon after she arrived. *Photos: Kate Kloza.*

RIGHT: GP Dr Brad Murphy with the signed door that flaunts his country music connections; and (ABOVE) with fellow Navy veteran and patient Gerry Fulton at the 2017 Anzac Service at Bargara, in the Wide Bay Coast region of Queensland. *Photo courtesy of Vic Sumner, Bargara Buzz.*

ABOVE: Paediatric and Child Health specialist Professor Elizabeth Elliott in Fitzroy Crossing; and pictured (INSET) with Aboriginal and Torres Strait Islander Social Justice Commissioner June Oscar. *Photos: Elizabeth Elliott.*

BELOW LEFT: Chester and Loie Wilson. *Photo courtesy of Leonie Eckel.* BELOW RIGHT: The quintessential country GP, Dr Chester Wilson provided medical services and much more to the Charleville community for decades before semi-retiring to the role of locum GP. *Photo: Loie Wilson.*

Dr Janelle Trees pictured with RAN Rob Atkinson (LEFT). Janelle initially struggled to get into med school and then became the first Indigenous person to graduate from Sydney University with honours in medicine. Now she's settled happily as the GP at the Yulara Health Centre in Central Australia. *Photos courtesy of Claudia Jocher.*

Not long after he graduated, Dr Bob Balmain was involved in a life-threatening traffic accident. His second chance at life underpinned his approach to delivering medicine to the people of South West Queensland during his sixteen years as Senior Medical Officer with the RFDS. (LEFT) Bob taking a call during a clinic in outback Queensland; and (BELOW) ready to fly. *Photos: Bob and Helen Balmain.*

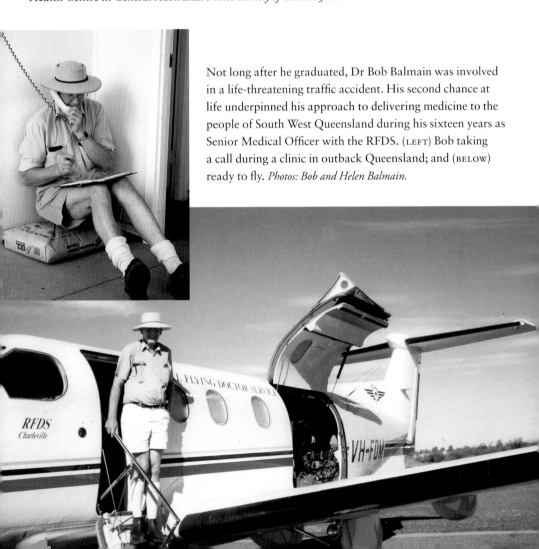

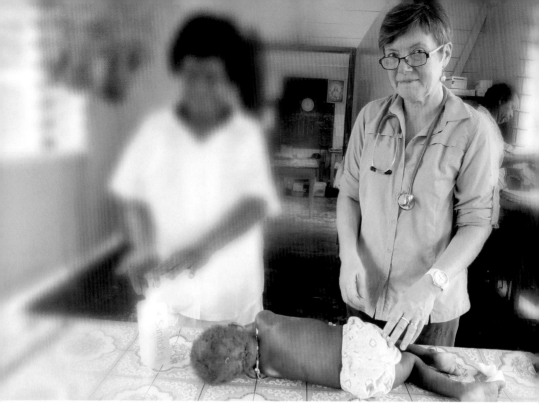

ABOVE: Dr Jenny Wilson treats a child while working within PNG. *Photo courtesy of Gayle Slonim.*

BELOW: Dr Paul Duff emigrated from Ireland to be a GP and ultimately a partner in a practice in Bright, Victoria. During the snow season, his practice provides medical services to the Mount Hotham Resort. *Photo: Paul Duff.*

After graduating and then completing her first-year residency at Royal Adelaide Hospital, Kate commenced work as a resident medical officer while trying to decide which career pathway she wanted to take in medicine. In the three years she worked as an RMO, she found she best liked the challenge and pace of emergency medicine and she enjoyed surgery, learning to do several basic procedures like appendectomies. However, she also discovered during that time that she didn't really suit hospital-based practice. Given her urban background, Kate was a little surprised to realise that something about the crowd scene no longer worked for her and, remembering Catherine Hamlin, she began to reconsider her options.

Hitting the internet, she started googling rural and remote practice, thinking she'd suss out what skills she needed to develop to take her overseas to some remote location that was crying out for doctors. While she was trying to decide if she could actually work in medicine without all the support networks that underpin urban practice, she realised there were remote places in Australia literally begging for doctors.

Then, searching for specific rural and remote jobs, she stumbled upon the Australian Antarctic Division (AAD) website. Although it was contrary to her vision of third-world opportunities, everything about Antarctica appealed to her. The pictures of the stations, the snow, the ice and the people stoked her sense of adventure and the idea of working as a solo doctor so far from all she knew fired her imagination.

Kate threw her hat in and went back to work in the emergency department. She wasn't sure she'd get an interview much less a job first time round, but hoped the AAD might explain the shortcomings of her application and alert her to the additional skills and knowledge she needed to accumulate to be successful down the track.

Two months later, the chief medical officer of the AAD Polar Medicine Unit (PMU), Dr Jeff Ayton, rang Kate to ask if she was still interested and invited her down to AAD headquarters at Kingston in Tasmania for an interview. The daylong meeting took place in two parts. The morning was devoted to Jeff and the selection committee asking her about her education and training up to that point, her experience and clinical skill set, her interest in Antarctica and the impacts on her future education and study. Kate was also asked to analyse and respond to some clinical scenarios as if she were practising in an extremely remote location.

During the afternoon she was assessed for suitability for station life, the key elements being her capacity to deal with stress, anger, extreme isolation, et cetera, and her willing-ness and ability to do jobs on the station outside of medical work. She was asked to consider her response to challenging situations that might occur with other people on the station knowing that relocation was not an option.

Following a comprehensive psych evaluation and a day-long medical assessment, both of which took place in Adelaide, Kate was delighted to be offered a job and tasked for next rotation at Casey Station leaving Kingston in November 2010.

In short order, she handed in her resignation, worked out her notice and packed up and stored all her worldly goods. She didn't even have time to go home to see her parents, although they flew down to see her in Hobart before she left for Antarctica. Kate relocated to Kingston for the pre-departure training, which was divided into two areas.

First up was medical training, conducted in Kingston by the PMU doctors and undertaken with the newly recruited doctors from all of the stations. The PMU has exactly the same medical equipment as the hospitals on every station so that doctors can learn to use and maintain these resources. The group also went to Royal Hobart Hospital to learn how to use the laboratory attached to each station medical facility. They did blood films and counts, bacterial cultures and growths and learnt how to make agar plates. Then they spent ten days at the dental school in Melbourne to learn dental procedures, and four to five days working with different physiotherapists in Hobart learning basic physio skills. They also had training in IT, e-health and the computer systems they would encounter; they learnt to take X-rays and to sterilise equipment; and they talked about polar-specific medical issues like hypothermia, frostbite and snow blindness.

In addition to all that, every expeditioner must complete community training, so the medical cohort also gained their certifications to ride quad bikes, work at height, drive forklifts and fight fires. They all learnt to tie knots, read maps and erect polar pyramid tents, and they attended HR sessions explaining the code of conduct, rules and expectations for living and working on an Antarctic station. Ready to give anything a go, Kate appreciated every opportunity in the comprehensive month-long training program and enjoyed getting to know all her fellow expeditioners, including mechanic Jose Campos, who became a good pal.

Early in November 2010, Kate and the senior communications officer, who like her had signed on to stay through the following winter and a second summer season, travelled in with sixteen summer-only crew, including Jose. The summer-only crew were scheduled to open up the station ready for planned summer work programs. The comms officer's skills were required because they'd be opening up the blue ice runway at Wilkins (about 65 kilometres from Casey Station) for incoming aircraft, and Kate was required because the AAD always employs two doctors during the busy summer months. As the Wilkins runway was not yet open, the new crew went in by plane to the American station at McMurdo, where they switched to a C-130 Hercules equipped with skis instead of wheels, enabling them to land on the small ski-way at Casey.

Flying into McMurdo and then landing later at Casey, Kate felt overawed and totally excited just to be in Antarctica. At the same time, while everything was new and fascinating and quite different to what she'd known before, Kate found it very easy to slot into the strict protocols and routines of the station, saying, 'Rules and regulations were all I had known so it wasn't hard to comply with them.'

Nevertheless there were some challenges, the greatest of which was getting over the awkwardness of toileting out in the field where there are no trees or features on the vast snowy-white landscape to provide privacy. Complicating matters, because expeditioners can't be leaving frozen pee all over the place, they must pee into a bottle (no mean feat for women) and take it back to the station with them. Down to earth and pragmatic by nature, Kate fast overcame any embarrassment about announcing that she needed to pee and where exactly she was going to do it so that those out with her could all face in the opposite direction.

Her good humour and natural, easygoing personality

pretty much guaranteed her popularity and she quickly became known around the station as the Mung Bean Queen, because she's vegan, or Tradie Katie because, clad in regulation Hard Yakka clothing, she was always keen to get on the tools and help out Jose and the other tradies. Ultimately though, for reasons that escape her now, she became known as Polarbird and then Dr Polarbird and the nickname stuck so well it has become her social media tag.

Professionally, Kate found it fairly easy to transition into her new role thanks to the warm welcome given her by Dr Kevin Harmey, who was reaching the end of his posting at Casey and looking forward to heading home after a year on the ice. By the time he left with the *Aurora Australis* in late December, Kate was well versed in the idiosyncrasies of her new work environment and familiar with all of the personalities with whom she lived and worked closely.

Apart from dealing with any injury or illness, Kate's role on the station was to look after everyone's general health and wellbeing and organise monthly medical examinations to pre-empt any brewing problems. Rumour has it she wasn't above confiscating all the Snickers bars on the station and using them as bribes to get everyone in for their check-ups!

There are also occasions when a doctor is required out in the field just in case they're needed or as part of a search-and-rescue operation (which is why there is always a second doctor during the busy summer season; the station complex can't be left without one). As well as search-and-rescue operations, Kate participated in search-and-rescue practice sessions, and was responsible for providing appropriate training and practice for lay surgical assistants so that they would be well

prepared for any circumstance any time they were needed in
the medical facility.

Even so, Kate had been told during her polar medical training that surgical emergencies rarely happen in the Antarctic
and that, statistically, it was very unlikely she'd have to operate
on anyone. She never for a second imagined that just six weeks
after she arrived at Casey, and three days before Christmas,
she'd be whipping out Jose's appendix!

Tasked with overseeing the fuel transfer, Jose had been
monitoring the exercise from the focsle of the *Aurora Australis*
since midnight on that December morning. By 4 a.m., all was
progressing well so he decided to take advantage of the offer
of a cabin and went to bed to catch a few hours' sleep.

He was woken a couple of hours later by a sharp stab of
abdominal pain, the first of many. Being as fit and healthy as all
expeditioners must be to join the Antarctic station crews, Jose's
initial thought was food poisoning. As the pain worsened, however, he realised it might well be something even more serious
and tried to get out of his bunk to go for help. The subsequent pain momentarily skewered him and hunched him over,
rendering him unable to stand straight and unable to walk.

Falling back onto his bunk, Jose contemplated the implications. He knew he needed medical help immediately, but
when he located the cabin phone he couldn't find a phone list.
His next best bet was getting himself up to the hospital one
deck above. After taking several agonising minutes to pull on
his boots – no bare feet allowed – and rug up, Jose dragged
himself out to the nearest stairs and hauled himself up, one

gut-wrenching step after the other.

Edging gingerly in through the medical facility doors, he was dismayed to find the doctor wasn't there. Nor was he in his cabin. Knowing no one on the ship, and being unfamiliar with the layout, Jose's only choice was to make for the bridge another two decks up. When he staggered onto the bridge clutching his belly, the startled ship's master and the voyage leader looked up from the chart table and asked him if he was okay.

With a small shake of his head he managed to grunt, 'I'm in a hell of a lot of pain.'

They got him seated and the master paged Dr John Cadden to the bridge. When John arrived, he asked Jose to describe the pain before helping him back down to the hospital. As they walked down, John asked him what he thought the problem was.

'I think it's my appendix,' Jose told him.

Once he'd got Jose into the hospital and onto an examination table, John checked his temperature and pulse rate then palpated his abdomen before calmly agreeing with Jose that it was indeed his appendix, adding, 'And I think it's ruptured.'

Jose remembers the brief stunned expression on Kate's face when she walked in shortly afterwards and found him stretched out on the hospital bed. For her part, Kate admits she was shocked to see him there, and looking so unwell. Despite that, her professionalism kicked in immediately as John quickly brought her up to date. He'd inserted a cannula into Jose's arm in preparation for the IV fluids and medication he'd need in the hours ahead and told her he'd given Jose some intramuscular medication to relieve his pain. John added that he had already spoken with Jeff Ayton, at the PMU in Kingston, who'd agreed that Jose was too sick to stay on the ship and directed he should be taken across to the medical facility at the station, which also had full operating capacity and, until the ship left taking Kevin with it, three doctors available to consult and perform the surgery they all felt sure was imminent.

Jose says, 'Kate came over to me and asked how I was feeling and told me not to worry. She tried to comfort me with small talk and jokes but her demeanour was quite different to the fun, happy Kate that I'd known the last few months.'

Given the amount of pain he was in, Jose couldn't walk so they had to stretcher him off the ship; even being lifted onto a stretcher hurt. The hospital has two big seaworthy doors opening out onto the sea deck, which enabled Kate and John, with the help of a couple of the crew, to carry him straight out and around to the fast rescue boat, a rigid-hulled speedboat that always travels on the *Aurora Australis*. They loaded him into it and locked the stretcher in place. Kate and one of the ship's crew hopped in with Jose and hung on as the davit arm swung the boat out over the side and lowered it onto the water.

They were whisked across the harbour to the wharf, where people from the station were waiting to help lift Jose into the yellow dual cab, rubber-tracked Hägglunds personnel carrier used for rescue work. The Hägg is incredibly rough and bumpy on anything other than snow; locked into a purpose-built place in the back cab, despite the analgesia Jose felt every excruciating little bounce as they slowly negotiated the 500 metres of snow-cleared road up to the Red Shed, the station's living quarters. Yet another group of stretcher-bearers were waiting to slide the stretcher out of the Hägg and across onto the verandah of the Red Shed, which was purpose built at the same level as the personnel carrier. Jose was carried into the station medical facility, where Kevin already had the clinical space prepared for his arrival.

Kate quickly found a vein and drew off some blood for analysis in their point-of-care laboratory. While she dealt with the lab work, Kevin attached a drip line to the cannula John had inserted into Jose's arm on the ship. Kate then commenced a new assessment before contacting the PMU to consult with them directly in her role as the current station doctor. Kate relayed all the newly acquired clinical detail plus her thoughts on Jose's condition to Jeff Ayton. He, in turn, spoke with an anaesthetist and a surgeon in Hobart who were familiar with the Antarctic medical context so that, between them all, they had the very best chance of a correct diagnosis and best possible outcome.

In the meantime Kevin continued monitoring Jose's condition, which was clearly worsening as his temperature and heart rate rose and his blood pressure began to fall. Four lay surgical assistants (a meteorological observer, a boilermaker, a plumber and an electrician who'd all undergone two weeks' training at the Royal Hobart Hospital) had been brought in to join the 'surgical team', their presence also ensuring that Jose was never left completely on his own.

Three and a half thousand kilometres south-west of AAD headquarters at Kingston and six hours away by plane, with no option for safe evacuation due to weather conditions and the seriousness of the case, after several hours of careful transfer, consultation and preparation, Kate got off the phone and

confirmed the PMU's decision: the three doctors would pro-
ceed to an emergency general anaesthetic and operate.

With his pain managed with morphine, Jose was encouraged
to contact his family back in Brisbane while he waited for
the inevitable surgery. Reluctantly he agreed, leaving them,
he says, just as shocked and worried as he thought they'd be
so many thousands of kilometres away. Although he saw no
point himself in worrying about something over which he had
no control, he did wonder what the next few days might bring.

Meanwhile, because of the limits on the station's response
capacity during an emergency, any high-risk work that might
engender another emergency had been stopped until further
notice. In addition, the fuel transfer was shut down and all
resupply transfers were halted. During resupply, no one works
outside the station parameters but if they had been, they'd
have been ordered back; during a medical emergency, the
station doesn't have a search-and-rescue capacity if someone
gets hurt or lost out in the field. All of the communications networks outside the Red Shed were shut down for the duration
to maintain confidentiality and to give the medical facility full
bandwidth to ensure the doctors would be able to speak with
the PMU throughout the procedure.

Needless to say, everyone on the station knew what was
happening and even as they continued low-risk tasks, all of
them waited with genuine interest for updates.

At some point, each member of the medical team slipped
away to change into appropriate theatre clothes and booties.
As the man whose desk stops the buck, Jeff Ayton says, 'I had

responsibility for directing what was happening down there. Kevin Harmey is a GP anaesthetist so it made sense that he should deliver the anaesthetic. Taking advantage of the availability of a third highly experienced rural general practitioner, I directed that John Cadden be brought over from the ship to scrub in and operate with Kate.'

Because they'd practised together before, Kevin had two of his regular lay surgical assistants (LSAs) to help him at the head of the table while Kate and John were assisted by two LSAs that Kate had trained with and then practised with since they'd all arrived.

While Jeff emphasises that the procedure was very much a team effort, it was Kate who would make the incision and commence the operation. Because of their location, laparoscopic, or keyhole, surgery wasn't an option and they knew the procedure would be a lengthy one. All of the doctors had discussed the procedure thoroughly, contemplating the steps Kate would take and any possible challenges. They were ready.

The team rolled Jose into the theatre, transferred him across onto the theatre table and scrubbed up. Already masked, Kate, John and the LSA who was assigned to be their scrub nurse donned their sterile gowns and gloves while the other LSAs tied up the backs of their gowns. The scrub nurse would be handing Kate whatever she required at the table while her second LSA acted as scout, fetching any extra instruments or resources they needed from outside the sterile area.

Lying on the table, Jose remembers seeing all their faces and chatting with them in those final moments of preparation and then, suddenly, they were gone. Having administered the anaesthetic, Kevin then intubated Jose and attached him to the ventilator, while Kate and John prepped his abdominal area with an iodine-based antiseptic and covered him with disposable sterile drapes to ensure a sanitised operating field.

Checking around to make sure everything and everyone was poised to go, Kate noted the time, took a deep breath and made the first incision through Jose's skin.

The instantaneous seep of pus-stained, bloody fluid confirmed that the appendix had indeed burst and was particularly nasty; operating was absolutely the correct decision and they all felt a tiny frisson of relief. Kevin called the PMU to relay what they'd found while Kate and John settled in to the job ahead.

The minutes steadily clocked over into one hour and then two before Kate finally clamped off the offending appendix, cut it off and oversewed the excision. After carefully checking the viability of their repair job, she and John then had to deal with the muck in the peritoneal cavity. While John carefully wielded the sucker nozzle, Kate gave the cavity a really good wash out making sure it all looked pristine before double checking again that everything in Jose's abdomen was back where it should be. Having counted and recounted all the swabs they'd counted in as the procedure progressed to make sure none were left behind, they began the process of closing him up.

They finished the surgery quite late and Kevin inserted a nasogastric tube to manage any post-operative vomiting Jose might suffer and to rest his gut, as well as a catheter so they could strictly monitor his fluid output. After consulting once again with the PMU, they loaded him up with broad-spectrum intravenous antibiotics to avoid any risk of sepsis.

Once the procedure was completed, John returned to the

ship to prepare to disembark and officially begin his term as second summer doctor while Kevin stayed with Jose as he recovered from the anaesthetic. He came to briefly, enabling Kevin to remove the intubation tube and ask him how he felt. Jose mumbled, 'Better . . .' and went straight back to sleep.

Kate offered to take the first shift caring for Jose, while she started the very necessary task of cleaning all the instruments. She explains, 'They can't be left with blood caked on them because they're really hard to clean then and you can't leave them soaking because they'll rust.' As she worked through the remaining hours of the night, she listened to the reassuring beeps of the monitor telling her Jose was just fine. The lay assistants had helped her clean the theatre but she then repeated the job on her own because, she says, 'There were so many of us in there first time round, I just wanted to be sure nothing was missed. We were a long way from anywhere down there and I wanted to be sure there was absolutely no risk of contamination next time we needed it.'

Summer in the Antarctic brings with it 24-hour daylight broken only by a kind of early morning haze. As Kate finished up and sat in the office writing up her notes, she noticed a full moon shining in the beautiful purple-pink 'twilight', all of which was reflected across the water. It seemed like a magical, perfect end to an extraordinary twenty-four hours.

When she went off duty at 8 a.m., Jose was drowsy and a bit sore but happy to tell her he was no longer in the agonising pain of the day before. Kevin and John both called to check on him throughout the day. Jose would surface and talk with them or the LSAs taking his hourly obs and then he'd fall asleep again.

With the crisis successfully resolved and everything back
to normal on the station, the bans on high-risk jobs related to
the resupply were lifted, enabling the refuelling of the station
tanks to resume and the handover to the incoming crew to
continue. All planned high-risk work on the station itself
remained on hold until after the resupply was completed and
the ship had been farewelled, taking Kevin with it. In between
shifts everyone on the station was getting into the Christmas
spirit and enjoying the pre-Christmas festivities.

Alternating so that one of them was always on duty to
keep an eye on Jose, Kate and John spoke with the PMU each
post-op day to advise them of Jose's status, also uploading
daily reports of his progress for their perusal and records. By
Christmas Day he was clearly recovering without complica-
tion so they removed the nasogastric tube, catheter and drip
and gave him a very light meal.

On Boxing Day he was allowed to have a go at walking
around. He didn't get far! Thanks to his classic appendix
suture line, stitched-up abdominal muscles and four days
restricted to bed, Jose recalls that his belly felt as though it
was going to rip open. He was allowed to sit in a chair though
and after another day twiddling his thumbs, convinced Kate
he could at least do paperwork. Determined to get up and get
going, Jose was soon up on his feet and mobilising around the
ward. Within a month he was back at work carrying out light
duties, although restricted to 10-kilogram lifts. Fortunately,
he had an engine to rebuild in the emergency powerhouse,
which kept him occupied for a while.

Jose stayed on until the end of summer then, deemed fully
recovered, left on the last summer voyage back to Australia in

February 2011. Meanwhile, Kate settled in for the long haul, staying right through winter with a reduced crew and then on through the following busy summer season.

Upon her return to Australia in January 2012, Kate went to the Flinders Medical Centre in South Australia to start training as a vascular surgeon. When she moved to Royal Perth Hospital to begin her second year she was struggling with what she imagined was a bit of post-Antarctic blues, saying, 'I'd had such an amazing time in Antarctica, living and working with friends, that any job was going to seem less exciting after that.' However, she was forced to acknowledge that she wasn't happy doing surgery and that vascular surgery, particularly, wasn't going to accommodate her growing passion for remote medicine. She applied instead to begin GP training and was accepted to start with GP training provider Adelaide to Outback in 2014.

While she waited to commence her training, Kate called Jeff Ayton to see if there was any work going with the PMU. Although they're not now, back then the PMU was responsible for the oversight and provision of medical support for the Australian Customs and Border Protection vessel and he gave her a job as the doctor on the *Ocean Protector*. Adding another unique experience to her CV, Kate did two 4-week voyages in northern Australian waters.

In due course, Adelaide to Outback placed her with Kadina Medical Associates in Kadina on the Yorke Peninsula in South Australia while she commenced GP training. It was a fantastic experience that strengthened her commitment to being a rural and remote GP. As soon as the applications opened she successfully applied to go to the Antarctic again and was sent to Mawson Station for another fourteen-month post-ing, completing her advanced specialised training in remote medicine while she was there.

Kate was very pleased to share the fun and satisfaction of living and working in the Antarctic again with several old friends, including Jose, who arrived at the beginning of her second summer to begin his third expedition to the polar region. Their trip was not without some significant drama to immortalise the memory.

Kate and thirty-seven expeditioners were aboard the *Aurora Australis* ready to return home when a blizzard howled in and pushed them onto the rocks after the icebreaker broke free from its moorings. When the storm eased, the thirty crew and all of the expeditioners were safely removed from the ship while the hull was assessed. Although there appeared to be little damage, the expeditioners – excluding Kate – were even-tually flown home. Kate stayed with the crew as ship's doctor and sailed with them to Fremantle for repairs.

In 2016, at the Rural Medicine Australia conference facilitated each year by the Australian College of Rural and Remote Medicine, Kate was recognised for her exceptional work as both the rural doctor she is now in South Australia, and as a remote Antarctic medical practitioner with the AAD. Receiving the Registrar of the Year award, Kate was applauded for her 'outstanding clinical skills and adventurous spirit'.

There is little doubt she'd apply to go to Antarctica again in the right circumstances, but her ultimate dream is to land a permanent job with the Royal Flying Doctor Service. For the latter half of 2016 and early 2017 Kate worked part-time at Kanyaka Surgery in Quorn in South Australia while she undertook a part-time contract with the RFDS flying clinic runs out of Port Augusta. She loves the job, the outback people they visit and the opportunity to practise the rural and remote medicine skills she honed in the isolated polar stations.

Excited by the possibilities with both the AAD and the RFDS, the one thing Kate Kloza is sure of is, whether she's on the ice or in a clinic in the remote outback, she has found her place in rural and remote medicine, far from the madding city crowds.

10

The Rock Doc

Dr Brad Murphy, Bundaberg, Queensland

It's just after 6 a.m. on a crisp Thursday in April. A group of about forty veterans is milling around on the walkway at Bargara, a small coastal town east of Bundaberg in the Wide Bay region of Queensland. The weather is starting to chill with the early whispers of winter and the vets have their collars turned up and their caps pulled low. They're shuffling their feet and talking quietly among themselves as they wait for one of the newest, and oldest, members of the group, Gerry Fulton, to join them.

He's not been with the group for long and Brad Murphy, Gerry's doctor and the one who encouraged him to join the weekly walk, is concerned that he hasn't turned up. Gerry was only minimally mobile when he started seeing Brad earlier in the year.

When Gerry first joined the group, he hooked an L-plate on his wheelie walker and attached a cardboard cut-out of a clock for a 'cruise control'. He soon advanced himself to P-plates, and though Brad's concerned, he is also pragmatic. Gerry is, after all, eighty-eight; he just might not feel up to it this morning.

Mindful of the time, Brad suggests the group head off; they'll do the walk and he'll check on Gerry at the retirement village later. As they set off down the walkway, Brad mingles among them open to conversation and queries, especially with the twenty or so vets he sees at his practice. Most of them are sporting the Rock Doc caps that come with being one of his patients.

As a veteran himself, Brad also draws strength from the group. It's a lovely informal way for them to connect with each other and the atmosphere is convivial and enthusiastic, reflecting Brad's firmly held belief that there is a strong connection between mental wellbeing and physical health.

Suddenly Peter, one of the vets, calls out, 'There's Gerry!'

Indeed, Gerry is rolling towards them on his wheelie walker, already on his way back. He's feeling so much better these days, he had left without them.

Relieved, Brad Murphy laughs as he sees that Gerry's chucked his P's . . .

It's twelve years since Brad graduated with a degree in medicine and at fifty-two years of age, he is finally living his dream. For as long as he can remember, he wanted to be a doctor. Born in Gunnedah, he grew up around the pub his Irish Australian parents owned in Manilla in northern New South Wales. The son of Catholics, he attended Marist Brothers High School in Newcastle.

In Year 10, despite his medical aspirations and good grades, Brad was advised by his science teacher that he should apply to learn a trade with BHP. He was already a naval cadet at TS Tobruk in Newcastle and Brad recalls one of his mates suggesting he be a medic in the navy. He'd been watching the new HMAS *Tobruk* being built at Carrington slipways and it seemed a natural progression.

Brad enlisted in the Royal Australian Navy and, on 7 January 1981, at fifteen years of age, boarded a plane to Perth where he joined HMAS *Leeuwin* as a junior recruit. When he was offered an opportunity to enrol in the officer candidate program, designed to help junior recruits matriculate with a view to university, he jumped at it, thinking he'd be able to get into medicine supported by the navy. Disappointingly, an untimely change of naval policy later denied him that option so he elected to return to his entry group and became a medic.

A few years later, Brad was based in Sydney and, in his role as a naval medic, was doing ride-alongs on weekends with the NSW Ambulance paramedics. He saw them using Narcan to resuscitate people who'd overdosed on heroin and thought, *I want to do this*. He says, 'These guys had stopped breathing. They were clinically dead but, with an injection of Narcan, they immediately woke up.'

He applied to join the NSW Ambulance service and then had to arrange his discharge from the navy, three years short of his nine-year contract. His commanding officer told him he'd be back inside three months and Brad agrees he probably would have been if he'd done anything other than join the ambos. He says quite earnestly, 'They provided me with the same kind of camaraderie as I'd experienced in the navy.

I still maintain contact with close friends in both the navy and Ambulance. When you trust people with your life, you're mates for life.'

Once he'd completed his formal ambulance qualifications in Sydney, Brad put his hand up for posting to his father's hometown, Hay, in the Riverina area of NSW. It was his first job as a professional working in a rural community. Steadfast in his belief that one should get involved in community activities, Brad was awarded the local Australia Day Award for Young Citizen of the Year in its bicentennial year.

Over the next few years, he advanced through several levels of training, including intensive care paramedics, ultimately supervising and instructing in clinical paramedicine. He was involved in establishing the existing paramedic training program in Queensland in the early 1990s, as well as the precursor training for intensive care paramedic support for the Queensland Police Special Emergency Response Team.

He'd have stayed in paramedics, but in the late 1990s he was poleaxed by Ross River fever. He was very ill for many months and because complete recovery took several years, by the time he was well enough to reconsider his future, his old job was no longer a viable option. Brad decided to change careers completely and focus on a multimedia pathway; exploring his options, he considered various university courses.

Chance being a fine thing, when he picked up the Queensland tertiary application booklet, it fell straight open to a page offering positions for the new School of Medicine at James Cook University (JCU) in Townsville. Even though he'd left school at fifteen, his experience and lateral training provided the wherewithal for him to complete the application and when Brad read that some places were specifically tagged for Indigenous Australians, he saw it as a sign and decided to give it a shot.

Discovering in his early twenties that his family belonged to the Kamilaroi people from northern NSW wasn't a complete surprise for Brad, his mother, Helen, or his sister, Kim. With a half-smile he says, 'Mum used to make jokes about claiming Bennelong Point.'

His grandmother, Hazel, however, did not openly accept the idea for many years. Brought up as a God-fearing white-Australian Catholic, she'd been conditioned to deny the truth from her early years. For Brad, though, the knowing filled an empty space in his heart and head and made complete sense.

His maternal great-grandmother finally revealed the truth at the very end of her life, telling him that her parents had taken to the road droving cattle to avoid her or her siblings being removed. As Brad retells it, 'They were so afraid their children would be taken from them, she had no father identified on her birth certificate and her parents completely denied their heritage to avoid the authorities of the time.'

Despite being quite fair-skinned, Brad was asked by an older Aboriginal healer at a health conference in Victoria several years later, 'What mob do you belong to?' When Brad asked him how he knew, the old man told him he saw his aura as he walked across the room. Brad says, 'It was like the final piece in a puzzle and that recognition provided authenticity.'

Unfortunately, it's such an incomplete story he's never been able to reconnect with any of his Aboriginal family but he is proud to call himself Kamilaroi and was particularly touched two decades later when his grandmother, Hazel, told him that she was proud of him for embracing the truth and for all that he'd achieved in the process.

It was Hazel's formidable commitment to community service and his mother's career as a registered nurse that motivated him to join a caring profession. He says, 'We were always encouraged to give back and the lessons of our childhood clearly shape who we become. I'm very proud of the lessons I was taught by my family.'

Consequently, as one of the first Aboriginal students to be accepted into the new School of Medicine at JCU and one of the first two to graduate at the end of 2005, Brad has made the very most of every opportunity.

Mentorship has been one of those opportunities. He says, 'I know from my own experience that good mentors make an enormous difference. I've been very fortunate to have some of the best.'

One of his mates and mentors is Bob Katter. Brad says Bob was vocal in his support of JCU's initiative encouraging Indigenous students into the med school and incredibly supportive of Brad himself, so much so that he was one of Brad's 'family' on the guest list at his graduation ceremony.

During his uni days Brad was keen to be involved in the medical school community at large, helping form the student representative body and also Club RHINO (Rural Health in Northern Outback, JCU's student health club). Thanks to a letter he wrote to then Australian Medical Association Queensland president Dr Bill Glasson protesting AMAQ's lack of interest in the JCU School of Medicine, he was invited to become the organisation's first JCU student representative. In 2003 he was presented with the Best Individual Contribution to Healthcare in Australia award by the AMA, and in his final year of medicine he became the chair of the National Rural Health Student Network, the collection of all student health clubs in all universities across Australia.

He also became a founding trustee of the Jimmy Little Foundation in 2006 after helping to develop and plan the establishment of the not-for-profit organisation, which is aimed at addressing and decreasing the incidence of renal disease in Aboriginal Australians. Brad says, 'I grew up listening to Jimmy Little on my grandmother's radiogram; he was a well-loved entertainer and definitely an amazing role model.'

Brad got to know Jimmy Little pretty well in the last years of his life and valued his advice and mentoring. He says, 'Uncle Jimmy was sometimes criticised for his lack of active involvement in some of the protest movements, but his strength was drawing people together. He used to say, "Don't ever confuse my gentleness for weakness." He never challenged or confronted anyone in a way that made them feel bad. That's a characteristic I've tried to emulate always and similar to one of the lessons I learned from Bill Glasson who always makes an effort to remember people, something that makes us all feel good.'

Brad spent several of his student pracs in Bill's ophthalmology clinics in western Queensland and was so impressed by his style and work ethic he was poised to enter that speciality himself. However, realising that it was Bill's art of blending medicine with community engagement rather than his own burning desire to be an ophthalmologist that influenced him was the turning point that steered Brad into rural general practice.

After a year's internship at Townsville Hospital, Brad went to Theodore in Central Queensland to work as well-known rural medico Dr Bruce Chater's registrar and relieving medical superintendent under the Remote Vocational Training Scheme, which allows graduate doctors to practise as registrars in rural and remote areas.

Eighteen months later, Brad was drawn to Eidsvold, an isolated town 200 kilometres south-west of Bundaberg with a significant Indigenous population in need of a doctor. As well as the opportunity to contribute to the community, Eidsvold had an added attraction . . .

There was a lovely story in *R.M. Williams OUTBACK* magazine a few years ago about Brad walking into the waiting room to call the next patient at a clinic in Theodore and hollering, 'Rally on the drum, ring on the bell. Come in, Emerald Brophy!' Emerald was sitting with her very close friend Jackie Beer, who Brad had met the day before. Two elderly ladies waiting to one side of them rolled their eyes. One of them patted Jackie's arm and said sagely, 'Our doctor's definitely a little bit different, dear.'

Laughing at the memory, Brad says he knew that Emerald was the daughter of Fred Brophy, of Brophy's Boxing Troupe fame, and he just couldn't resist trying to impress Jackie with Fred's traditional rallying cry.

Brad had met the Brophys not long after he arrived in Theodore in January 2007. Fred says he was sick of being sick and Brad made him well. 'Then he started looking after my fighters as well.' Their mutual friendship became even easier after Brad moved to Eidsvold, which lies directly on the road between the Brophys' two pubs; it also brought him closer to Jackie, who later became his wife.

Brad started going on tour with the troupe and the Brophys say he's like one of their family. Fred nicknamed him the Rock Doc because, he says, 'As well as the boxing, he loves country music and he used to hang out with all those country singers. He'd look after 'em. You know, Adam Brand, Steve Forde, Adam Harvey, Troy Cassar-Daley . . . he loves all that stuff.'

Apparently they love him back. Adam Brand says, 'Yeah, the Rock Doc is somewhat of a legend amongst my close circle of friends. We can always count on him if we need help.'

As well as the personal opportunities, moving to Eidsvold was also a wonderful opportunity for Brad to find his feet as a lone GP. He was employed by Queensland Health as the medical officer at the Eidsvold hospital with right to private practice. Typically he did morning and evening hospital rounds and worked in his practice throughout the day. He'd work on call for twenty-four hours a day for twenty-two days, then a locum would relieve him while he took ten days off to go to Bundaberg to visit Jackie and her young son, Travis. Brad's daughter, Kiah, joined them in Bundaberg as often as possible.

As a lone doctor, with every little unexpected call for his attention adding to his already busy day, as often as not, Brad would be running late. Convinced that people need to be as relaxed as possible, and being the country music fan that he is, the Country Music Channel played on the big wall-mounted TV in his comfortable waiting room, which generally suited his rural clientele.

Aware, however, that country music on its own was never going to be enough to get some men into his surgery, Brad started a men's health group, initiating health checks down at the football oval one evening a week after training. It's not a new concept but, as he says himself, 'There's no point in reinventing the wheel. If initiatives work, especially in the bush, then we should be embracing them.'

One such initiative that Brad instigated while he was in Eidsvold was the first accredited mobile GP service in Australia, aptly called the Rock Doc van. It had sleeping quarters up one end and a small, well-appointed consultation area up the other. At the end of January each year, he'd take Jackie and their kids down to Tamworth for the Country Music Festival to check out his various muso friends, many of whom are still in the habit of ringing him from 'wherever' for medical advice and a quick cure for a bad cold or a lost voice, especially just prior to a big gig.

As well as Fred Brophy's, the van door flaunts signatures from some of the biggest names in Australian country music: Uncle Jimmy of course, Adam Brand, Beccy Cole, Kasey Chambers, John Williamson, Adam Harvey, 'Buzz' Bidstrup from GANGgajang, Shane Nicholson . . . the list goes on. There's even a Queensland governor on there. When Brad retired the van a few years ago he kept the door, which takes pride of place in his office.

Throughout the year, locum permitting, he'd take the Rock Doc van on tour with Fred's troupe and provide a mobile clinic service outside the tent as well as any first aid inside. Brad loves the ambience and the entertainment and even though the van has been mothballed, he hasn't. He particularly loves going to the Birdsville Races with the troupe and the first Saturday in September is always blocked out of his diary for the purpose.

His role in the tent is to stand just outside the corner of the makeshift ring with his medical kit handy and a towel over his shoulder to mop up any 'blood, sweat and tears'. The fact that there is rarely any need for his skills doesn't stop him playing the part, and at the end of each round, the towel is handy for flapping a breeze over the nearest panting boxer.

One of Fred's mates said to Brad once, 'I didn't realise you were a real doctor.'

When Brad asked him what he thought he was, he replied, 'I thought you must have been a geologist.'

Astonished, Brad said, 'You've seen me stitch someone up. What did you think I was doing?'

'Oh well,' the man said, 'you know Fred. He has some unusual, though interesting, friends . . .'

Back in the day, in Eidsvold, Brad also used the Rock Doc van to venture away from his bricks-and-mortar practice to take the good health message to anyone who cared to listen. He took it out to a couple of the district's furthest properties for community events to offer a service, and some days he'd park around town in the hope of capturing the attention of members of the Indigenous community who were less likely to front up to the surgery. He explains, 'Going into a surgery is just too confronting for some people whereas the van had a different feel.'

Through consultation with the community and with all the relevant stakeholders in the surrounding North Burnett area, Brad was able to significantly enhance access to health care, especially for those suffering chronic disease. On a roll, he also established a roster of visiting or telehealth specialist services that ensured enhanced health outcomes for his patients. In fact, he's never been able to resist starting, promoting and getting involved in any project that's going to advance the cause of Australian health generally and Indigenous health in particular.

Which is why, at the same time, Brad was treasurer of the Rural Doctors Association of Queensland and is still one of three trustees of the Jimmy Little Foundation. While still a GP in training, he was also the founding chair of the National Faculty of Aboriginal and Torres Strait Islander Health, which focuses on raising general practitioners' awareness of Indigenous health needs and advocating for political change and resources.

Towards the end of 2011, three and a half years after he arrived in Eidsvold, Brad was driving home to Bundaberg to spend his days off with Jackie at the end of a long and very busy 22-day block when he woke up off the road heading for a tree. Heart pounding and breath frozen in his throat with shock, he managed to pull up in time but it was definitely a catalyst for change.

Realising that 'you are a long time dead', the near miss was a wake-up call that not only made him realise he couldn't sustain the 22-day blocks of work, especially on-call 24/7, but also made him reassess his capacity to contribute effectively when he was fatigued.

He resigned and left Eidsvold soon after. He and Jackie moved into the house between Bundaberg and Bargara that is now Ashfield Country Practice and Brad opened for business in the front room in July 2012. By the winter of 2013, they had bought their home in Bargara and officially opened the practice in the expanded and converted old house.

At Ashfield Brad's been able to create the same gentle-paced, family friendly atmosphere in his waiting room that he's always aspired to, minus the CMC on the wall; his staff get to choose what music's channelling into the room. Set on half a hectare with an empty 12-hectare block right beside it, the house he and Jackie originally bought now resembles a country homestead complete with stylised kangaroos created out of scrap metal on the lawn. There's a very colourful 80-metre concrete rendition of a rainbow serpent slithering through the garden and their big water tank features handprints of patients incorporated into a painting by a local Indigenous artist.

The garden is a tranquil, peaceful space that appeals to the veterans and Aboriginal and Torres Strait Islander peoples who make up about 80 per cent of Brad's client list. In one corner of the garden, they are building a memorial for veterans. When the *Tobruk* was decommissioned in 2015 and Brad heard she was being scuttled off Bundaberg for use as a dive ship, he successfully requested some pieces of her that will be incorporated into the memorial. It adds a touch of 'full circle' to that part of his story.

There's also a barbeque area where vets and families gather regularly for a feed and a chat. It provides more opportunity for men's health business in an informal forum. Brad says they make the most of any chance to promote discussion about healthy life choices. He loves telling people that he inherited the siltstone they've used in their garden from his late father-in law, Mick Beer, who used to joke that Brad would have the only doctor's surgery in the world with a Beer garden. Brad adds, 'It does give us an opening to discuss sensible drinking.'

They have a second doctor in the practice now, which is good for business and good for life balance. Dr Jeannette Wimbus is a young third-generation Bundaberg woman who proudly claims Australian South Sea Islander and Torres Strait Islander heritage, adding, 'and a lot of my family is Aboriginal'. She joined Brad in the practice in 2016 and is particularly interested in encouraging Indigenous people to be proactive about their health rather than waiting until something is really, really wrong.

Just after Jeanette joined them, Ashfield Country Practice was reaccredited as one of the first private Indigenous health services in Australia, leading the way in formal accreditation of focused Aboriginal and Torres Strait Islander health services. It's a distinction Brad's very proud of.

Appreciating his own opportunities, Brad subscribes to the notion of paying it forward as well as back. Emily Samuels is a young Aboriginal woman who met Brad when she brought her mother into the clinic in 2012 just after Brad and Jackie moved there. Because they were operating in a room in their house, Emily wasn't even sure it was a real practice but as they sat in the waiting room, she overheard Brad ask how to do something on the computer.

She piped up and suggested he press 'such and such a button'. As he glanced over to thank her she said jokingly, 'If you're ever looking for anyone to help . . .' Brad asked her if she was serious. Shocked that he'd even asked the question, Emily replied hopelessly, 'Not really.' The product of a really tough childhood, Emily had little education, having left home at thirteen and lived the best way she could, wherever she could, in the intervening years. In her twenty-odd years, no one had ever given her a break and she says she was just about at her lowest that day in the waiting room.

Still amazed at the changes in her life five years later, Emily says Brad and Jackie took her in and gave her a hand up. 'They gave me a job as their receptionist and supported me through TAFE as I learned my basic literacy and numeracy skills; enough for me to do my receptionist training Certificate III.'

Emily now works four days a week and goes into the surgery on her fifth day so she can study because she doesn't have a computer at home. She's doing a Certificate IV in Aboriginal and/or Torres Strait Islander Health. Jackie, who is godmother to Emily's three-year-old daughter, is helping her with her studies and between them their plan is that she will be able to work as an Aboriginal health worker.

With awe in her voice, Emily says, 'I really don't know where I'd be if I hadn't met Brad that day. He and Jackie have been so supportive and encouraging. Normally I wouldn't even have been there that day as I don't really spend much time with my mother. I just thought I should make sure she got to the doctor.'

Like Emily, Shayne Brandon says Brad and Jackie have given him hope where there was none. At thirty-five, Shayne is a young veteran who was a combat systems operator in the Royal Australian Navy, before he was discharged 'medically unfit' on 28 February 2017. He'd been in the navy for sixteen years and developed the back problem that provoked his discharge. In addition, he developed concurrent major depressive disorder and anxiety disorder. Like many veterans, he self-medicated with alcohol.

Out of work and unwell, Shayne returned to Bundaberg, where he still had family. A good army mate who'd moved to live at Bargara encouraged Shayne to go along with him to the Thursday morning walking group, where Brad was recommended to him as a GP who was both a veteran and a compassionate doctor and advocate for veterans.

Shayne had been told prior to seeing Brad that he shouldn't try to work for at least twelve months but, he says, 'Brad suggested I get straight into it and offered me a job working in reception.' He now works two days a week in a job he shares with another staff member. Shayne's life is far from easy, but he says quietly, 'I know now I'm not as broken as I was told. I'm one of the luckiest post-career vets because of the support they've given me.'

While it's true they virtually created jobs for Emily and Shayne, Brad and Jackie agree it's almost easier to get doctors than the kind of great loyal ancillary staff they have. As he has done in the past, Brad has urged all his staff to step up and own their workplace; he values their input and applauds their successes. Barbara Coyne, another member of the growing Ashfield Country Practice family, started with them as registered nurse and now looks after all their nursing care and coordinates all their veterans affairs.

Jackie was a regional bank manager before she and Brad launched this new enterprise. With his full support and encouragement, she resigned from that job and took over the role of practice manager. With a Bachelor of Commerce (Accounting), a Master of Management and the Leadership Journey Program through the Australian Graduate School of Management already under her belt, Jackie completed a Diploma in Practice

Management and was named Queensland Practice Manager of the Year in 2014. She is currently the treasurer of the Australian Association of Practice Management Ltd.

Meanwhile, Brad has stepped back from active involvement in some of his bigger commitments like the Jimmy Little Foundation, though he still contributes to a medley of organisations, committees and events and has little spare time. In 2009 he accepted an appointment as an Associate Professor of Aboriginal and Torres Strait Islander Health in the Faculty of Health Sciences and Medicine at Bond University, a role he is soon expected to replicate at his alma mater, James Cook University. In 2016, he was named Indigenous Doctor of the Year by the Australian Indigenous Doctors' Association, an award he was very humbled to receive.

As has always been his way, Brad continues to focus on providing a warm, comfortable and safe environment for his patients to share their concerns and challenges, whatever they might be.

Gerry Fulton is one of his biggest fans. An Irishman who'd come to Melbourne as a 22-year-old 'ten pound Pom' in 1950, Gerry joined the Royal Australian Navy in 1952 and served on an aircraft carrier deployed to the Korean War. He first met Brad when Brad was doing a locum in Bundaberg just before he opened Ashfield Country Practice.

Gerry was tickled to discover they were both navy veterans and when he heard at the beginning of 2017 that Brad had opened his Ashfield practice, he immediately rang to see if he could get in. Emily apologised, telling him that Brad was fully booked up and not currently accepting new patients. Gerry was obviously very disappointed, so she asked him if he happened to be a veteran.

'Oh, I am,' said Gerry.

'In that case he'll fit you in. He likes to look after veterans.'

Delighted, Gerry went to see Brad in February 2017. At that time he could barely walk a few hundred metres and was feeling quite isolated even though he'd lived in his retirement complex for more than two decades. 'It's got so big,' he says. 'There are 400 people there now.'

Since seeing Brad and joining the Thursday morning walks, an RSL initiative to get vets exercising and connecting, Gerry has gone from strength to strength. On Anzac Day he walked in the parade, a feat that would have been impossible a month before. It's something Gerry thinks about when he's out walking every morning. He proudly wears his Rock Doc cap as he walks 2.5 kilometres from the cenotaph and then back again. Of Brad he says, 'I've never met a better doctor. He is the most wonderful, caring man.'

Brad says he considers it an honour to care for Indigenous Australians and veterans. As he did at the 2017 Bargara dawn service, he often recites the Ode, which he says captures the essence of everything that's important to him:

> *Age shall not weary them*
> *Nor the years condemn*
> *At the going down of the sun*
> *And in the morning*
> *We will remember them*
> *Lest we forget*

In many ways, Brad's life is complete. Living with Jackie at Bargara and working in his practice at Ashfield is enabling him to achieve a healthy balance, while practising exactly the kind of medicine he dreamt of back when he was a youngster stepping onto a boat instead of into a university.

11

All the Little Ones

Professor Elizabeth Elliott AM, Fitzroy Valley,
Western Australia

Elizabeth Elliott is Professor in Paediatrics and Child Health at the University of Sydney and Consultant Paediatrician at the Sydney Children's Hospitals Network, based at Westmead. She is also Honorary Professor at the School of Public Health in the University of Sydney's medical school and at The George Institute for Global Health. And that's just her day job. Her list of qualifications and accomplishments is formidable, her reputation global and her demon worker gene finely honed.

In 1993, Elizabeth founded the Australian Paediatric Surveillance Unit, a national research resource that facilitates the study of rare childhood diseases. One of her particular areas of interest is fetal alcohol spectrum disorder (FASD), the term for a range of disorders arising from birth defects caused by prenatal alcohol exposure. With colleague Professor Carol Bower from Perth, Elizabeth initiated a national study on FASD epidemiology in 2000. Recently, also with Carol, she was responsible for facilitating a national collaboration to develop an Australian diagnostic tool for FASD.

Elizabeth's research encompasses all aspects of the disorder and she now heads the New South Wales FASD diagnostic service at Westmead, chairs the government's FASD Technical Network to advise on strategy and policy and is leading work to develop a national website about FASD and a national register of cases.

So when the women of Fitzroy Crossing in the Kimberley region of Western Australia began to suspect a connection between alcohol abuse in pregnancy and the issues they were seeing among children in the community, and put out a call for partners to help them combat the growing problem, Elizabeth Elliott was the obvious person to contact. For Elizabeth, choosing to get professionally involved in the Fitzroy Crossing community was a straightforward decision; she was asked so she went.

In the winter of 2007, overwhelmingly distressed by the very high number of deaths in the Fitzroy Valley in the previous eighteen months, two local Aboriginal leaders and Bunuba women, June Oscar and Emily Carter, decided enough was not only enough, it was way, way too many. Included in the number of deaths were thirteen suicides in thirteen months. June and Emily undertook to stem the flow of alcohol that was destroying people in the Valley communities. Together with other leaders in the Marninwarntikura Fitzroy Women's Resource Centre and a small group of men who supported their purpose, they called for significant alcohol restrictions.

Despite fierce opposition from many in the communities, they lobbied the West Australian liquor licensing board strenuously and successfully for a complete ban on takeaway sales of all spirits, wine and full-strength beer from the two pubs in Fitzroy Crossing, restricting community access to takeaway light-strength beer only.

Serendipitously, in September that same year, Elizabeth Broderick was appointed as the Sex Discrimination Commissioner with the Australian Human Rights Commission. One of the principal responsibilities of the role is promoting gender equality and Elizabeth was determined to consult with real Australian women and men across the length and breadth of the country. Two months later she embarked on a listening tour around Australia with her twin sister, Dr Jane Latimer, a physiotherapist and Professor of the Sydney Medical School at the University of Sydney who was, at the time, working at The George Institute for Global Health. Fitzroy Crossing was one of their destinations.

Located 2500 kilometres north-east of Perth and 400 kilometres east of Broome on the Great Northern Highway, Fitzroy Crossing is a long, long way from anywhere remotely urban. Even in the dry 'winter' season from April to September it's very warm. Throughout the long wet-season months of summer, it's tropical; with humidity usually high to very high and most days averaging 40 degrees, it's achingly, sweat-drenchingly hot.

When the sisters arrived and met June and Emily and heard their story, they committed to help them raise awareness of the plight of their community and their efforts to turn the tide of alcohol and the violent abuse and self-destruction that followed. Consequently, Jane co-produced a documentary about the Fitzroy women's fight to save their community with film-maker Melanie Hogan.

Yajilarra – To Dream: Aboriginal women leading change in remote Australia was previewed in 2009 at a function at Yarralumla hosted by the then governor-general, Quentin Bryce, and premiered a couple of weeks later at a function at the United Nations Commission on the Status of Women in New York hosted by Elizabeth Broderick and the then minister for the status of women, Tanya Plibersek. June Oscar and Emily Carter led the discussion that followed the screening.

Buoyed by their reception, June and Emily returned to the Valley, keen to build on their success. However, even though it was clear that the restrictions were making a difference, as documented in a formal evaluation by Notre Dame University, they soon realised they had a new crisis to resolve. Many of the older kids were misbehaving, skipping school, getting into drugs and glue sniffing. Even more worrying, when they looked around at the younger children of the community they noticed that something was wrong; some of them looked different, had small heads and weren't growing well, and many were struggling at school. Although alcohol-related injuries and alcohol-fuelled domestic violence incidents had markedly decreased, it appeared a whole new tragedy was emerging.

The women in the community held a bush meeting to discuss ways to address the problem. June Oscar, Maureen Carter from Nindilingarri Cultural Health Services and others initiated a strategy which they called *Marulu*, a word in the Bunuba language meaning 'precious, worth nurturing', to reflect how they feel about their children. They wanted outside

partners to help advance this strategy and approached Jane
Latimer.

Jane was acquainted with Elizabeth Elliott through the
University of Sydney and knew about her research and clinical work on FASD at the Children's Hospital at Westmead in
Sydney. At June's request, Jane contacted Elizabeth, explained
the women's observations and asked her if she'd be interested in going to Fitzroy Crossing to help them decide how to
respond to this new challenge.

Elizabeth was not only interested, she was willing and able
to lend a hand.

By this stage of her career, years of experience in dealing
with trauma in emergency departments and paediatric intensive care units has broadened the scope of her natural empathy
and understanding of other people's challenges and had
strengthened the fabric of her resilience. Nevertheless, she was
shocked the first time she went to Fitzroy Crossing.

Even though she'd spent time in Central Australia, had
travelled widely and worked in India, Elizabeth's personal
background is very much an urban one. As she and Jane drove
into the town, she was struck by the extremely obvious picture
of disadvantage hovering around them on shimmering waves
of Kimberley heat. It was dry, dusty and desolate. The local
supermarket had been burnt down, its ruins a memorial to
appallingly poor access to decent, nutritious food. There was
no such thing as a coffee shop.

After meeting June and Emily, she learnt that only 7 per
cent of the houses, most of which were overcrowded, had
access to the internet. Few locals owned cars and, she quickly
discovered, only two public bus services a day go through

Fitzroy, from Darwin to Broome or vice versa. Both buses pass through the town in the middle of the night, meaning anyone wanting to get out of Fitzroy Crossing waits in the dark, hoping the bus will stop and not run over them.

And then there were the town's two hotels, the Lodge and the Inn, one on the north-eastern outskirts of town and the other on the south-eastern edge. Both overlook the Fitzroy River, from opposite banks, and although they're owned by the same company, they compete to attract every passing tourist dollar. Even though the publicans adhered to the new laws prohibiting anyone from taking anything other than light beer off their premises, they objected to restricting the grog.

June had set up meetings with leaders from the Bunuba, Gooniyandi, Walmajarri, Wangkatjungka and Nyikina peoples – the five language groups who call the Valley home – and representatives from a range of Aboriginal community organisations. After June introduced her to the group, Elizabeth shared her experience of FASD and she and Jane discussed with them the risks, benefits and implications of a project set up to investigate the prevalence of FASD in the Valley. The leaders agreed collectively to go ahead and in the months following initiated a research partnership between Marninwarntikura Fitzroy Women's Resource Centre, Nindilingarri Cultural Health Services, The George Institute for Global Health and the department of paediatrics and child health in the Sydney University medical school. They called it the Lililwan project, *lililwan* being a Kimberley Kriol (mixed language) word meaning 'all the little ones'.

When Elizabeth and Jane later visited Fitzroy Crossing to undertake wider community consultations, they took with them Dr James Fitzpatrick, then a trainee in paediatrics, who had worked in the Valley and who'd recently approached Elizabeth to ask if she would supervise his PhD. The three began consultations with schools, health services, police and community groups in Fitzroy Crossing to explain the proposed project.

Having entree into communities that don't usually allow visitors was a privilege Elizabeth particularly appreciates even as she acknowledges that, in some ways, that's part of the problem, 'because outsiders have absolutely no true idea what life in remote communities is like nor do they know the people who live in them'. Their consultation confirmed community concerns that some of the children were exhibiting effects of prenatal alcohol exposure.

Funding for the first year of the Lililwan project was secured thanks to a private philanthropist, and June, Maureen Carter, Elizabeth, Jane and James were appointed as Lililwan's chief investigators. Their target group was kids who were born in 2002 and 2003. The team made it very clear from the beginning that in their dealings with families and the broader community there would be a policy of no blame, no shame. Their focus was the welfare of the children and they committed to be understanding and not judgemental.

In the first stage of the project, James or one of the other investigators, with Indigenous community volunteer Meredith Kefford and a team of Aboriginal 'community navigators', interviewed all of the mothers and/or carers of the seven- to nine-year-olds they could locate, using a diagnostic questionnaire that they had modified to accommodate local language and cultural requirements. Their purpose was to identify each child's exposure to alcohol during pregnancy, how much the mothers had drunk and how often, and what their particular concerns were about their child or children. They documented which language group each child and mother belonged to, where they lived and in what circumstances – how many people lived in their house and what their relationship with the other occupants was. The survey established the details of family separation, identified who was in jail and noted the presence of drugs and alcohol in the house.

Basically they found that 55 per cent of the mothers of children in the seven to nine age group had drunk alcohol during pregnancy and that the most common pattern was at least ten drinks two to three times a week and up to four to five times a week. This very high level of drinking reflects the community's history of trauma and disadvantage – and women did not know it could cause their babies harm.

With some hard data in hand, Elizabeth and Jane accompanied June and Maureen to seek government funding for the next stage of the project. When they returned to Fitzroy they had formed a team made up of paediatricians, psychologists, physios, a speech therapist and an occupational therapist, and began the long process of visiting all of the children in the target group in their home environment.

Loading up their hire cars in Broome with camping gear and enough supplies to ensure they weren't an unnecessary burden on their hosts, the team set off, accompanied by local people with knowledge of the languages and cultural protocols they would encounter.

They saw virtually whole classrooms of kids who were disruptive, who had problems with attention, hyperactivity, and little chance of learning the basic skills of reading and writing. There were also kids with birth defects, whose brains had been injured so dramatically their heads were physically smaller than they should have been.

While most of the team stayed in the Valley, visiting each community for four or five days at a time, Elizabeth, Jane and some of the other specialists came and went as work and family responsibilities permitted. As the mother of three teenagers, Elizabeth found being so far away and completely out of contact at times was a juggling act, but one that she and her husband, David, a paediatric psychiatrist, were prepared to accommodate. 'Fortunately,' she says with a smile, 'David is very capable.'

During their time in each community, the team would physically examine the kids and treat them for whatever they found as they went. In retrospect, Elizabeth says, 'It was quite a novel way to approach child health care because we worked as a team so whatever specialist care they needed was available then and there.'

Staying in the communities for several days at a time gave the team a very real feel for the conditions in which people lived; the distance on dirt roads, overcrowded housing, the unbelievable heat (even though visitors were rarely there over December and January), the lack of appropriate fresh food, the absence of viable communications, the threat of dangerous snakes and crocodiles, the lack of continuous services and, all too often, the lurking threat of violence. Even after the alcohol restrictions came in, every now and then someone would go to Broome or Derby or Kununurra and sneak back grog.

As they worked through the communities, the team all

supported and learnt from each other. They case-conferenced each child, coming to a joint decision about diagnosis and the resulting management plan. They were looking for FASD but, making the most of their multidisciplinary expertise, treated whatever they found as they went: asthma, injuries, eye complications, hearing difficulty, malnutrition, skin complaints et cetera. They called it 'action research'.

Having made many referrals to health services during the project, they did an audit of services in the Valley, which Elizabeth says highlighted a number of deficiencies, one of them being the lack of Aboriginal health workers (AHWs). 'They're exactly what's most needed on the ground,' she says, adding, 'the problem is, they are now required to go to Broome to do the training and they don't want to leave their communities and children. They could easily be taught the skills needed in their local clinics. They need to be able to identify that there *is* a problem with a child (or an adult) and alert the medical service. They could be taught to treat minor injuries, give kids their vaccinations, supervise medications, recognise substance abuse, treat skin conditions; any number of minor medical concerns that otherwise go unmentioned because, for various reasons, many people don't want to go to the clinic.' In recognising the seriously ill child, AHWs could also save lives.

The lack of AHWs made follow-up care problematic and the team found the solution in teaching schoolteachers what specific kids needed. For instance, the physios taught the teachers exercise regimes that would help different kids develop motor skills.

Because the doctors made an 'official' diagnosis of FASD, some of the children were able to access extra funding for additional assistance in the classroom – but the problems continue to feel almost insurmountable. While the kids who have disabilities are regarded as special or different rather than disabled, having nearly 20 per cent of the kids diagnosed with FASD and challenged by the associated learning, developmental and/or emotional problems threatens daily to overwhelm the people who are caring for them. And, according to Elizabeth, nearly all of the children in the age group they studied, even if they weren't exposed to alcohol in utero, had some level of early life trauma that could contribute to their neuro-developmental problems.

On the upside, when they completed the original questionnaire, the team found that relatively few of the mothers used drugs. About 13 per cent of the mothers they assessed smoked cigarettes and about 13 per cent smoked a bit of dope but there didn't appear to be any other drug use at the time. On the downside, although the men they interviewed were honest about their alcohol use, they were unable to gather much specific information about the fathers of the kids directly involved in the project because most of them weren't currently living with the mother or able to provide child care.

In an adjacent project, Elizabeth participated in work facilitated by Aboriginal-health researcher Heather D'Antoine in Fitzroy Crossing and in communities in two other parts of WA to find out why women were drinking in pregnancy. Invariably drinking was found to be related to stress resulting from the trauma of historical abuse, being among the stolen generation, removal from land and the prohibition of speaking language;

in short, considerable feelings of displacement and disconnection from country and culture.

Until a referendum in 1967, when a majority of Australians voted to amend the constitution to allow the Commonwealth to recognise Aboriginal people as citizens by including them in the census, and to legislate specifically in regard to their needs, most remote Indigenous families lived and worked on cattle stations in exchange for basic rations, and a camping ground accommodated their extended families. Most lived in the old ways, hunting and gathering from the land around them, land to which they felt culturally connected. Following the referendum, one of the legislated changes was that Aboriginal workers must be paid money for their labour. However, the majority of station owners calculated that they couldn't afford to pay. As a consequence, most families were pushed off the land and forced into camps on the outskirts of towns like Fitzroy Crossing with people from other language groups, a long way from their traditional hunting grounds.

Elizabeth interviewed a woman in her eighties who remembered the first time alcohol came into her community. She told Elizabeth that only people who registered for citizenship were allowed to buy alcohol but they inevitably brought it back to the community and shared it around. They had no idea it was harmful even though, the old woman told Elizabeth, she could see the harm and never touched alcohol herself.

Some of the parents of the target group of children in the Lililwan project, who were alcohol affected themselves, were children of the stolen generation, displaced from their country and traditions by an authority they had no capacity to repel, so they were using alcohol to deal with their distress. Reflecting on their situations, Elizabeth says, 'You can't ignore your past. You carry it with you.'

This is a truth very much at the forefront of Elizabeth's mind in her work with the Australian Human Rights Commission assessing children in immigration detention centres. Even as she recognises the need to protect our borders and check people for security and health risks, Elizabeth laments our behaviour towards children in detention and was a passionate advocate for their immediate release long before the eventual liberation of most child detainees in April 2016. 'The whole refugee situation is a major problem for which there is no easy solution, but detaining people, particularly children, in totally inappropriate settings without assessing their claims is causing serious harms. They, too, will be forever scarred by this experience. No one sees their faces or hears their names and because they are out of sight and out of mind; it's as though they don't really exist.'

Drawing some distinct parallels with remote Aboriginal communities that are also out of sight and easily out of mind, Elizabeth voices her disappointment that Australia has got itself in this position in the first place, saying, 'We have Aboriginal people living in desperate conditions and [the way we are going] we are not going to close the gap any time soon.' With a troubled look in her usually calm, warm eyes, she adds, 'We have to be careful not to normalise their situation; to make sure we don't get less impacted by the trauma. That said, the Fitzroy Valley has strong leadership and they have a good governance structure that enables them to identify their priorities.'

Fitzroy Crossing is indisputably one of the leaders in

innovation. Other communities have found it much more difficult and have tried with varying degrees of success to instil
the restrictive alcohol strategies that have worked so well in
the Fitzroy Valley. According to Elizabeth, the difference lies
in the good working relationship between the five language
groups who'd been thrust together at Fitzroy Crossing. 'They
decided they would work together to achieve their outcomes
and have equal say, whereas some other communities outside
the Valley don't have that level of cohesion.'

Thanks to the action taken by women like June, Emily and
Maureen, Fitzroy now has a new child and family centre, a
social enterprise art program and a domestic violence shelter.
It is gratifying, too, to see that many children in the Fitzroy
Valley are doing well.

Elizabeth continues to visit the Valley at least twice a year.
She has spent a lot of time with June Oscar, who has done
so much to try and turn things around. June's contribution
to her community and her commitment to the health and
wellbeing of all children, particularly those with FASD, was
recognised when she was awarded an Order of Australia (AO)
in 2013 and then named Western Australia's Local Hero in the
Australian of the Year Awards in 2016.

More recently, June was appointed as Aboriginal and
Torres Strait Islander Social Justice Commissioner and commenced work at the Australian Human Rights Commission in
April 2017. While much has been achieved through community
self-determination and there are many Aboriginal musicians,
linguists and artists who will ensure cultural knowledge is pre-
served, when June and her colleagues view the children and
young people who are already impaired by alcohol they agree

it's overwhelmingly depressing. They know that much of that cultural knowledge is going to pass by these children, another lost generation.

Sadly the cycle is hard to break. As Elizabeth points out, in the Lililwan cohort 'over half were exposed to high levels of alcohol and one in five fulfil the diagnostic criteria for FASD. So if a fifth of kids are running riot in class, it makes it pretty hard for the others. Many of these kids end up getting into trouble with the law quite young and the whole community suffers; the capable kids get caught up in that.'

Five years after the project began some of the Lililwan cohort are on drugs, glue sniffing, pregnant, in jail, disabled from car accidents, desperate, dead. The problems don't just go away and, Elizabeth says, they are starting to see ongoing problems in adolescents. Although the team made lots of medical referrals, they had always known that some would never be actioned. They had discussed this possibility with community leaders right at the beginning but pushed ahead in order to identify problems early so that there was a chance of them being successfully treated. And although some referrals didn't happen, they've been able to use the data to lobby for more funding for services.

The team's reporting has also been helpful in that they put all the documentation of clinical assessments and management plans into each child's electronic health records. The parents or principal carers were given a copy of the reports written in lay terms and, with their permission, the reports also went to the school and to the relevant health services, effectively providing a multidisciplinary assessment that might have taken those same services years to negotiate and collate. The team also trained a lot of people, both local and visiting. A number of medical students, psychologists, young doctors and allied health workers have benefited from the training and Elizabeth would dearly love to see increased numbers of locally trained AHWs.

Progress has been made in other areas, too. In consultation with local women, Elizabeth has recently introduced a parenting program to assist and support parents in the Valley in dealing with the difficult child behaviours identified in Lililwan. Funding is always a conundrum but she has a wish list that begins with a government-funded multidisciplinary paediatric team based in Broome rotating through all the communities, taking a frequent and really holistic look at all kids, interacting with the schoolteachers and being part of the local service provision. And if that's not possible, she'd like to see the same multidisciplinary team doing the same thing on a fly-in fly-out basis; going back to communities continuously so they get to know the people and, just as importantly, the people get to know them.

Back in Sydney, Elizabeth's days are generally long and incredibly busy as she moves between her patients at Westmead, her research work, teaching at the Sydney Uni medical school, writing medical texts and articles, and conversing with the vast number of people who seek her expert opinion.

While the obvious effects of alcohol (and drugs) on behaviour are well documented, one of the things Elizabeth is currently researching with labs in Sydney and Melbourne is the influence that excessive use of alcohol might have on gene expression and function. It is already well known that the earlier people with brain injury are diagnosed and the better the intervention, the more chance they have of re-establishing brain connections, especially in young brains that have a lot of plasticity. Knowing how alcohol impacts the genes will hopefully help understanding of brain recovery in babies and very young children suffering from FASD.

The opportunity to participate in the Lililwan project has enriched Elizabeth's life in many ways, not least through the friendships she has formed with the women in Fitzroy Crossing who are trying so incredibly hard to turn things around for their families. Working with children who live in such desperate circumstances, including those in immigration detention, incurs a price though, and Elizabeth admits to crying on more than one plane trip home.

When she came back from Christmas Island, the Human Rights Commission sent a psychologist to interview her and the group who went with her. The psychologist was experienced in vicarious traumatic stress and Elizabeth remembers telling her, 'I'm fine, I'm used to working in ICU and neonatal units seeing trauma and kids dying and I've worked in developing communities quite a lot in Asia and I've worked in Aboriginal communities . . .'

The psychologist went around the table and asked each of them what they were like the week after they arrived back. Reluctantly they all confessed to varying degrees of distraction and inability to concentrate. The psychologist then explained to them how processing intense grief and trauma witnessed in other people disrupts cognition and normal thought processes and how much harder it is to process that grief and trauma when it occurs in defenceless children.

While Elizabeth works at maintaining her coping mechanisms by keeping physically fit and pursuing many interests, she worries about the people who work in remote communities all over Australia, particularly the young, single women who travel long distances to get there, who are working a long way from home and living in pretty ordinary circumstances. She worries that they are not emotionally well prepared for the challenges they'll face, remembering how tough it is starting out . . .

Apart from long, gruelling hours and heavy workloads, most young doctors are exposed to some quite dreadful things. Elizabeth remembers one week when she was a young resident working in intensive care when a child died every night. She also remembers that no one discussed it with her. 'You go home and feel guilty and blame yourself and wonder what you could have done better. We don't do debriefing very well in our profession.'

In regard to the Lililwan project and the extreme disadvantage they continue to witness, Elizabeth says the team members talk about it among themselves but not in any formal way and she wonders constantly how people living the life survive. People like June, who are seeing the disintegration of their young people and are trying to hold it all together, especially as they know they have a whole generation who may never be able to care for themselves.

Despite that, the people of the Fitzroy Valley are resilient, staying firm in their commitment to restricted alcohol access and continuing to work towards resolving the challenges faced by all the little ones diagnosed with FASD. Elizabeth believes the Lililwan project has been successful because it was prioritised, initiated and driven by the local community. Her admiration and respect are clearly obvious as she says, 'The women were incredibly courageous to stand up and tackle a problem that was taboo in light of much opposition. This is a great example of self-determination and the result was improved outcomes for mothers and babies in the Fitzroy Valley.'

For as long as June and the people of the Fitzroy Valley need her particular skills and knowledge, Elizabeth Elliott will continue to support them with every resource at her disposal.

12

The BFGGP

Dr Chester Wilson OAM, Charleville, Queensland

Late one Thursday afternoon, just a week before Christmas in 1997, I was in our kitchen doing odd jobs in preparation for a few days' shearing and enjoying the kind of family's-all-home peaceful school-holiday afternoon that boarder parents particularly appreciate. My husband, Ian, was up at the shed with our son, Chris, waiting for the shearing team to arrive. Our eleven-year-old daughter, Chloe, was lying on her bed reading a book while I'd put a pudding in the oven and moved on to ironing clothes for the week ahead.

Our serenity was suddenly shattered by the ceaselessly blaring horn of a station vehicle coming fast. Knowing it could only be trouble, we both ran out to the gate. As Ian pulled up, it was obvious he was okay but beside him Chris lolled white-faced, hair matted and filthy, his clothes drenched in dust; he was nursing one arm and vaguely rambling.

As I gently felt Chris's head, soft and squishy on top and

dinted at the back, Ian quickly explained that Chris had been riding around the horse paddock fence at the shearing shed and somehow came off his motorbike. He couldn't remember what happened but had managed to walk into the shed and find Ian.

Chris was breathing but semiconscious with a thready pulse. We lived 130 mostly dirt-road kilometres from Charleville. With an RFDS base there as well as our local medical practice, we tossed up between Flying Doctor or hit the road. An hour from sundown, and sure that we could be well on the way before the plane got in the air, we opted to drive to town. I rang our local GP, Chester Wilson, who very calmly directed, 'Bring him straight to my house.'

We transferred Chris into our 4WD wagon. Chloe jumped in the front with Ian and I cradled Chris's head and tried to keep him awake as he lay across the back seat drifting in and out of consciousness, surfacing only to ask if his motorbike was okay and if he was going to die. It was terrifying. As the top of his head got softer and squishier, any useful nursing knowledge I might have retained completely vanished . . .

The minute we braked in the driveway at the Wilsons' house, Chester's tall, bearded form emerged from the early evening gloom and he gently but decisively took over. Two decades on, the relief is still a vivid memory.

An Ipswich boy, Chester Wilson was born into a family of doctors going back generations, and never imagined he'd do anything else. He graduated from the University of Queensland Faculty of Medicine in 1972 and undertook his

two years' residency at Hornsby Hospital in Sydney. He spent
the next few years working in rural medicine in Queensland,
New South Wales and South Australia and was looking for
an opportunity to return to Queensland when a serendipitous
detour in his travels led him to Bourke in far north-west NSW.
He called in to visit a mate, who alerted him to the fact that
world-renowned outback surgeon Dr Louis Ariotti was looking for a fourth doctor to work as an assistant medico in his
practice in Charleville in South West Queensland.

Chester rang ahead, arranged an interview and drove up
to Charleville, where he chatted with Louis while eating the
Ariottis' homegrown grapes on their back verandah. A long
and steadfast friendship was born and, having delivered two
handwritten sentences to formalise his application, Chester
got the job.

Back then, Charleville was a vibrant medical town with
110 beds in its education-oriented training hospital, a busy
RFDS base and a big private medical practice owned by Louis,
Dr Dorothy (Dotty) Herbert and Dr Ron Parker. Louis's reputation was such that he attracted medical students, trainee
doctors and patients to Charleville from all over Australia,
indeed from all over the world. He worked through a busy
theatre list at the base hospital three days a week plus
emergency surgery. When he finished operating, and on the
other two days and Saturday mornings, Louis would return
to the surgery downtown to see a long waiting-list of patients,
often working late into the night.

Chester was to start in August 1978, after he had married
his long-time sweetheart, Loie. However, his appointment was
fast-tracked after Dotty Herbert suffered serious injuries in a

gliding accident. He agreed to start three months earlier than planned and moved out to Charleville on his own.

When he sauntered purposefully back into town in May and then popped up in a consulting room, the locals were agog. Standing 198 centimetres tall in his bare feet, Chester Wilson is hard to miss, but it's not just his height and flourishing beard that attract attention. Getting around, as he mostly does out of hours, in elastic-sided work boots, Stubbies and a faded blue shearer's singlet, he doesn't exactly look like a doctor. Like Chinese whispers on bingo day opinions sizzled around the community, jumped the nearest party line and segued onto the airwaves during the morning galah session down at the RFDS base. 'Oh my God! Have you seen the new doc?' – and then, depending on who was asking – 'He looks like a truckie/ navvy/lumberjack.' The south-west corner of Queensland ran hot with rumour and speculation . . .

With no accommodation immediately available, for the first few weeks Chester boarded with the recovering Dotty Herbert and spent many of his off-duty hours keeping her company. Dotty just loved Chester and appreciated the assistance he gave her as she recuperated from her injuries. As her many friends called to visit her, they also got to know and like the friendly young GP and quickly shared their approval around the community.

Sticking to their original wedding plans, Chester and Loie were married in Gatton in July. After their honeymoon, Loie joined Chester in Charleville and won them both even more fans with her gentle heart and sweet smile. The love affair was mutual, as Loie says so many people helped them when they needed it. With a wry smile she admits they were both really naive when they came to Charleville, with very few relevant life skills. Laughing, she says she'd never had to cook before because she'd always lived in nurses' quarters; her first cooking lessons came from her local butcher, who'd sell her a cut of meat and then give her instruction on what to do with it.

On the other hand, her extensive qualifications as a registered nurse, midwife, maternal and child welfare nurse and paediatric nurse were considered a major bonus and, as soon as she had them settled into the two-bedroom house that accompanied Chester's job, Loie was quickly snapped up by the base hospital where, for the next couple of years, she cheerfully specialled little kids who needed one-on-one nursing.

When he first accepted his job, Chester imagined he might learn some new operating procedures to add to his skill set. However, while he did perform surgery himself some of the time, Lou Ariotti had such respect for his skill as an anaesthetist that when they were both in theatre Chester generally found himself honing his already excellent gassing skills. As Lou wrote in his memoirs, 'Generally, I arranged my operation list so that he gave the anaesthetics for the more complicated and major procedures.'

Within six months, Ron Parker retired and Chester and Loie accepted an offer to buy into the practice. What they didn't realise when they agreed was that it also meant they had to move out of the house that had been theirs to use while Chester was an employee. Consequently, they had to go back to their bank manager and ask for an even bigger loan, one the manager was only too pleased to provide. Contrary to public perception, doctors don't all make a bootload of money and certainly Chester and Loie never have. Loie remembers,

'It was very tough and we never really knew what our income would be. We worked on an overdraft for years and the bank, much to their advantage, was happy to keep it that way!'

In 1981, the Ariottis opted to move into a smaller residence. With baby Geoffrey on the ground and daughter Naomi on the way, Chester and Loie decided they needed more room, so they sold the little house they'd bought three years before, hitched their overdraft up another couple of notches and bought the Ariottis' rambling old Queenslander. Set on the bank of the Warrego River, this home became heartland for the Wilsons and their kids. Ultimately, it also became a refuge for an assortment of animals. As a registered wildlife carer, Loie was regularly called upon to rescue defenceless bundles of fur and she was rarely seen without a tiny bottle and teat in hand ready for some small body's next feed.

Two years after Naomi was born, Chester and Loie welcomed Elise to their family, and two later, baby Jimmy. As the kids grew up, the Wilson household became a magnet for a vast network of young neighbourhood friends. It was not unusual for extra kids to stay overnight with them and one young lass, Rose, whose family lived a long way out of town on a property, lived with them during the school term so that she could go to high school.

As their old Charleville neighbour Carmel Pfingst remembers with a burst of laughter, 'They are the friendliest people I know. They never worried about who people were or where they came from. They'd just welcome them all. What's more, Chester would ring up on a Friday afternoon and say, "We're having a few people over for dinner tonight, Carmel, and we thought we'd have it at your place!"'

Despite his ambling affability, Chester is, in reality, very sharp and misses very little that's going on around him. He's composed, kind hearted and quick witted. He's also very, very clever. His extraordinary intellect wrapped itself around the intricacies of computing long before most people knew what a computer was. Fascinated by the potential, in the late 1960s he had taken a year off from his medical studies and switched to computing, and when he came to Charleville, he brought one of the town's first computers with him. Typically, he let any interested high school kids loose on it, teaching most of them to understand computing and code. Thanks to him, one young lad in particular turned out to be such a wizard with computers he went on to pursue a career that led him to Silicon Valley.

In later years, as Chester expanded his collection of electronics to include assorted sound systems, he continued to share his expertise and resources with the wider community. In his spare time, such as it was, he amplified everything from dance music for local weddings to conferences, and never missed the annual eisteddfod, the Anzac Day service or any end-of-year functions for the schools. As usual, he always had a group of willing high schoolers around him, eager to learn all they could from him and happy to teach him everything they knew.

Loie says Chester has, pretty much, been living three incarnations during his current lifetime: the main medical one that landed him in South West Queensland in the first place, the computing and electronics one, and a muso one that regularly puts him on stage with the Australian bush band Ned and the Kellys.

Ned and the Kellys was spawned in 1990 in the aftermath of the devastating Charleville floods. As the water rose above the previous high-water mark, Lou Ariotti assured Chester that their old house had never been flooded. Nor had most of the rest of the town and yet, in the early hours of 21 April, while the Wilsons watched from the safety of the rumpus room they'd built in the attic two years before, the Warrego River surged 30 centimetres through their home and most of the town went under water. Nearly all of the 3000 residents of the town were evacuated out to the RFDS base at the Charleville Airport. Chester and Loie shipped their kids out to Brisbane then, while friends from elsewhere cleaned their house, they spent many long hours in those first post-flood days attending to people until the army took over all the medical needs of the community.

In the wake of the deluge, a handful of local blokes got together to make some music for the huge recovery party that followed the clean-up. Chester heard them practising and offered his banjo and ukulele playing to the cause. He also plays guitar, bass guitar and piano. The band was a rip-roaring success and to everyone's delight, Ned and the Kellys have been hugely popular ever since. They've released two CDs, and enjoyed two tours to Ireland and one to Norfolk Island, gathering an international following. The locals love it and often brag about Chester, claiming him like a tourist attraction. 'See that big fella up there with the beard and the banjo? He's our doctor!'

While he's a sociable man who has always enjoyed his various active roles in the community and the company of the people who crowd his day, Chester has also always needed some aloneness to centre his being and renew his spirit. Although he appreciated living on the Warrego, it was the

Ward River, 20 kilometres west of town, that provided the balance in his life. Smiling sweetly, Loie says, 'In another life, he'd be a perfect beach bum!' For as long as she can remember, Chester would disappear out to the Ward on his one afternoon off each week. For most of the year and certainly all of the long summer months, he'd strip off and swim a kilometre or two up and down the river, enjoying the peace and solitude.

One afternoon he came across a man who'd left his mates at their camp and putted down the river to fish. When Chester swam into view he was sitting in his tinnie desperately trying to restart the outboard. He'd been at it for a while and his relief was obvious. A stranger to the area, he wasn't even sure quite how far he'd travelled. Ever ready to assist anyone in need, Chester offered to help by slinging the boat rope over his shoulder and towing the man back up the river.

As Chester pushed him into shore below their camp, the grateful man begged him, 'Come up and have a cold beer!'

Treading water and rumbling with laughter, Chester replied, 'I'd love to, mate, but I'm afraid I can't; I've got no clothes on!'

For many years after Dotty Herbert's retirement, Lou Ariotti and Chester were the only permanent doctors in their practice and subsequently, after Lou retired in 1989, Chester was often on his own. It had become much more difficult to attract doctors to remote practices and, while he had doctors come and go for short periods of time, he was the only one who stayed. Of being on call 24/7, he says, 'It's never worried me being out through the night. In fact, the government telling everyone that "doctors' surgeries are shut at 3 a.m. so go to the hospital" has not been good for any of us. It's often easier to deal with something yourself at 3 a.m. than come into a busy day and try and sort out what other people have done with your patient in the middle of the night.'

In the thirty-five years he practised in Charleville Chester acknowledges that, from snake bite to drug and alcohol abuse, terminal illness to car accident, heart attack to chicken pox, he saw pretty much everything there is to see. In time, he delivered the babies of babies he had delivered and he doctored several branches and generations of the same families. He's also 'doctored' the odd other thing!

Howdy and Jay Bryant used to own a cattle station north of Charleville and west of Augathella. A registered nurse in her younger days, Jay rang Chester one lunch hour to ask if he had a colonoscope (a telescopic tube inserted via the rectum to investigate the large intestine) they could use to find a nut that had dropped into the final drive of their very expensive bulldozer. Immediately grasping the concept, Chester enthusiastically replied, 'Yes, I've got an old one of Lou's we no longer use. I'll come up after work.'

Taking his daughter Naomi for company, he drove the 120-odd kilometres up to the station late that night, inserted the colonoscope into the final drive and located the nut, which they then managed to hook out with a piece of wire. It saved the Bryants many thousands of dollars in time and money since the alternative was to pull the machine to pieces. Two decades later, Chester and Loie are still working their way through the last bottle of their favourite hot toddy tipple that Jay sent them as thanks . . .

'Getting to know people really well is part of the picture for a rural doctor,' Chester says, 'and some of the people we've known have become an important part of our family.'

The Wilsons named their youngest son, James, for one of their favourites, Jim Irving. Jim and his wife Erla lived at Barwhinnock, a property 140 kilometres north-west of Charleville, in the days when party-line telephones, with several homesteads linked to the same line, were the norm in the outback. When a party line rang in or out to the exchange, the different morse-code rings could be heard by all the properties on the line.

Jim Irving had lung cancer, but was managing well at home until he vomited up quite a lot of blood very late one night. Erla immediately rang Chester, who responded that Jim needed to be transported to Charleville urgently. Chester had barely put the phone down when it rang again. It was John Turnbull, from Bayrick, the property next door to Barwhinnock. 'We heard the phone ringing so late and figured someone was in trouble,' he told Chester. 'We have a good airstrip here and it's known to the Flying Doctor. We'll go across to Barwhinnock and bring Jim and Erla here. We can set up lights and clear the roos . . .'

The RFDS landed at Bayrick, with Dr Margie Henderson on board. As she walked across to the car, being a polite old bush gentleman, Jim got out and stood waiting for her. 'How are you, Mr Irving?' she asked. Though clearly very pale, very weak and very shaky, he replied, 'I'm very well, thank you, Dr Henderson.' Listening on, Erla said later, 'I could have killed him myself right there and then!'

As rewarding as working in a small rural community

among people who are your friends is, though, it can be a double-edged blade, especially around the complex issue of confidentiality. Chester says, 'You can never, *ever* talk about some things, even non-medical things, because you never know who's related to whom.' Carrying the burden of people's problems goes with the territory, but Chester says having a large medical family helps; if he needs to debrief, he talks to other doctors including, on occasion, those he's related to. He has generally avoided downloading to Loie so that she's been able to conduct her relationships in the community without the weight of prior or privileged knowledge. That has guaranteed some surprises for Loie, who laughs at the memory of one of her very close friends stopping her one morning outside the bakery to tell her, 'I'm so excited! Your husband is wonderful! He is the best doctor! I'm pregnant!'

Sharing news with people you know well is another challenge for a country doctor, especially when it's bad news. For Chester, it's been both harder and easier being the one who has to tell friends bad news. While it grieves him, he also knows those same friends probably find it easier to accept that news from someone they know and trust.

Several years ago, Chester got a phone call alerting him that another of the Bryants, John, was on his way to the hospital in a serious condition after collapsing near one of their properties south of Charleville. When Chester met them at the hospital he quickly recognised the severity of the massive heart attack John had suffered. John's wife Jo was in town that day teaching at one of the schools when she was informed. Looking back, she says, 'Arriving at the hospital, I had no idea that John's situation might be very serious until I saw Chester's face; then I knew it was critical.'

Grateful that he was there to explain everything to them and to organise John's evacuation to Brisbane, Jo says it made a big difference that Chester was someone she knew well and someone who, she knew, loved John.

With the shocking news already reverberating around the south west, John was flown out with the well wishes of many on his tail. He had another heart attack in transit but was hanging in when Jo and their family arrived at the Holy Spirit Hospital at Northside very late that night. He spent nearly four days in ICU but never regained consciousness and by the morning of the fourth day, they knew he wasn't going to make it. John died that night.

My family's connection with Chester is wrapped around the wonderful care he gave to various members of our clan. Although we regularly accessed the monthly RFDS clinic that took place on the next-door station, Chester was always Ian's GP of choice and he played an integral role in the birth of our son Chris, administering the general anaesthetic that preceded his delivery by emergency caesarean. And years later, it was he once again who gave assistance when Chris came off his bike up near the shearing shed.

As soon as we arrived at his house, Chester quietly and capably took charge. He checked Chris's vital signs, assured us he would be okay and directed us to meet him at the hospital. After Chris had been admitted, examined and X-rayed, Chester explained that there were no fractures in Chris's skull or neck and that the soft squishiness on his head was caused by blood that had accumulated between his skull and scalp; it would dissipate in due course. His wrist was bruised and strained but not fractured. He was okay, though Chester kept him in for observation overnight. Glued to the side of his bed, I stayed with him while Ian and Chloe headed home to find the blackened shell of the pudding in the still hot oven and the iron poised and ready for its next steamy sweep . . .

Chester let us take Chris home next day with orders to keep him quiet for a few days and to buy a helmet! Although both of our kids had worn helmets when they learnt to ride motorbikes as little tackers, Chris hadn't been wearing a helmet that day. None of us ever wore them. We wore big shady hats with our long pants and long-sleeved shirts. We weren't ignorant of the dangers but we'd always considered the searing inland sun to be our greatest threat.

In fact, it was an ants' nest that had caused Chris's accident. He never saw it and only remembers flying through the air, but when Ian tracked down his bike the next day he saw the ant bed and Chris's body impact on the road about ten paces away. He found the bike off the road, lying against the broken roots of a fallen tree.

Happily, Chris is now a grown man with small children of his own. He still rides motorbikes and no doubt so will they, but always with a helmet.

In 2008, just before Chester's sixtieth birthday, Loie insisted that she and he have a serious conversation about their future. She very much wanted to move closer to their several grandchildren but more significantly, after thirty years, she knew they were both feeling the pressures of running a virtually single-doctor business, though Loie is quick to point out that single doctor did not mean single person. 'We had the most wonderful staff who fully supported Chester, sorting out all the day-to-day issues of a busy practice, juggling patients and paperwork and all the details that keep a big procedural practice running smoothly.'

The loyalty of their staff was one of the main reasons why Loie wanted a well thought out plan, so that the staff would know exactly where they stood. Because she'd never managed to get a five-day plan out of Chester much less a five-year one, when they had that conversation she stipulated 1) that they make a plan for retirement by his sixty-fifth birthday and 2) that they had to stick to it!

Reluctantly admitting that Loie was right, Chester agreed that when they retired they would probably have to leave as they both knew that he would never be allowed to properly stop working if he stayed. In a country community, there are always people who'll ask the doc for medical advice down the street, in the supermarket or at a party. Eyes twinkling mischievously Chester says, 'Sometimes I'd be sitting on my back verandah, buck naked, drinking coffee and enjoying the peace of a Sunday morning off and someone would drive right in and come and consult me about their problem.'

Loie began planning their withdrawal while Chester continued to work and ignored the impending move as much as possible. Then one morning in 2012, a year out from their proposed departure, Trevor Eckel, Ned and the Kellys' guitarist and one of Chester's closest mates, came to see him for a consultation. When he finished his examination, Chester referred Trevor to a gastroenterologist in Toowoomba. Wishing against instinct that he was wrong, Chester's worst fears were confirmed when the specialist diagnosed cancer of the oesophagus with secondaries. Trevor wasn't expected to live out the year. He and his wife Glenda prepared for the worst but hoped for the best. Their three daughters moved closer to home and collectively they planned to make the most of whatever time they had. In the short term, Trevor responded to treatment better than expected and the months rolled on into a second year . . .

Unbeknown to Chester, as the date of his retirement drew near, the Charleville community was planning a surprise fare-well. Gleefully in on the secret and supported by the rest of the band, Loie told him it was a fundraiser for the Save the Bilby Fund and that Ned and the Kellys, with Trevor on lead guitar as usual, would be playing at the event. It was the only sure way she could think of to get him there.

'Chester Wilson – This Is Your Life' was a wonderful gather-ing of family and friends sharing anecdotes and reminiscences from the thirty-five years of his tenure. Chester was truly surprised and delighted. However, his euphoria was tempered when he found Trevor backstage standing alone and gazing at a blank wall just before the band went on stage. It took Chester a few seconds to engage his attention and although he got him out on to the stage, for the first time in his life Trevor played out of sync and had to stop.

Once again shepherding him through the medical path-ways, Chester sent Trevor back to Toowoomba for the head scans that showed secondaries in his brain. After surgeons successfully removed the tumours his clarity returned, but his days were clearly numbered. Trevor slipped his hobbles a few months later.

Coming to terms with the initial knowledge that he couldn't fix Trevor, Chester says, 'In the end, you know you just have to accept some things and do the best you can. You have to enjoy life the best way you can because you never know what's ahead.' He knew for sure then that Loie had been right to insist they move on.

When Chester closed the door of his surgery for the last time on 13 December 2013, the day before his sixty-fifth birthday, he had to store the electronic charts of the 7000 patients still on his books, although Loie says only about 1500 of them were current. That's a big workload by anyone's measure and, at the time, he was still administering occasional anaesthetics for emergency procedures up at the hospital.

Despite five years' warning, replacing Chester was always going to be problematic and boldly illustrates the challenges of attracting and retaining doctors in rural and remote Australia. Although it's traditionally a retrieval service that offers clinic runs to remote areas, the RFDS Queensland Section initially agreed to open a clinic with a view to providing two doctors on a rotational basis to fill the vacuum. However, that proved to be unsustainable and early in 2016 Queensland Health took over. They rotate doctors through the clinic and the Charleville hospital on a roster system that provides a medical service but no guarantee of seeing the same doctor.

Meanwhile, Chester and Loie are now firmly settled in their new home. Their grandchildren regularly descend on them for visits but otherwise they have come full circle back to just themselves, when Chester's at home. Not yet ready to stop working completely, he's been doing locums where he's needed and is getting a regular dose of the outback when he rocks back out to Cunnamulla to provide relief at the local clinic. He continues to be fascinated by coding and writing computer programmes and will join the Neds any time they've a mind and opportunity to jam.

The big friendly giant GP and his good wife have found life outside rural medical practice is an adventure that's waited for them to have time to join in. Early in 2017 they took off together to Epping Forest National Park in Central Queensland for a month to volunteer their time looking after northern hairy-nosed wombats. They both loved it and as he cheerfully moseys into his sixty-ninth year, it looks as though Chester Wilson has found his fourth life!

13

Desert Doctor

Dr Janelle Trees, Yulara Health Centre, Northern Territory

Late in the morning on another shatteringly hot desert day, a seriously ill tourist was brought into Yulara Health Centre, where Dr Janelle Trees was on duty. The man had been out on a 10-kilometre desert walk when he began to feel unwell. He and his partner both thought he must be dehydrated, so he kept drinking more and more water. Now he was barely conscious.

A remote area nurse (RAN) brought the patient's point-of-care blood results to Janelle, who instantly recognised hyponatremia. The man had an acute sodium deficiency and was in immediate danger of brain damage or death. He started having seizures as Janelle called the Royal Flying Doctor Service to come and retrieve him and spoke to the emergency department at Alice Springs Hospital, over 450 kilometres away. The isotonic saline infusion that he needed, only available in the strictly supervised confines of intensive care units, was not on hand in the small remote health centre.

While they waited for the plane to arrive, Janelle and her RANs responded quickly but very carefully. One of the nurses inserted a cannula into a vein and put the man on a slow saline drip while Janelle gave him a judicious dose of a diuretic drug to help his body to excrete the excess fluid, and a dose of IV medication to control the fitting and calm him. Through a nasogastric tube into his stomach, they fed him small amounts of salty water. He vomited most of it up again later, but by the time the flying doctor arrived his sodium levels had begun, very slowly, to rise.

The RFDS evacuated him to the intensive care unit at Alice Springs where, Janelle was pleased to hear, he recovered well. As dire as the man's condition had been, it is not an unusual clinical scenario for a Central Australian doctor. In this particular situation it had been exacerbated by the fact that the man had not eaten dinner the night before or breakfast that morning and he'd drunk eight or nine litres of water, clearly not knowing that something so good and integral to survival can poison you in excess.

'Finding balance is the challenge of our individual lives and our societies. But balance is a relative thing,' Janelle says, adding quite seriously, 'As well as your water, take a pack of salty chips with you when you travel in the desert. It could save a life.'

As an adult, Janelle Trees is a very proud Thungutti woman. As a child, even though she grew up in an extended Aboriginal family, she had no real awareness of being Aboriginal and no idea what racism or prejudice meant. Until she was four, Janelle lived with her parents and her younger brother in a converted garage out the back of her nana's house. She had cousins and a couple of aunties also living with her nana and people would come and go, camping in the living room.

'We were loud and friendly and communal,' she says with a twinkle in her hazel eyes. 'My nana was the matriarch and ruled the house (and much of the street). She grew vegies and there were chooks and dogs. I didn't know any different from how we were, but I thought our family was lucky and good.'

Her parents eventually got their own house out in the little community of Heathcote in the Sutherland Shire south of Sydney and welcomed another son to the family. Growing up, Janelle thought she wanted to be a hairdresser or a dancer. The generally accepted career choices for females were nurse, teacher or secretary. Janelle never wanted to learn to type and she didn't want to be a nurse because she remembers thinking as early as four years of age that it was all just a bit disgusting.

She considered being a teacher like her mother so after she'd finished school, she enrolled in an arts degree and went to university. Leaping with great interest into her big new academic arena, Janelle learnt a whole lot more than she'd anticipated. It was her first exposure to alternative ideas and lifestyles, but while the experience sparked a new self-awareness, she eventually ditched uni without completing her degree and meandered through a series of casual jobs.

She got her forklift driver's licence, she was a spruiker in a carnival and a belly dance teacher. She was an agricultural worker who picked grapes and chopped weeds out of rows of beans and she worked in a factory. Her first really official job was putting zinc and metal plates together, making tank batteries for the army, but when the boss told her they weren't

supposed to employ young women and asked her if she could
be pregnant, Janelle followed her mother's advice and never
went back. Not knowing for sure what she wanted to do with
her life, she opted for broad experience and tried a bit of retail
and hospitality work.

Eventually, Janelle found a job she really liked, working
for a beautician who trained her as a massage therapist. Being
a healthy, strong young woman, she quickly found her rhythm
as she listened to the stories clients shared with her. She felt
the energy flowing around people's bodies, and began to
believe there was a strong connection between the stories and
the massaging that helped move and create that life force. She
discovered she wanted to learn and understand more about
that connection.

In 1983, Janelle boarded a bus in Sydney and travelled
via Queensland to join over 700 women who set up camp
in the red spinifex country outside the Joint Defence Space
Research Facility at Pine Gap, near Alice Springs in Central
Australia. The first significant event protesting the location of
an American base in Australia, Pine Gap women's peace camp
began on 11 November, Remembrance Day, and ran for two
weeks, during which women from all walks of life and cultural
backgrounds sang and danced their way into the national and
international media spotlight. It was an important moment in
Janelle's personal journey to discover who she really was and
what her connection with the earth was; she began to know
herself. She volunteered her massage skills in the healing tent
and was introduced to traditional Aboriginal and other healers, as well as to the brutality of the police, who beat some of
her sister demonstrators severely.

Afterwards, she hitchhiked to Adelaide, where she stayed for a couple of weeks before hitching back to Sydney via the Wangaratta ConFest, where some kind people welcomed her to their campsite, and gave her a blanket to sleep under. The bush conference cum music festival, initiated in the late 1970s by former deputy prime minister Jim Cairns as a forum for individuals to collectively consider alternatives to accepted social norms, felt very uninhibited to Janelle. She felt she had a licence to express herself with a new kind of energy and freedom, and saw her massage work as a tool for healing.

Despite her fascination, however, massage was very hard work. Before long she had her small son, Anton, to carry around as well. One day during an acupuncture treatment to relieve the muscular pain in her back and arms, Janelle noticed that her mood had suddenly lifted. It begged the question, could acupuncture be used to treat depression? Janelle believed so, saying, 'It's safe, it's drug-free, it's cheap and it's legal.' The experience prompted her to enrol to study traditional Chinese medicine, an endeavour that took her four years.

After she graduated, Janelle set up an acupuncture clinic in Sydney. A lot of her patients were on a lot of medication, which worried her. Some elderly patients were taking many different tablets and she couldn't help but wonder how they interacted, how they affected their bodies, whether they were counterproductive and in fact damaging. A voracious reader, she consumed books and articles by science writers. She wanted to learn more about science and the possibility of taking people off some of their medicines.

At the time, Janelle was involved with a group planning an anti-racist action in response to management of one of the inner-city pubs banning Aboriginal people from drinking there. The action group planned to occupy the hotel and, keen to build the crowd, they were promoting the event among university students.

One evening, after she had closed the clinic for the day, Janelle was going around a residential university college letting students know about the coming action. She knocked on the door of one of the rooms and was surprised to be greeted by two Aboriginal women. The way Janelle tells it, her mouth hit the floor. It had never occurred to her that any of the students in that elite college would be Aboriginal.

Amazed, she asked them what they were doing there.

'We live here,' one said. 'We're studying medicine.'

'What? You can do that?' asked Janelle.

The women smiled. They were sisters, young, relaxed and confident. 'Yeah, we're doing it. We'll be doctors in a couple of years — the first Indigenous graduates in medicine at this university.'

Janelle promptly asked herself, *Why not me?*

She applied to that same university since there was clearly a precedent for Indigenous students in medicine, but was discouraged when the person reviewing her application suggested she should become a nurse or a health worker. Janelle couldn't understand why it was okay for the sisters to be there but not her.

Sorely disappointed but not deterred, she applied to a different university, where the dean of science told her they were prepared to admit her to medicine, as long as she could gain a credit or higher average in maths, chemistry, biology and physics.

Science was a long hard slog for Janelle. Physics and maths were a struggle. She'd never done calculus and not much trigonometry. Many maths concepts were new to her. She did biochemistry twice and chemistry two or three times.

Unlike most of her peer group who all looked fifteen and seemed to be able to just get on and do whatever they needed to do, Janelle questioned everything. She read books on the history of maths and physics so she could understand what it was she had to learn.

At the time, she was living in housing commission accommodation, working part-time, bringing up Anton and going to demonstrations. Janelle's relationship with her son's father, who was, she says, 'an intelligent, kind and caring man', had ended around the time she began her science studies. She'd come to realise that she was attracted to women, and believed that her immediate future was a journey she best walked alone, albeit with young Anton, who went to university with her at times. Janelle says he was particularly fascinated by the anatomy library, with its gruesome collection of body parts in jars. With a smile, she says, 'Luckily, he turned out alright – not weird at all!' Blessed with the same intelligence and compassion that underpins his mother's character, Anton now works with families, helping parents to keep the care of their children.

It took Janelle a while, but she obtained a Bachelor of Science with honours in the history and philosophy of science and technology. It was more than enough to ensure her entry into medicine which, after the long slog of her science degree, was less challenging. Janelle graduated with honours from Sydney University in 2005, the first Indigenous person known to do so. She spent her internship and resident years working in the Illawarra region south of Sydney in New South Wales.

Getting out of Sydney and going to live and work in rural and regional areas felt a bit like going home. But rewards for overworked, enthusiastic, exhausted interns and residents can be rare. They were trying years; long hard hours learning lessons about life and death and the challenges of medicine.

Still single, although she dated when she was free from her harrowing schedule, Janelle didn't meet anyone special until 2006, when she met Claudia Jocher on an online dating site.

Claudia, a photographer, was living at the time in the Black Forest in Germany, the country of her birth. She and Janelle began exchanging emails and confidences and steadily built a strong and enduring friendship. They met for the first time face to face when Claudia came to Australia to care for Janelle after the particularly distressing loss of one of her patients. Their relationship deepened and they married in New Zealand in 2007.

Claudia had travelled around the world and had been to the centre of Australia, but not to remote Aboriginal communities. That year, Janelle took her on a tour. They went to Fregon, a community in the Anangu Pitjantjatjara Yankunytjatjara (APY) Lands in north-west South Australia to visit friends who were *ngangkari* (traditional Aboriginal healers). Janelle knew the *ngangkari* through the Australian Indigenous Doctors' Association, of which she was a foundation member back in 1997. She says, 'It is a great source of strength having contact with other Indigenous doctors.' Janelle and Claudia's tour also took them to Uluru and to Mutitjulu, the community of the traditional owners of Uluru and Kata Tjuta.

Mutitjulu lies in the late-afternoon shadow of the monolith that draws up to half a million people to Anangu country each year. Although it's a dry community, closed to the public, and one must have a permit to enter, its proximity to the first-world indulgences of the tourists staying at Yulara Resort, about 20 kilometres north-north-west of Uluru, makes the restrictions difficult to enforce and corruption a constant and insidious trespasser.

Mutitjulu was purported to be the catalyst for the Northern Territory Emergency Response, usually called 'the intervention', which hit when Janelle and Claudia were still living and working in the Illawarra, planning their trip. Even so, Janelle says, 'It was like a bulldozer pushing through. It was devastating for Aboriginal people. Because doctors were meant to be mobilised with the troops to occupy Aboriginal communities, all Indigenous doctors felt it keenly.

'It was a terrible time. I don't believe there was ever any justification for the intervention. Of course there are ongoing emergencies in Indigenous health, especially in rural and remote areas, but there is also urgent need in urban areas. The intervention was never about protecting children or advancing Aboriginal peoples' health. It was all about social control and rolling back land rights.'

Janelle and Claudia's first visit to Mutitjulu took place about six weeks after the intervention and Janelle says the community was a ghost town. Tersely she describes the only new construction in town: 'a great big barbed wire fence built around the child care centre . . .' The federal police were there and the clinic was staffed by just one locum RAN and a man who, Janelle was told, had left his corporate job to make the most of the opportunities presented by the intervention.

Distressed by the sight of the fence, Janelle was standing unhappily considering the injustice of it all when Claudia came up to her and said, 'You know, I think when it's back more to itself, we could probably live here.'

They returned to the ocean view at their lovely, peaceful house on the escarpment in the Illawarra and Janelle went back to work. Memories of Mutitjulu lingered though. She spent the next couple of years working in emergency departments and in rehabilitation and palliative care. Palliative care helped her to recognise that her strength as a doctor lay in her capacity to work in a slow, thoughtful and connected way, with her patients and her colleagues.

Reading a newspaper one morning, Janelle spotted an ad for the position of doctor at Mutitjulu and said to Claudia, 'I think we should apply for that.'

The timing just felt right. Janelle felt well qualified and prepared for the role and knew she would be well supported by the RANs at Mutitjulu. She had learnt to trust nurses implicitly. Reflecting on her enormous respect for them she says, 'Nurses taught me so much as a junior doctor.' Janelle also imagined there would be Aboriginal health workers in the clinic; however, having successfully applied for the position, when she and Claudia arrived in April 2011, she found there were none.

Sadly, the Mutitjulu they returned to was, Janelle says, 'an unbelievably beautiful place with the damage of dispossession evident everywhere'. It was a challenging contract but rewarding for Janelle, who felt as though she was where she needed to be, not just for the work she could do and the care she could provide, but also for herself. She feels very much at home in the desert, finding a level of peace there that eludes her in a city setting. She believes that much of the disease and dysfunction that plagues Indigenous Australians can be attributed to the relatively recent and ongoing invasion and dispossession of their lands, adding that 'This is true of Indigenous people around the world.'

Born into the fifth generation in her family since the British arrived, she says, 'My great-great-grandmother saw them come. My great-grandmother was taken to be a domestic servant and witnessed the killing times. The clan were dispossessed of their land in Grandad's youth.'

People in the APY Lands, she says, were more recently challenged and dispossessed. 'I can hardly begin to comprehend, let alone articulate, the mental, physical, emotional and spiritual attacks sustained by the Anangu – the people of the APY Lands.'

Chronic illness as a result of exposure to western culture is endemic. Diet-related diseases like diabetes and heart disease are widespread and mental illness caused by substance abuse is prevalent. After more than 40 000 documented years of existence, these illnesses are relatively new to the Indigenous Australians who suffer them and especially to the Anangu. Janelle says, 'There are people my age (in their fifties) who saw the first white people come to the APY Lands.'

And yet, she continues, 'They are remarkably resilient. They have their own healers. My aim was to work cooperatively with traditional healing to help in any way I could, whether that involved medicines, referral for surgery or listening. Helping people to heal is all any doctor can do.'

Much as they enjoyed Mutitjulu, after a couple of years Janelle and Claudia found themselves confronted by the sinister machinations of corruption. They stood up publicly to support a group of people within the community fighting against a land grab by outsiders and suddenly found themselves the target of burglary and home invasion. In the end they felt forced to leave.

Unsure where to go next, Janelle opted to do some locum work. She and Claudia spent a couple of weeks on Christmas Island and then went to the Cocos (Keeling) Islands before relocating to Newman, a mining town in the Pilbara in Western Australia. It proved to be one of her most challenging contracts. Although she says mining companies are a lot more fastidious about workplace health and safety in the modern era, accidents still happen and she did see traumatic injuries, including amputations. The mental health issues were also confronting. Janelle explains, 'It's a very strange environment and people work extremely long hours, day after day.' She looked after employees who worked for thirty days straight; some of them would break down.

It was a tough schedule and Janelle was ready for a change when Claudia heard via a friend that a GP in a very remote part of Tonga wanted to go on maternity leave and was looking for people to cover her. Janelle had already been to Tonga a few times with Claudia, who had been going there for years to photograph the whales and who has friends there who are 'family'. She put up her hand and said she'd do five months.

They went outside tourist season, between December and April, when it rains incessantly, especially in February and

March, and tropical cyclones are not uncommon. During Janelle's locum, there was an outbreak of a virus of unknown origin with flu-like symptoms similar to dengue fever. Many people were very ill and while most recovered quickly, some were struggling with debilitating joint pain. Some patients even became disabled. And she had no way of making a diagnosis.

Janelle says there was an obstructive bureaucracy in Tonga who wouldn't assist her to diagnose the virus because it was just before the coming tourist season. She found out that bloods that had been taken to go to New Zealand or Australia were being held up in customs for weeks so they couldn't be tested.

With no way of knowing what the mechanism of the disease was, Janelle wrote to the doctor she was working for, then reached out to anyone who could help her learn more about the virus. She did wonder whether she should be isolating herself from Claudia and even if they should leave. Learning that there were doctors around the Pacific who were monitoring outbreaks of any viruses in the region that were endemic, she managed to get on their email list.

Eventually she got an email from a public health doctor on Tonga who'd heard from a source in Japan that an aid worker who'd been working in a nearby island group had been diagnosed with chikungunya virus, a mosquito-borne virus related to zika. Its African name means 'to become contorted' because of the severe joint pain people suffer. While there is no specific treatment, once they knew for sure what they were dealing with, doctors and other health workers were able to treat the symptoms.

Knowing the Tongan people are very good at community

organisation, Janelle says, 'If they'd been told early enough they would have taken all the appropriate precautions but they just didn't know. It might have been a much less extensive outbreak had they been told. The Tongan government had been informed that the virus could be headed their way, but did not launch an anti-mosquito campaign.'

Returning home at the end of their unexpectedly challenging five months, Janelle was drawn back to central Australia. She went to work at the remote West Australian community of Tjuntjuntjara. She and Claudia felt privileged to be allowed to stay there and Janelle enjoyed looking after Anangu people again. When a job came up with the Northern Territory health department for a post at the Yulara Health Centre, they decided to return to the place of the big red rocks.

The health centre at Yulara provides medical care to the 1200 people who live in town to service the resort and the 4000–5000 visitors staying or camping there during the tourist season. About 30 per cent of patients are Indigenous people who travel from all over Australia to work at Yulara.

Working with a fantastic staff that includes three RANs, a second part-time doctor and Claudia as an on-call ambulance driver, Janelle loves her job. She says, though, 'It's frustrating how ill-prepared and ill-equipped some people are when they come to the outback and some tourists do have a culture of entitlement.'

Not long ago, a girl on a school trip to Yulara was brought into the clinic suffering hyponatremia in similar circumstances to the man on the desert walk. Thankfully, she was conscious and not having seizures, but her situation was exacerbated by the fact that she was starving herself. As Janelle was inserting a cannula into her arm to give her a bag of intravenous saline she heard one of the RANs speaking on the phone with the girl's worried father.

The nurse explained to him that Janelle had put his daughter on a drip and was getting her to eat salty chips and a banana to give her some potassium. The nurse continued very politely to tell him, 'No, that's how we do it here. No, there is no hospital; the nearest one is 450 kilometres away. However, there are two highly qualified, highly competent remote area nurses on call overnight and Dr Trees can be called out of bed if necessary. Yes, the teachers can see if her heart is beating fast again. Yes, if she eats she will get better. I will check on her tomorrow. No, we really are very remote. Thank you and welcome to the outback.'

Understanding that city people in particular don't comprehend what remote means doesn't make it any less frustrating. Janelle says one of the testing situations the clinic staff face is tourists who travel without extra medications and then expect to be able to fill their scripts in the small geographically isolated town, where there is no pharmacy and pharmaceutical supplies are limited.

Mostly though, she is immensely satisfied with her work and loves seeing a tangible outcome for her effort. Although she's not routinely available to patients out of hours because she doesn't do call, the RANs know that Janelle will always come if they ask her to, just as she knows they won't ask unless it's urgent or a situation they need extra hands to manage.

They called her in one night to help with a baby girl who'd

had fifteen bouts of diarrhoea and was quite flat. She had a high fever, her eyes were sunken and she was lethargic. The nurses had been called out to a motor vehicle accident about an hour's drive from the health centre. Following the murder of remote area nurse Gayle Woodford in South Australia in March 2016, the Northern Territory government had adopted the principles of 'Gayle's Law', decreeing that all RANs (and health staff) must work in pairs. Both RANs went to the accident and Janelle and Claudia went to the health centre to treat the baby.

Janelle quickly checked the baby over. Finding no viable veins, she knew that she might have to resort to an intraosseous infusion, inserting a needle straight into the bone marrow in the baby's femur so they could get some urgently needed fluids into her system. Saving it as a last resort in such a remote location, Janelle and Claudia rattled through all the nasogastric tubes they could find until they located the smallest of them all. Dipping the tip of the tube in iced water, as nurses had taught her, so that it was easier to feed in, Janelle gently inserted the tube into the baby's nose and down into her stomach.

Hoping the tube was safely in her stomach where she'd directed it, Janelle fed the first tiny amount of saline into the tube. Reassuringly, the baby didn't mind. Janelle showed her mother how to fill a syringe with small amounts of salt and sugar solution and drive it slowly into the tube.

Slowly and steadily they managed to get the baby's fluid levels up. By the time the RFDS plane arrived, her little veins were full enough for the flying doctor to get a cannula into her arm and attach her to IV fluids. Janelle was relieved that they had managed the situation without having to resort to

the invasive process of an intraosseous infusion. Hearing later
that the baby, who had bacteria in her blood, made an excellent recovery was also very gratifying.

Sometimes doctors in remote areas are called upon to do
things they're not specifically trained for, which is challenging
but equally rewarding. One day a man was brought into the
health centre with a fractured and dislocated ankle. His toes
were starting to turn faintly blue, indicating his circulation
had been compromised. Not being trained for orthopaedics,
Janelle contacted the RFDS but, unfortunately, right on the
tail of her call, they got another call-out to a road accident
involving children.

The RFDS doctor asked Janelle if she could reduce the
dislocated ankle, thereby returning it to its normal position,
which would restore circulation to the foot. After consulting
with both an emergency doctor and an orthopaedic specialist in Alice Springs, Janelle took a deep breath and, assisted
by one of the RANs, returned both bones back to their correct
location, and was rewarded with a flush of pink toes. It was
an adrenaline-inducing moment because she was well aware
that she might just as easily have stuffed it up and the man
might well have lost some toes or even his foot if his circulation hadn't been re-established. As it was, she averted a crisis
and the RFDS was able to go directly to the kids who were
injured and needed evacuation.

Now into their third year at Yulara, Janelle and Claudia feel
at home living in the Red Centre. They both love the starkly
beautiful desert landscape and the flora and fauna of the area.

A big-hearted woman who needs big skies, big landscapes and daily encounters with nature, Janelle particularly is connected to country there in a way she wishes all Australians could understand. 'Having connection to country helps people to feel looked after. They feel nourished when the earth in that place looks after them. All country people feel it. It's why they live there.'

She continues, 'If you've had a butcher bird come and sit in front of you and you feel like it's trying to talk to you – and that's something that's happened often enough – then you just accept that the butcher bird talks to you. It becomes part of your everyday reality. That kind of spiritual and cultural understanding about place is something all Australian people need to understand. It's not unique to the Indigenous people here; it's the same for immigrants who come from the mountains of Iran, from the desert of Sudan or from the centre of Europe. Connection to country is not exclusive to Aboriginal Australians but until non-Aboriginal people living on this big island understand that this is about them too, we're not going to get anywhere.'

Being out in remote Australia, Janelle feels like she's in her right place. She's living the lifestyle she wants with the woman she loves and, when she's not providing emergency medicine to people in strife, she's doing the thing she enjoys most: providing slow, thoughtful, caring medicine to people who really need her.

14

Second Chances

Dr Bob Balmain, RFDS, Charleville, Queensland

A bit after mid-morning on Friday, 20 March 1993, Bob
Balmain and the Royal Flying Doctor team were conduct-
ing a routine clinic at Jackson Oil Fields, 160 kilometres west
of Thargomindah in far South West Queensland, when Bob
answered a call from Suzanne Gibbes, the matron and lone
nurse at the Thargomindah hospital.

Suzanne told him that Robbie Fraser had come off her
motorbike on Nooyeah Downs Station and that Scott, Robbie's
son, was bringing her in to the hospital. Suzanne said she would
call again as soon as she had a chance to check Robbie out.

Bob alerted the flight crew that they were on standby for
immediate departure to Thargo, depending on Suzanne's first-
hand report on Robbie's status.

Suzanne and her husband, Ted, were ready and waiting
with a stretcher when Scott's car screamed to a halt in front of
the hospital. Robbie was unconscious and, although it's not an

expression she would normally use herself, as soon as Suzanne saw Robbie's racoon eyes, the deeply bruised-looking sockets indicating severe brain trauma and a possible fracture at the base of the skull, she knew Robbie was in deep shit. She called Bob back immediately and asked him to come. Bob didn't hesitate; he knew that if Suzanne said it was serious then it was.

Once they'd transferred Robbie onto the emergency room trolley, Suzanne quickly triaged her as Scott gave her as much detail about the accident as he could. Suzanne's assessment included scoring Robbie on the Glasgow Coma Scale (GCS), which ranges from a lowest score of 3, indicating severest brain injury, to a highest score of 15, indicating full consciousness. When Bob walked in thirty minutes later Suzanne gave him all her current observations plus the alarming news that Robbie scored 3 on the GCS.

Doing his own assessment, Bob was relieved to note 'no other trauma and no localising neurological signs', meaning that Robbie exhibited no evidence of neurological damage affecting other regions of her body, for instance notable weakness or paralysis of her extremities.

Nevertheless, 3 was a terrifyingly low score, so much so that when Bob completed his assessment and consulted with doctors in the neurological unit at Royal Brisbane Hospital they advised him there was not much point in flying Robbie to Brisbane. Bob told them he was bringing her and hung up.

Once upon a time, Bob Balmain had been given his own second chance at life and there was no way he wasn't going to ensure that every patient in his care had their own crack at 'second chance'.

———

Bob was born and spent his childhood in southern Scotland, initially around Dumfries and later Kelso. His grandfather was a British Army officer whose wife, Alice Fairbairn, came from Woomargama Station north of Albury in New South Wales. Alice had returned home to have her son so Bob's father was technically an Australian; he was also an officer in the British Army, but after his discharge he turned to farming.

Growing up, Bob's one burning ambition was to move to Australia to live. Although towards the end of his schooling he did vaguely consider the merits of medicine, any fledgling aspirations he had were completely overshadowed by his determination to migrate to the great southern land. Barely two weeks out of school, and travelling as a participant in the Big Brother Movement, which facilitated the migration of young men from the UK who were looking for new opportunities in agriculture in Australia, Bob sailed to Sydney in 1961.

He was met at the ship by a stock and station agent who, having arranged for Bob to go and work on a dairy farm at Deniliquin in the Riverina area of NSW, put him on a train going west. Bob's brother Andrew was already working in the Riverina so he had some family support on the ground.

Several months after his arrival, Bob scored a job as a jackaroo at Wonga Merino Stud. With a laugh he admits he was the quintessential Pommy jackaroo when he arrived, but he was so keen he soon learnt the skills he needed to lose his green edge. He spent three years at Wonga, during which time he met a young nurse named Helen on the bank of a dam at the next-door stud, Pooginook.

Bob's mate who was jackarooing over at Pooginook was celebrating his engagement to Helen's friend, and the girls had driven up from Mildura where they were undertaking their 'staff nurse' year, having completed their general training at Royal Melbourne Hospital the year before. Love blossomed between Bob and Helen and, better yet, survived his transition to a new job at The Well, an outstation of Noondoo in the Dirranbandi district in South West Queensland, where he worked as overseer before being promoted to manager.

In 1967, Helen moved back to Melbourne and the Queen Victoria Hospital to get her midwifery qualification. Bob wore out his Ford Falcon ute driving the 1400 kilometres overnight from The Well via Bourke and Cobar to Melbourne so he could see her as often as possible. They married at Wagga Wagga in 1968 after Helen graduated as a midwife.

By the time the 1970s kicked in, Bob says he could see the writing on the wall for the merino industry and, believing there was no future in it, began to rethink his options. Ten years after he'd first briefly considered the prospect of medicine, Bob started to think about it seriously. He and Helen had two children and he knew it wouldn't be easy, but when the company he worked for changed hands, they decided to give it a red-hot go.

They moved to Brisbane, where Bob got a job as a cellarman throughout the day and enrolled in evening classes at Kelvin Grove High School to prepare to sit for his senior exams. He matriculated at the end of 1971 with a high enough score to get into an undergraduate degree in medicine at the University of Queensland. He was just turning twenty-eight when he started.

Working and studying was tough but Bob was determined, and he graduated at the end of 1977. His first job placement as a resident was at the Toowoomba Base Hospital, where he was due to commence work on 2 January 1978. New Year's Day was a Sunday that year and Bob and Helen and their two children, Geoff and Wendy, went to an evening church service to give thanks for their good fortune.

Bob was driving home from church with Geoff in the back and Wendy sitting between her parents on the bench seat in the front when a car slammed into the driver's side. Apart from a broken leg Helen was okay, as was Geoff, but Wendy slid under the dashboard and sustained some nasty but not life-threatening injuries. Bob, on the other hand, took the full brunt of the impact, suffering a head injury involving a brain-stem injury and major concussion, bilateral fractured arms, and a fractured femur, tibia and fibula in his right leg, plus the consequent tissue trauma.

Unconscious, Bob was taken straight to his new workplace, where he was intubated in casualty before being admitted to the intensive care unit. The doctors told Helen that he needed to be stabilised before they could try to deal with any of his fractures, but she suspects the real reason they didn't oper- ate immediately was that they didn't expect him to survive the first night.

However, this particular man is nothing if not determined and even in a coma, on a ventilator via the tracheostomy which was inserted two or three days later, he was fighting. Ten days after the accident Bob was still alive and stable enough to have plaster of Paris back-slabs bandaged to his arms to immobilise them and his leg pinned and a traction splint applied. At two weeks he came off the ventilator and started to wake up a bit. Helen laughingly recalls, 'One of his first conversations was about the dream he'd just had that he'd had a baby.' Although he remembers none of it, Bob says he just kind of realised one day that he was still alive.

Three months after he was admitted to the Toowoomba Base Hospital, Bob was transferred to Princess Alexandra for two weeks to be assessed for rehab. He didn't want to be there and the Princess Alexandra doctors agreed he would probably do just as well in Toowoomba. Bob promptly went home on crutches and Helen looked after him.

Thanks to Dr Des O'Rourke, the medical superintendent at the time, for the three months that Bob was in Toowoomba Hospital, Helen and the kids had been able to stay in one of the doctors' flats provided by the hospital. They'd sold their house in Brisbane prior to moving so they had some funds immediately available and Bob had sickness benefits to help support them. Even so, while his professional future was uncertain so was their financial future, although neither Bob nor Des O'Rourke appeared to have any doubts he'd fully recover.

By October, Bob's tracheostomy scar was still not closed, he was wearing an eye patch and walking with a stick, but Des put him to work in casualty as a 5/7 resident, meaning that he only worked a five-day week and was not on call. Bob did that until the end of 1980, by which time he was considered well enough and experienced enough to be promoted to a senior resident position.

The family stayed in Toowoomba until the end of 1981, when they went to Bundaberg for a year and then Charleville Base Hospital for two years. In 1984, Bob returned to Toowoomba Base Hospital for a year as a registrar, during which time he trained in anaesthetics and obstetrics.

Three years later, after placements in Chinchilla and

Longreach, Bob successfully applied for the job of flying doctor with the RFDS base in Charleville. Having secured his dream job, he stayed there for sixteen years, undertaking all the regular clinic runs that are core business for the RFDS, and pretty much all of the retrievals. Even though, statistically, 75–80 per cent of RFDS retrievals are undertaken by a lone flight nurse, in Bob's day he always went as well, especially when the emergency was as serious as Robbie Fraser's accident was.

Robbie and Scott had been riding home from shifting cattle on Nooyeah Downs, their 84 000-hectare sheep and cattle station, when they split up. They'd been out since daylight to beat the expected heat of the day and were about 30 kilometres from the homestead when Scott turned off to cut across country to check some waters, while Robbie rode home along the 'safer' route of the Thargo–Bulloo Downs road which cuts through Nooyeah.

About 10 kilometres from the Nooyeah homestead, Robbie's wide-wheeled Yamaha TW200 motorbike, which had been bought specifically for its stability, hit a boulder buried in the bulldust. Fifty-eight-year-old Robbie was thrown head and arm first onto the road.

Few people use the road other than the Frasers in the course of their station business but, with exquisitely lucky timing, their only neighbour, Ian Glasson, was travelling between his properties in a truck and found Robbie very soon after she hit the dirt.

Had Ian not been on that road, Robbie would not have been missed until after Scott got home and called her at her house to check she was safely back. Even then, knowing that she might have had a flat tyre or even found a job that needed doing on the way, he wouldn't have worried immediately. He'd have given her half an hour perhaps, then called her on the radio.

As it was, he'd just walked into the house and drunk a glass of water when Ian called him on the two-way radio that remote station people invariably carry and said, 'You'd better get down here. Your mother's had a bad prang and she's not in a good way.'

Leaving his wife, Paula, in charge of the radio and telephone, Scott chucked a couple of blankets and a pillow in their Holden station wagon and took off. When he found them, Robbie was standing on her feet beside Ian but looking very unwell. Knowing better than anyone her resilience and determination, but fearing that she might fall, Scott talked her into sitting and then lying down. She had skin sheared off her face and all down one arm and she was drifting in and out of consciousness. Scariest of all, he could see blood trickling from both ears and her nose.

He called Paula on the radio and directed her to ring Suzanne Gibbes at the Thargo hospital to explain what had happened, tell her about the blood and ask her to get the Flying Doctor in the air and on its way. Paula also rang Scott's sister, Jocie, who lived about three hours away on a station between Hungerford and Bourke, to let her know what had happened.

While Suzanne was alerting Bob Balmain at the clinic in Jackson Oil Fields, back at the accident site, Scott put the back seats down in the wagon and folded the blankets longways down one side of the extended space to cushion Robbie. He and Ian manoeuvred her into the back, lying her on the

blankets on her 'good' side with her head on a pillow and the
spare tyre chocked in behind her so she wouldn't roll around
as Scott drove, flat out, straight to Thargomindah.

Because Ian Glasson had found Robbie almost immediately
and because Scott was able to get her to town straight away
and because by good fortune the RFDS was already only a
twenty-odd minute flight away, Bob was attending to Robbie
within two hours of the accident, an advantage that undoubt-
edly paid dues in terms of her recovery.

Reflecting that 'one of the benefits of studying anaesthetics
is having the capacity to put people to sleep for the duration of
their evacuation', Bob recalls that once he had confirmed his
decision to fly her to Brisbane despite her GCS score of 3, he
put Robbie to sleep, intubated her, attached an Air-Viva bag
to the tube in her throat and started hand-pumping the bag
to push air into her lungs. Because they didn't have an ambulance, they loaded her into the back of Scott's car and took her
to the plane, attached her to the inflight ventilator, gave Scott a
seat up the front with the pilot and took off.

When they landed at Eagle Farm Airport, they transferred
Robbie and the ventilator to the waiting ambulance, then
Bob and the flight nurse accompanied her to Royal Brisbane
Hospital, where Bob, as was his habit, personally handed her
over to casualty staff. Robbie was transferred back onto an
Air-Viva while they admitted her, and Bob and the flight nurse
retrieved their ventilator and returned to the plane for the
flight home.

Scott followed them in from the airport with his cousin
who, coincidentally, worked in air traffic control and had been
waiting for him when they landed. It was still daylight when

Scott walked into the casualty department at Royal Brisbane Hospital and found his mother lying on a trolley, pushed up against a wall with a handful of other patients, while a nurse took her observations, wrote details in her file and occasionally reached over to squeeze the Air-Viva.

Scott recalls his horror when he saw that his mother was only getting a sporadic pump of the bag and that nothing appeared to be happening, but the nurse told him he had to complete his assessment before he could send her to X-ray. The hour and a half they waited for any action was such a stark contrast to the immediate response they'd had a thousand kilometres inland at their local clinic and with the RFDS. Robbie appeared to be deteriorating before Scott's eyes and his frustration led him to bomb the nurse, telling him where she'd come from and how badly she'd been injured; that she needed attention now! The nurse appeared to have no understanding of Robbie's situation and even less appreciation for Scott's distress.

Finally, they wheeled Robbie off to X-ray and sent Scott home for the night. When he returned to the hospital first thing next morning his mother was lying in Intensive Care in an induced coma. The ICU doctor told Scott she had a base-of-skull fracture and seven fractures on the right-hand side of her skull radiating out from her ear. He explained that, in theatre the night before, they'd drilled a burr hole through her skull to relieve the pressure on her brain and she needed to remain in the intensive care unit (ICU) for a couple of days.

Jocie and her husband Stuart had arrived in the early hours of the morning, having had to wait until extended family arrived to look after their baby boy and the property before driving the twelve hours to Brisbane. She and Scott spent every waking hour beside Robbie's bed, not knowing if she would pull through.

Scott says, 'They tell you to talk to unconscious patients just as though they're listening to you, you know; to include them in the conversation. But you can never really tell if they're hearing you or not.'

The day the medical staff brought Robbie out of the coma she was lying in ICU looking pretty shattered with two black eyes in her swollen, skinned face. It was a long slow process but, although she could hardly see through her eyes when she eventually opened them, Scott says, 'You wouldn't believe it but she seemed 100 per cent okay. She knew who we were.'

When they moved Robbie out of ICU and into a room with a lot of other people, however, they realised her short-term memory was out of whack – she knew all the details of her life but thought it was the 1970s. She was also amazed to learn she'd fallen off her motorbike and couldn't comprehend that she was in a hospital in Brisbane.

Jocie recalls her mother kept thinking she was at the airport. 'I used to ask her if you could land a jumbo jet in there and she would look up and down the line of beds in the ward and say, "Well, probably not . . ."'

Robbie spent six weeks in hospital, during which time she underwent further major surgery to stop cerebrospinal fluid leaking out of her nose and gradually recovered her physical health. Over that period her memory perception also progressed until it was accurate, but she never remembered anything about the accident itself.

She went home to Nooyeah and slowly made a complete

recovery, although she had a carer living with her for quite a long time as she wasn't allowed to drive for six months or ride a bike for a year. The first time Robbie went in to Thargo to see Bob Balmain at his routine RFDS clinic at the hospital, Suzanne apologised to her for cutting off all her clothes, including what looked like a brand-new set of undies. With a return of her old sense of humour, whenever Robbie saw Suzanne after that, she'd tease her that she owed her a new bra and a new pair of knickers.

As for Bob, seeing Robbie for her post-accident check-ups was particularly pleasing. Each time she arrived looking a little better than the last was a nod to his insistence that they take her to Brisbane for specialist care. And every time she left to return home to Nooyeah, he had the satisfaction of knowing that his skills and experience had saved and sustained her life so that she could have her second chance.

It was by no means the last time Bob would feel that same sense of accomplishment.

Bob was in the Royal Flying Doctor base in Charleville on the morning of 29 January 2000 when he got an urgent phone call from Neen Hawkes, the registered nurse at the Yaraka health clinic in central western Queensland. She was alerting him that her friend and neighbour John Paul Tully had been in a serious motorbike accident at Mt Marlow Station and that she was on her way over. Bob assured her the plane would be on standby, that they would await her update from the scene of the accident and that he would come immediately if she needed him.

After she hung up, Neen grabbed her nurse's bag, whooshed her two young daughters Holly and Jess into the car and, guided by her husband, Hawkes, who'd been in a plane returning from Mt Marlow when he heard the calls for help over the radio, she hightailed the 30 kilometres across country to the accident site. As she drove she called Andrew McCarthy at the Yaraka police station, confirmed she was on her way and asked him to stand by to act as a relay to Bob at the RFDS base in Charleville.

Although he doesn't remember anything much about the collision, John Paul Tully does recall they'd been mustering since daylight with Hawkes spotting from the air. He remembers calling his wife, Sue, on the radio and asking her to come out and pick up any sheep struggling in the piercing summer heat. He remembers they collected a few and put them through to the next paddock, after which Sue followed him down the fence line.

As she drove, Sue was thinking about her and John Paul's wedding anniversary the next day and hoping they'd have an easier day, when she glanced over to see if she could see Jason Kruger, the station overseer, on his bike with any more sheep. As she looked back at the road, she realised too late that John Paul had pulled up in front of her. Despite slamming on the brakes, she could not avoid hitting him.

On impact, the back wheel of his motorbike was caught up under the bull bar, hard against the front of the left-hand front wheel of the Toyota utility. Jammed upright by the bull bar, the bike crimped in the middle, lightly pinning John Paul, who was flung back across the bull bar then forward again like a rag doll.

By the time Neen braked beside the Toyota, a handful of people who'd heard the panicked cries for help on their two-ways had turned up to help. At her first direct sight of him, Neen noted that John Paul didn't look good. Quickly organising a couple of men to keep supporting him in place on the bike, she checked his vital signs and established an intravenous line to keep him hydrated. Although he was badly dazed, he was initially more or less coherent but as Neen checked him out a little more thoroughly, she ascertained that he had a definite fracture of one arm, a possible brain injury, a very probable spinal injury and possible internal injuries.

Being the person on the ground with appropriate medical training, Neen was in charge of the situation. As well as managing John Paul's status she needed to support Sue, who was in shock. She quickly sent Hawkes up to the homestead to get their RFDS medical kit, some blankets and pillows, and the Tullys' Landcruiser wagon so they could use it to transport John Paul to the plane when it arrived, and then she sent her daughter Holly to their car to radio Andrew McCarthy, who was waiting at the police station to hear her assessment of the accident.

Though still in primary school, Holly and Jess were both accustomed to going to emergencies with Neen. They knew how to do things to help their mother and Holly capably told Andrew, 'We're at Mt Marlow and Mum needs the oxygen and a stretcher from the clinic urgently and Mum says can you call the RFDS and tell Dr Bob it's bad and she'll call again soon with some details but can he come PDQ.'

Shortly after, Andrew called Holly back to tell her that he was on his way with the things her mother needed from the clinic and that Bob and the flight crew were boarding the plane.

Even without knowing exactly what the situation was, Bob says Neen's request for assistance was always enough to get him in the air. 'It was reassuring knowing Neen was at the scene, as she always did everything exactly as I asked and would report back exactly what I needed to know.'

Neen's completed assessment was relayed to Bob via the police station as the plane was about to take off. While John Paul was still conscious, Neen felt compelled to get him off the bike. However, through the relay, Bob said, 'Do not move him before I get there and follow the ABC of first response: airway, breathing and circulation' – which Neen did.

Neen organised a rotation of helpers to continue to brace John Paul, relieving them as soon as their arms tired so that he always had firm, steady support. As soon as Andrew McCarthy arrived with an oxygen cylinder, she set John Paul up with the oxygen mask to help maintain his blood oxygen saturation. All the while, she checked his vital signs every fifteen minutes.

In the meantime, one of the men had nosed another vehicle around in front of the bike and a couple of them rigged a tarpaulin between the vehicles to provide shade for John Paul in the rapidly rising late-morning mid-summer heat.

Then they settled down to wait, knowing full well that all around the district, people were glued to their two-way radios, waiting with them.

As the minutes crept by, the sun rose higher and got much hotter, glaring fiercely across the open plain. All the while, Neen was outwardly confident and reassuring but inwardly feeling sick because she knew that John Paul was critically compromised and, even with the RFDS on the way, they were a very, very long way from the kind of medical intervention he would need. She didn't really think John Paul would survive.

Keeping up her appearance of calm confidence as time slipped away, Neen told only Andrew that John Paul was steadily deteriorating and that they were getting low on oxygen. In a relay to Bob in the air, she told him that John Paul was suffering increased periods of apnoea (when he would stop breathing momentarily), and his level of consciousness was deteriorating so much that she'd begun to assist his breathing manually with an Air-Viva bag. Bob sent her back a message of reassurance and an estimated time of arrival from the pilot.

Finally, out of the south-east they heard the first faint buzz of the plane. Thinking back with a glimmer of tears in her eyes, Neen says, 'I'd never been so pleased to hear the sound of an aircraft in my life.' It took another fifteen minutes for the plane to land on the airstrip up at the homestead and for Hawkes to bring Bob and the flight nurse down to the scene of the accident.

'Dr Bob stepped out of the car, came straight over and said in his calm, gentle voice, "It's okay now, we'll take over." It was such a relief to have him there,' Neen says. Quietly taking up the story, Bob says he could see it was a difficult and stressful situation, but that Neen had it all well in hand.

As Neen handed over to Bob, she couldn't get a viable reading on John Paul's blood pressure, his heart rate was 100 and the oxygen cylinder was pretty much empty. Bob sedated John Paul and then directed several men to lift him very carefully, using full spinal precautions, up and off the bike and onto the stretcher on a tarp on the ground.

Bob then thoroughly examined him, got him stabilised, put him to sleep for the journey, intubated him and connected him to the Air-Viva, pumped by the flight nurse, all the while explaining everything to Sue, who was clearly distressed. 'He was just wonderful,' Neen recalls.

They loaded the stretcher into the back of the Landcruiser and Hawkes carefully drove Bob and John Paul (with the nurse tucked in beside him pumping the Air-Viva) back to the plane while the pilot and Sue followed in another car. As soon as they loaded John Paul into the plane, Bob transferred him onto their inflight ventilator.

Having called ahead to the Royal Brisbane Hospital, the plane landed and refuelled in Charleville, giving Bob a chance to restabilise John Paul on the ground before they continued on to Brisbane.

Ultimately John Paul's injuries proved to be extensive. His lung had collapsed, his spleen had ruptured with accompanying blood loss and he had a spinal injury but he survived thanks to Neen Hawkes' first response, and to Bob, whose anaesthetics skills enabled him to safely manage John Paul's evacuation from Mt Marlow right through to the casualty department of the Royal Brisbane Hospital. Viewing the world from his wheelchair seventeen years later, John Paul continues to conduct a productive and very happy life with his second wife, Shelley.

In a tribute to Dr Bob Balmain, shared in her own story 'Outback Angel' in *Nurses of the Outback*, Neen says she is grateful for the years that she worked with him when she was the lone RN at Yaraka and he was the flying doctor based in

Charleville. 'I admire and respect him so much. Dr Bob taught me procedures that enhanced my ability to care for the people of the Yaraka community until he could get there; skills that stand me in good stead today. He knew my capabilities and he knew just how much I could manage on my own. I couldn't have asked for a better medical back-up or a finer professional mentor than Dr Bob.'

For his part, Bob very much enjoyed his sixteen years with the RFDS in Charleville, and particularly the six years when his wife, Helen, flew with him as a flight nurse. Attending regular clinics all over South West Queensland and up into the centre of the state was an adventure they both treasured. Because of his background in the sheep industry, Bob could relate to the circumstances in which most of his patients lived and worked and because of his personal experience of critical injury he could empathise with those people whose lives were literally in his hands when he went to rescue them.

Reflecting on his experiences with the uniquely unrushed tone that reflects both his UK childhood and his thoughtful, deliberate nature, Bob says, 'As far as I was concerned, it didn't matter how low they were, if the patient was alive when I got to them, my job was to keep them alive until we delivered them to the specialist care they needed.'

Although, in the end, some of his retrieval patients didn't survive, Bob Balmain is deeply satisfied that not one of them died on his watch.

15

Nomad Locum

Dr Jenny Wilson, sometimes South Australia, often elsewhere

In 2015, Dr Jenny Wilson was out on patrol with a health team and overnighting in a village on the tiny, remote island of Emirau in Papua New Guinea's New Ireland Province when she woke shivering with fever. Lying in her cot on the south-western edge of the North Pacific, her first thought was that she was incredibly fatigued.

It was her second excursion to PNG as a volunteer with the same aid organisation but, even without her rising temperature, quite unlike her first. Just after she'd arrived in Kavieng – the capital of New Ireland – to assume her role as team doctor some weeks previously, the project manager of her group made the decision to move to another role with a different organisation. Even though he was still around and did offer some advice he would not be going out on the patrols he'd teed up and Jenny was dumped in the deep end. For all intents and purposes, she had to organise the patrols herself:

the staff, the logistics, all the preparation that ensures a safe, secure mission. And then, when they came back in, she had to clean everything down and prepare it for the next patrol, which would take place as soon as she reported on the one just done and organised the new one. It was a gruelling schedule and she was exhausted.

But that didn't explain the fever. Jenny's second thought was that she might have contracted malaria; she was momentarily relieved when she tested herself and it proved negative.

Unable to leave her bed, she sent the rest of the patrol off to provide a clinic around the other side of the island then, as her fever worsened, she worked her way through the other possibilities. That was when she noticed the scratch on her ankle where her sandal strap had rubbed through and, on closer examination, the enlarged glands in her groin. Ruefully acknowledging that it probably hadn't helped, she remembered the swim she'd had in a river pool the day before.

Realising she had an undefined infection, Jenny treated herself with some oral antibiotics and paracetamol and hoped all would be well.

Within twenty-four hours, she realised it wasn't . . .

Growing up in suburban Adelaide, Jenny Wilson very much wanted to live on a farm and admits with a wry smile, 'I wondered why my parents couldn't just pack up and go to the country and buy one.' When she was six, her father went overseas on a round-the-world ticket. Of that memory Jenny says, 'I was so impressed I decided there and then that, as soon as I was old enough, I was going to do that too.' Needless to say, economic comprehension accompanied maturity, but both dreams lingered.

By the time she was a Year 11 student at Cabra Dominican Convent, Jenny knew she wanted to help people and was thinking about being a nurse or physiotherapist. As a devout Catholic with an older sister who'd already joined an order, she was also juggling those possibilities with the idea of becoming a nun and even doing some kind of aid work. Then one of her best friends told her she was going to do medicine. It was a bit of light-bulb moment for Jenny, who really wasn't at all sure what she wanted but thought, *That sounds like an interesting thing to do. Maybe I'll become a doctor . . .*

And so she did, although it wasn't a smooth pathway. In fact, she hated her first three years at the medical school of the University of Adelaide. Having been in the top three in her year at school she was suddenly thrust, she says, 'into a very bright, highly competitive group of students who all appeared to know exactly what they were doing while I felt completely out of my depth'. Adding to her consternation, Jenny found she couldn't organise her thoughts fast enough in a university exam room and struggled to write the excellent responses she could and did write in her assignments because she had time to think about them.

Barely seventeen when she started uni, Jenny was dealing with all the usual teenage insecurities and uncertainties even while she was testing her parents with the first tendrils of 'attitude'. Adding to her woes, in her very first year she had a serious accident. Her boyfriend of the time was teaching her how to ride his motorbike around the ring road at the uni. Jenny was riding on her own, went too fast, drifted onto the wrong side of the road and a car hit her. As she went over the handlebars she remembers thinking, *Mum and Dad are going to be* really *mad at me now*.

The silver lining was the novel insight it gave her into the flip side of medicine. During the six weeks she spent in hospital with her fractured leg she learnt a lot about the value of good nurses and the arrogance of some doctors. In the first couple of days, every time the orthopaedic surgeon came around she told him her ankle was hurting. He told her the injury was to her shin and that's where the pain should be. She'd sustained some nerve damage and lost a little feeling in her lower leg so she figured maybe he was right, but when they took the cast off she had a pressure sore on her ankle from the tight bottom edge of the plaster.

When the nurses noticed staining coming through the plaster over the point where her shin was crushed, the registrar on duty ordered a window be cut into it. They found her shin skin was not healing and he decided she'd need a skin graft. Morning and night, the nurses had to debride the proud flesh forming on the surface of the wound to prepare it for the graft, and each time they gave her a shot of pethidine even though Jenny assured them she didn't need it. The registrar insisted she did. Jenny says, 'There was something odd about him insisting I have the pain relief when I didn't think I needed it and I wasn't especially surprised to hear he was later charged and deregistered for drug misuse.'

After she was eventually discharged, Jenny was able to resume her studies but hobbled about for the rest of the year with her leg in plaster. Once out of the cast she could get out and about more easily and began to enjoy her social life, even though she was still not enjoying medicine. As she ventured into second and then third year, she was beginning to question a whole lot of things about her life.

When she entered fourth year, Jenny was still living at home and scrapping more and more often with her mother, who always wanted to know where she was and what she was doing. Unhappy at home and at uni, Jenny began asserting control over the one thing she felt she could: food. A few months later she went to a doctor because she hadn't had a period for some time and was further disenchanted with the medical profession when he said to her quite flippantly, 'Well you're not pregnant . . .' She already knew that!

Many years later she realised she'd been anorexic, but at the time Jenny only knew that she needed a complete break. The dean of the faculty agreed that she should take the rest of the year off and then re-evaluate. Jenny moved out of home and found work in a nursing home, which she really enjoyed. By the end of the year, she was feeling so much better, she decided to go back to uni and finish what she'd started.

As turning points go, it was a doozy. Entering fourth year for the second time, Jenny found her new cohort weren't anywhere near as competitive and they were a lot more fun to be around. They were more social, much more down to earth and she felt as though she finally fitted in. As a consequence she relished the rest of her uni years, which became even more interesting as they undertook clinical placements and began to practise practical medical skills.

Jenny graduated at the end of 1978 and spent her intern year at Flinders Medical Centre in Adelaide. She had never completely abandoned her dream of living in the country, so when she broke up with her boyfriend at the beginning of her RMO (resident medical officer) year, she applied for a job at Cessnock, a large country town in the Hunter Valley in New South Wales. Having enjoyed that experience, she still had to complete her RMO year and moved to Nepean Hospital at Penrith on the outskirts of Sydney.

Four years after she graduated, Jenny finally took off with a view to travelling as far as her dollars would take her. She and a friend wandered through Indonesia for a month savouring the different cultures, languages, colours and food before Jenny continued on alone through Malaysia, Thailand and India where, three months down the track, she joined a Topdeck tour to London. Meandering through Pakistan, Jordan, Syria and Turkey into Europe and then on to the UK, constantly fascinated by the medley of peoples and places that corresponded with the changing landscape, Jenny consolidated her capacity for self-sufficiency and resilience.

When she finally arrived in London she was well and truly ready to work again and pleased to be offered a job in a rural hospital, where she was able to start doing anaesthetics. Jenny planned to go on from there and perhaps learn some paediatric medicine but she had such a great experience working with the anaesthetics specialists there she decided to stay. They were so encouraging about her potential, she sat the first part of her anaesthetics specialist exams and, when she passed, was pleased to be appointed as a registrar.

As life rolled on, she made some great friends, caught up with some old uni mates and met her future husband, Colin. He was working as an anaesthetic assistant and they quickly became a couple. Her life became a little less studious and as soon as she said 'Yes!', they filled out the paperwork and married three weeks later.

Meantime, as she partied with her friends and listened to what everyone else was doing, Jenny realised she didn't really want to become a specialist at all and nor did she want to stay in England. She'd never given aid work a crack and the idea still lured her. When she failed her second exam, she had the perfect out.

Jenny and Colin had saved enough money to keep themselves for quite a while, so Jenny successfully applied to go and work in St Mary's Hospital, a small privately run bush hospital at Melmoth, about 200 kilometres north of Durban in South Africa. Colin's qualifications were not recognised in South Africa (or Australia) so he went as her partner knowing he wouldn't be able to work in his usual role.

As well as providing outreach services and an occasional mobile vaccination clinic, the 110-bed hospital catered to, more often than not, around 150 inpatients, sometimes two to a bed, sometimes with people on the floor. There were a lot of white people living in the area, but St Mary's was specifically for Zulus, some of whom would walk for days to reach help. The fact that they were required to pay a fee for services seemed contradictory to Jenny and she soon discovered her new medical colleagues felt the same.

The CEO of the Anglican organisation running the hospital was a Scottish missionary who took a very hardline stance on the matter of patient payments. If people couldn't pay, they had to be on death's door to get in and then he wouldn't let them be discharged until someone came and paid their dues. He had guards on the gates to make sure no one got away.

Apart from the disagreements that arose because of the CEO's insistence on patient payments, Jenny loved the work. As one of only three doctors she was incredibly busy dealing with lots of traumatic injuries, terrible infections and chronic illness. As Jenny says, 'all the usual things you see in a developing country that you don't see in the first world. It was such a contrast even to the white population in South Africa. We had a dedicated tuberculosis ward that was always full and yet we'd hear the [white] president and minister for health on the radio saying TB had just about been eradicated.'

Day after day, patients arrived with serious and sometimes critical injuries as a result of violence, some of it against women but mostly from men fighting. Jenny recalls that the police weren't interested, adding, 'If someone was critically ill there was no rescue service or retrieval service for the Zulus. They just watched them die.'

Even more challenging were the kids who died, particularly those who succumbed to preventable diseases like measles; beautiful, chubby babies who died because there was no available treatment. Then there were the kids who died of gastro, or something much worse because they'd been taken first to the local witchdoctor and given a home remedy of strong bleach solution poured into the rectum. When that had the inevitable dire consequences, the parents would walk hours and hours to the hospital in the hope that the doctors there might be able to help. It was just one more heartbreaking characteristic of Jenny's new environment.

Shortly after they arrived in Africa, Jenny realised with great delight that she was pregnant. Nine months and one week after she and Colin were married, in the very early hours of the morning, Tom was delivered at a much larger hospital about 80 kilometres away in Eshowe. Jenny had hoped to have an epidural but her labour was so fast (four hours) she didn't need it; so fast, the doctor only just made it into the labour room!

Jenny happily recalls that as she later lay nursing Tom in bed in her east-facing room, his arrival was heralded by 'the most magnificent African sunrise. It seemed a very fitting start to the day'.

Their joy resonated around the hospital after Colin went into the cafeteria where all the nurses and docs were having breakfast and told them she'd had a baby boy. The room erupted with ululation and cheering.

Back home in the grounds of the bush hospital, Jenny enjoyed great support from the medical superintendent and his wife, who lived next door with three young children. Despite their geographic and cultural isolation, Jenny found that 'living in a communal environment surrounded by so many supportive people was very special'.

With Colin on hand as house husband, Jenny was able to go back to work when Tom was six weeks old. She says everyone made it so easy for her. If she was on the wards she could slip away easily to feed Tom, but if she was rostered in outpatients, the nurse would just tell everyone she was going to feed the baby and they all understood; as often as not they cheered!

Jenny learnt an enormous amount from both the doctors and the nursing staff at the hospital. The latter were, she says, 'very supportive and empathetic with their people. And they were so skilled. They were allowed to do far more than nurses back here in Australia.'

Some months after Tom's birth, the hospital's governing board started advertising for a replacement for the medical superintendent, whose three-year contract was drawing to a close. In the meantime the CEO continued to upset the doctors with his attitude towards Zulus who couldn't afford to pay for treatment. When the hospital celebrated St Mary's Day that year, the doctors did a humorous skit about a warrior with a spear going through his chest arriving at the outpatient's desk and being turned away because he didn't have enough money. The CEO and the board weren't amused and the incident led to even more antagonism between management and the doctors. The situation deteriorated when the board accused the doctors of tearing up potential applications for the med super job and trying to set up jobs for their mates.

The med super's three years finally clocked over and, sadly farewelled by Jenny and Colin, he and his family returned to England. When he wasn't replaced and then the other doctor decided he couldn't continue working for such a corrupt board, Jenny was left in an untenable position and opted also to resign. As the only doctor left it would have been incredibly difficult to stay, but as the only doctor with an eight-month-old baby it was impossible. Learning later that some of the board were sacked did little to relieve Jenny's regret at having to leave, but she was pleased to hear that the new board quickly got everything up and functioning well again.

Meanwhile, with a husband and baby her family had never met, Jenny realised she was ready for home. After a couple of weeks' holiday in Malawi, they returned to England so that Colin could apply for Australian citizenship. They decided he would work while she had some time off to be a full-time mother to Tom, which went really well for a few weeks. Then, out of the blue, Colin became ill. He was a bit feverish but, exhausted from sleepless nights with a teething baby and a recent history working with people who were *really* sick, Jenny told him quite unsympathetically, 'You'll be right, just go to work.'

She was mortified when he was sent home with a diagnosis of malaria. Colin recovered but they'd not given a thought to malaria prevention when they went to Malawi and they both paid dearly for it. Tom went into day care and Jenny went back to her old job with the anaesthetics specialists until, nine months later, Colin's paperwork finally came through.

After nearly six years away, Jenny flew into Adelaide with her new family at the end of 1988, not only to see her parents and introduce them to Colin and Tom but also to share the good news that she was pregnant again. After a few weeks reconnecting with extended family and friends, Jenny applied for a job at the medical centre at Goolwa, a small country town about 80 kilometres south of Adelaide. She had baby Joe a month or so after she started work there and, with Colin continuing in the role of house husband, returned to work after six weeks. Happy to be in a rural setting, Jenny stayed there for a year before moving to Lakes Entrance in Victoria, where she worked as a rural GP for four years. It was perfect while the boys were so young, but then she started getting itchy feet again and hankering to do some more aid work.

Colin didn't share her enthusiasm, but he was content to care for the boys wherever Jenny wanted to be. Unfortunately, she couldn't see a way to take her whole family to a third-world country and continued to feel unsettled. Agreeing that she should follow her heart, they decided to return to Adelaide to give the boys time to get to know her family again while she undertook a year's training in obstetrics, a prerequisite to pursuing aid work.

A year later, with GP obstetrics under her belt, Jenny found a job ad for a locum at the hospital in Cooktown in Far North Queensland. With a beaming smile of reminiscence, she says, 'It was the best three years of our lives.'

The boys roamed everywhere in safety with the local kids and never wore shoes the whole time they were up there. They enjoyed going to school and made lots of great mates, while the whole family loved sharing their days with the assortment of intriguingly lateral people who called Cooktown home.

Professionally, things got off to a rocky start when, despite his assurances to the contrary, the medical superintendent pulled the pin the very day after Jenny started. She became med super and had to search for a second doctor to start asap.

The majority of Jenny's work in Cooktown was with Aboriginal and Torres Strait Islander peoples. The hospital served Hope Vale to the north and Wujal Wujal to the south and Jenny travelled to each every week to provide clinics. Once she appointed a second doctor they were both flat out busy, but as happy as. At the hospital, Jenny says, 'We had wonderful nursing staff who had the skills to deal with a lot of medical matters themselves. If they knew I'd been up all night, they wouldn't call me in unless it was absolutely necessary; life and death stuff.'

Well accustomed to managing trauma injuries after her time in Africa and finding the tropical slant on chronic illnesses fascinating, Jenny's appetite for aid work intensified. She loved her time in Cooktown and they left only because Tom needed to go to high school. She explains, 'There were great teachers there but not good subject choices and we didn't want to send them to boarding school.'

Instead, Jenny resigned her post, enrolled Tom and Joe at the Cairns School of Distance Education, and they all set off around Australia for twelve months. Jenny did a handful of locums along the way, including three months on Christmas Island, where the boys went to CI District High School, which catered to primary and secondary students. It was well before the establishment of the first 'temporary' detention centre, therefore quite peaceful, with none of the challenges of asylum seekers arriving by boat. They all loved living among the colourful and diverse languages and cultures of Christmas Island's Chinese, Malay, Eurasian and European resident population.

Working at the fairly new hospital on the island, Jenny says mental illness was the most significant problem she encountered, adding that it was difficult to deal with in such isolation – although she admits twelve weeks is a relatively short time to gain a comprehensive understanding of any community's health status.

After wandering home via southern Western Australia and the Nullarbor Highway, Jenny and Colin decided to put down roots somewhere the boys could complete their secondary education without disruption. Jenny had previously done a locum in Kapunda, near the Barossa Valley in South Australia, and knew it had a great high school with an excellent principal. The fact that she could practise both obstetrics and anaesthetics there appealed to her; knowing as well that they were only an hour to her family in Adelaide was all icing on the cake. She successfully applied for a job and stayed there for eight years, time for both Tom and Joe to graduate and move on to university.

At the end of those eight years, Jenny's feet were positively twitching, and simmering underneath it all was her undiminished desire to do more aid work. She was worried, however, about leaving the Kapunda practice in the lurch.

Her dilemma was resolved in the most confronting way when Colin was unexpectedly diagnosed with multiple sclerosis. Jenny realised she needed to be able to work much more flexibly and together she and Colin decided that they would travel while he was able. Jenny returned to undertaking locum appointments for several weeks or months at a time to make enough money so that they could go wherever they fancied. Then once each year, with Colin's support and sometimes his company for a short while, she went off to do a stint of aid work.

The first time Jenny went to New Ireland Province in Papua New Guinea, she went for four months. The province incorporates numerous small islands as well as its namesake New Ireland, a skinny strip about 350 kilometres long that forms the north-easternmost border of PNG. It's home to about 190 000 people, most of whom live in coastal villages, although there are some villages up in the mountains that run like a spine along the length of the island.

The project manager of Jenny's first tour had organised the health patrol schedule well. The team, which included a dentist, a physio, an HIV worker, a nurse and a pathologist as well as Jenny, would travel out to the designated villages, staying for two or three nights at a time to provide clinics and health checks. Travelling in and out was often difficult and sometimes downright dangerous, especially negotiating the muddy, eroded tracks into the mountains. Communications and electricity are pretty much non-existent in these areas but the aid workers kept on going because the need for their help was ceaseless. Jenny was called upon to deliver babies, fix fractures, drain abscesses, stitch wounds (usually inflicted violently), and treat seriously ill babies and/or children, all without any of the resources she would normally have access to in Australia.

While there are health workers living in many of the villages, their morale is often very low because they are not well supported, never well resourced, and often they were never well trained in the first place; they just do the best they can in the most difficult circumstances. And any resources they might have take between a long time and never to replace. A major part of the patrol team's role was to train, upskill and support the health workers as much as possible in the short time that was available, but such assistance is intermittent at best, and the level of disadvantage in the villages immense.

Chronic illness is endemic and traumatic injury from neighbouring warring tribes is a constant challenge, but the thing that really dismays Jenny is the lack of obstetric support for women, who sometimes walk for days to get to a health centre to deliver their babies. Infant mortality is improving thanks to people like her but it still compares poorly to western statistics. 'And yet,' Jenny says, 'because this is life as they know it, they make the best of it and are generally happy, welcoming people.'

On that first trip, Colin joined Jenny for six weeks and

really enjoyed the experience. He was going to fly up during her second trip, too, but it didn't work out and she spent five months up there on her own, including the night when she woke shivering with fever on Emirau Island, sixteen hours by direct sea route from Kavieng on New Ireland and days away from home by plane.

Although the patrol had travelled to Emirau on a specially chartered boat, Jenny knew the island had been used as an American base during World War II and that it had a viable airstrip – had she had the capacity to call someone in Kavieng for help. However, she didn't and when her condition deteriorated despite the oral antibiotics she was taking, she did the only other thing she could. She ordered the nurse on the patrol team to mix an IV antibiotic out of the medical kit with some local anaesthetic and inject it intramuscularly twice a day.

It was a painful process but it halted the onslaught of the infection. With everyone checking on her and delivering cups of tea and water to keep her fluids up, Jenny's fever slowly abated and she recovered enough to make the return journey by sea directly back to Kavieng. After some further rest and recuperation, and with a totally refreshed appreciation for the gift of life, she was able to resume her duties for the rest of the tour.

Completely undaunted by her experience or by the isolation and challenges of New Ireland Province, she says she would go back again, though never for more than four months at a time; that's long enough. She definitely plans to continue aid work of some description and to that end chooses to do locum work so that she can take off when the right opportunity presents itself.

Working on a two-week-on two-week-off rotation, Jenny administers anaesthetic in Port Augusta and in between, when it suits her, she takes locums around the inland. It's not always an easy pathway. Sometimes she will be relieving an overworked, overstressed permanent GP; at other times she will be walking in to situations where there has been no regular doctor, which means no continuity and, all too often, things not followed through. It takes time to build a viable patient profile when previous treatments are unfinished or paperwork is incomplete because of the carousel of changing medicos. The upside is the permanent staff, principally nurses, who are, Jenny says, 'mostly extremely accommodating, who try to help as much as possible. I've met some generous, incredibly supportive people; the kind who restore your faith in humanity.'

While working two-on two-off allows her to feel some degree of attachment to the Port Augusta community, it comes with a measure of disconnect. Even so, it's a schedule that suits her purpose; Jenny going off to do locums or aid work suits her and Colin as a couple too because, they agree, it makes them more appreciative of each other when they're together.

It also works for Colin as he negotiates his journey through MS. Occasionally there'll be a challenge that they manage between them, but on his own, he is able to sustain an optimum level of independence. Jenny particularly admires the way Colin maintains his good humour and just gets on with life, saying, 'He finds a way to go forward. He played guitar but lost touch in his fingers so now he plays ukulele which is great since there's a uke group in Kapunda . . . it gets him out and about.'

While home base is still Kapunda, a transition to Adelaide has been in the pipeline for some time and will transpire when the time is right, so that they can be nearer their sons and grandchildren and so that Jenny can help her sister to care for their ageing mother. Her father's death in 2017 added wings to their intent.

As she contemplates her journey thus far, Jenny Wilson is thankful for many things, not least her family and the life she's been able to live. She's grateful to have been in the places she's been and to have met the people she's met in her role as a doctor.

With a warmth and humility that belie her talent and dedication, she says, 'It's a great privilege to be a doctor, to be a part of people's life cycle and to hear their stories. Bringing babies into the world and being there with people as they are dying, being entrusted with such important milestones in their lives, are the very best things about being in medicine.'

16

High Country Medicine

Dr Paul Duff, Mount Hotham, Victoria

One very cold but clear night many years ago, Dr Paul Duff was on call in the Mount Hotham medical centre in Victoria's north-eastern high country when a three-week-old baby was brought in by her mother. Swiftly assessing the very sick infant as seriously ill, he immediately organised an ambulance and a nurse escort to evacuate the mother and baby down off the mountain to Wangaratta, 135 kilometres away to the north-west.

Fifteen minutes later, Paul was horrified when the ambo walked back in reporting that the ambulance had conked out a couple of kilometres down the road. All but pushing the ambo out the door and into his own 4WD wagon, Paul drove down to where the mother, baby and nurse waited in the fast-cooling confines of the immobilised ambulance. As they transferred all the emergency equipment into the back of his vehicle, the nurse settled herself in the back seat beside the mother. With no car seat and time being of the essence, the nurse held the baby and directed Paul to 'stop friggin' around and get going!'

Knowing well the dangers of the steep, slippery road, he set off, white-knuckled hands gripping the steering wheel as he carefully negotiated that terrible descent . . .

Paul and his wife moved to Australia many years ago, but his lilting accent lingers as he says with a grin, 'Catherine and I migrated here from Ireland twenty-six years, one month and fourteen days ago. The 13th of July 1990.' It's not that it's been so awful he's counted the days; he's just always been terrifyingly good at maths and mental arithmetic.

As the children of the senior sergeant of police in Ballycastle, a small town in County Antrim on the north-east coast of Northern Ireland, Paul and his siblings grew up in the local police station. When Paul was about ten, his father was transferred to another town and, not wanting to leave Ballycastle, his family moved out into a private house. This was before the worst of the conflict that became known as the Troubles seriously commenced in the early '70s and Paul remembers being aware that there were violent incidents happening, but it didn't impact on them directly and he doesn't recall ever feeling scared or even worried about it. There was nowhere in his village he was afraid to go.

Until he was thirteen, Paul was really keen to become an airline pilot so he was studying two languages (French and German) and physics, but the language teachers were so bad there was no hope of him getting his O levels. His English teacher encouraged him to do medicine instead, saying, 'My brother's a doctor and he has a great life!' Paul talked it over with his parents, who thought it was a good idea. His mother told him if he became a doctor he'd surely be able to afford to buy his own plane! Paul just wanted a good job that was going to make him some decent money so he changed to biological sciences.

People in Northern Ireland at that time were either devoutly Catholic or fiercely Protestant and never the twain mixed, although small towns didn't have quite the level of sectarianism evidenced in the bigger towns and cities. The schools were technically segregated but there were a couple of dozen Catholic kids at the Protestant school in Ballycastle, although none vice versa until Paul's older brother became the first Protestant in history to be allowed to go to the local convent. Following in his brother's footsteps, Paul also went to the Catholic school, where he was able to achieve the A levels he needed to get into Queen's University in Belfast to do medicine.

Once qualified, he did his internship at Whiteabbey Hospital just north of Belfast prior to relocating into the city to the Royal Victoria Hospital. From that base, he spent two and a half years training in general practice as he moved through various medical and surgical rotations, including six months' paediatrics at the Royal Belfast Hospital for Sick Children and six months at the Royal Maternity Hospital.

While he was working in Belfast he met and married Catherine, who'd completed her nursing training there. Paul maintains they came to Australia for the adventure. Catherine says it was because of their mixed marriage: 'He's Anglican and I'm a Catholic.' In reality they came because chance threw the right hand . . .

Always intent on general practice, Paul never considered specialising but instead successfully applied to work in a private practice in Oxfordshire, a rural county in South East England. Still a bit of a wild Irish lad despite his qualifications and his marriage, in his spare time Paul had developed a passion for snow skiing and he and Catherine spent many of their days off whipping across to the ski fields of Europe.

Coincidentally, both of his bosses in the Oxfordshire practice had been to Australia; one of them even had an Australian wife. The other had worked in Omeo in East Gippsland. When they told Paul he wasn't ready for partnership and that he needed to back up and 'get the fire out of his belly', they also suggested he go to Australia because there were ski fields there. As luck would have it, someone in Bairnsdale in Victoria was advertising for a doctor.

Early in 1990, Paul wrote to the Bairnsdale practice expressing his interest. Before the advent of emails, written communication travelled by air or sea mail so he expected to wait for a reply, but when the answer came several weeks later, it came from the town of Bright 230 kilometres further north. The doctors at Bairnsdale had found someone for their practice but knew that Bright Medical Centre was looking for a doctor and had sent his letter on. The Bright doctors wrote to ask him if he'd like to come and work in their practice starting the following January, explaining that it included a satellite practice at Mount Hotham.

As soon as he realised that Mount Hotham was a ski field with a resort, Paul was hooked.

———

Keen to get on their way, in July 1990, the Duffs moved to
Brisbane, where Catherine was able to get a nursing job and
Paul locum work. They both worked all after-hours shifts,
which was a slog, but only for three and a half days each
week, giving them ample time to venture out and about anywhere that took their fancy and suited their timeframe and
budget. Then, as planned, in the first month of 1991 Paul
and Catherine escaped the Queensland summer and moved
to Bright for what they agree was 'the most wonderful ten
months'. Paul loved working in the country practice and getting to know regular patients. And as the snow season revved
up towards the middle of the year, whenever he wasn't working, he skied. When the snow was done, he and Catherine
explored north-eastern Victoria and as much of Australia as
they could.

As their tenure drew to a close, they planned their return to
the UK, thinking they'd go home for a visit and then maybe try
Canada next or perhaps New Zealand. When they researched
the possibilities, there was no work available in Canada apart
from Labrador and Saskatchewan, neither of which appealed
to them, and they thought New Zealand might be too small.

As it turned out, a week after they arrived back in Ireland,
Catherine's father had a heart attack and her sister was diagnosed with breast cancer, so they stayed in the UK. Paul got
a job as a GP in an urban practice in Wiltshire and hated it,
observing grimly, 'It was soul-destroying.' He keenly wanted
to come back to Australia.

Reprieve came when he heard that the locum who'd
replaced him in Bright was leaving and the practice partners
asked him if he'd like to come back. Nearly a whole, long year

after they'd left, with both Catherine's father and sister well on the road to recovery, they returned to Australia. Aware that it might not live up to their rose-coloured expectations, especially having viewed it from the depths of despair in Wiltshire, Paul and Catherine were delighted to find it even better second time around. Well acquainted with what they were coming to, and to whom, Paul was much more assured and better prepared for rural general practice.

Despite being only a couple of hundred kilometres from Melbourne as the crow flies, Bright is 320 kilometres by road, so it is very much a rural community. Paul knew very quickly that he'd found his particular paradise and, like his colleagues, became a member of the Australian College of Rural and Remote Medicine and the Rural Doctors Association of Australia, availing himself of the networks and support those organisations provide so very comprehensively to their members

Catherine also found her feet in their new home. She got a job working as a psych nurse 60 kilometres away at Beechworth, until the first of their children, Madeleine, was born. After their son, Michael, was born and when she was ready, Catherine was employed in Bright working in family therapy.

Meanwhile, Paul had marked his place firmly in the Bright Medical Centre practice. Having returned to Australia with no plan to leave ever, he worked for the practice until he and Catherine got permanent residency in 1994, after which the doctors offered him a partnership.

Unlike many businesses, being a partner in a rural or remote medical practice has nothing to do with seniority and everything to do with permanency. With a laugh, Paul expresses a truth that will resonate with every rural and remote doctor in the country: 'It's about the other docs tying you to the place so you won't leave!' But he's not complaining and he's never regretted his decision to buy into the practice.

Located in the Ovens Valley between Mount Buffalo and the Bogong High Plains, Bright is an old town drenched in farming and gold-mining history. It has a permanent population of a couple of thousand people, which is boosted all year round by tourists, thousands of whom trek there throughout summer and autumn to enjoy the changing colours of the masses of European trees planted there in a century past. Many visitors hike or cycle the various mountain paths, while others are drawn by the promise of fabulous food, including locally manufactured chocolate, interesting and delicious wines from local vineyards and even a trendy brewery. And then there are the snow bunnies on their way to winter at the resorts.

As soon as the snow season kicks in, the four senior doctors, including Paul and his partner, and two registrars in the Bright practice rotate through the satellite clinic at Mount Hotham for seven-day blocks every four or five weeks. There are always two of them up there working alternate 24-hour shifts, technically from 1 p.m. to 1 p.m., but when it's really busy there is, in reality, an hour or two extra either side. The roster gives the doctors a break from their normal routine at Bright and means they can ski when they come off their shift, enjoy a night out with friends if they've a mind to and ski again next morning before they go on duty again. It's an impeccable balance that suits everyone and ensures the resort is well covered medically.

There are also two permanent nurses who come in to Mount Hotham for the season. Both are partners of ski instructors who work at the resort throughout the Australian winter then head to the Northern Hemisphere as soon as the season ends. Like the doctors, the nurses work 24-hour shifts that give them time on the ski runs and every second evening off.

The medical centre is right in the middle of the resort and is open from 10 a.m. to 5 p.m. seven days a week. It's a private practice with no bulk billing and must pay its way. In the last couple of years, the resort board and government have provided the clinic with some much-needed equipment the Bright medical practice couldn't have afforded to install up there just for four months' use, and they are now well resourced with a lot of very modern paraphernalia. Without the additions they'd have continued to use the old equipment, which would have been perfectly acceptable, but this is so much better.

The clinic has a doctor's room cum office, but is otherwise an open-plan area resembling an emergency department in a small public hospital. If there's a major traumatic incident, both doctors will be on hand. When they set the rotation rosters back at the Bright Medical Centre, they try to ensure they have one doctor up there who's experienced with anaesthetics; should there be a call-out onto the slopes, that doctor goes because he or she will be better equipped to manage respiratory complications skilfully while the other one prepares the emergency room. Alternatively, the senior doctor goes . . .

Every day, all day, the ski patrols are on the move up and down the mountain keeping an eye on everyone and policing the speedsters. If someone falls over, hurts themselves and can't get up, either their friends will help them or, if they're on their own, another skier will check on them; it's the unwritten rule of the snowfields. That first responder will remove the injured person's skis and stand them crossed over in the snow, the international ski sign for help.

As soon as other skiers see the X they'll wave down a patroller, if they can spot one close by, or ski on down to the bottom of the run and tell the lift operators, who'll radio the on-duty communications officer at resort headquarters, advising them of an accident and its apparent location. If a ski patroller hasn't already called in from the site of the accident, the comms officer – whose job includes knowing which slopes the patrollers are all on – will radio and check if any of them is above the accident and able to ski down, or calculate which two can get to the top and ski down or, on occasion, across to the site quickest. The first patroller will go directly to the injured skier, assess the situation and report to HQ who, having warned the medical centre of an incoming trauma patient, will coordinate the retrieval. The second patroller will ski or snowboard down with a sled. They'll immobilise the patient, give them some pain relief and sled them down to the bottom of the hill and the nearest ski lift.

Meanwhile, the lift will have been completely stopped while a metal basket is slung over the back of a lift chair and attached, one of only two circumstances in which its machinations are halted; the other is when someone falls off, usually a kid trying to get on. The patient will be transferred to the basket and transported to the top of the lift, where an ambulance will be waiting to take them to the medical centre.

Having been advised about an incident on the mountain, the on-duty doctor and nurse at the centre will be functioning with a heightened sense of awareness, keeping one ear on the turned-up two-way radio for progress updates. Once the ambulance arrives, they'll receive and treat the patient in exactly the same way any emergency department would.

The medical staff at the Mount Hotham clinic deal with an extreme range of traumatic orthopaedic injuries: dislocated shoulders, broken collarbones, broken fingers, broken wrists, broken arms, broken legs, torn knee ligaments and sometimes even death. In the course of any season they'll treat more fractures than the average GP does in a year.

They also see some very serious head injuries, although Paul thinks the head injury toll has gone down a bit since people started skiing in helmets. He says, 'There's no research been done on it, but the helmets seem to be helping in the lesser traumatic incidents like where a skier might fall and their ski might flip up and whack them in the back of the head. The helmet will be saving them from the stitches that would have been required without it. However,' he muses with a bleak look, 'they certainly haven't made any difference to the serious trauma accidents like when a skier slams into a tree at 80 kilometres an hour . . .'

As often as not, though, it's a simple reduction and plastering of a broken limb. If it's an arm or a collarbone the person might choose to stay on and enjoy the ambience, if not the slopes, but some people, especially with leg injuries, will need to be transferred off the mountain. In regards to their geography, Paul says most people aren't fazed by their relative remoteness during an accident, but most of them will want to be transferred back home depending on where home is.

Once in a while there'll be a major incident that puts the

whole resort on high alert. In most instances, the ski patrollers are so well trained and equipped they can deal with any
emergency, but there have been rare days when someone is so
seriously injured a doctor has had to go down onto the slopes
and provide advanced critical care. In that situation, the doctor will intubate the patient, get a drip line in and running
so they can administer whatever drugs are required intrave-
nously – and if it's a really complicated, complex retrieval
they'll sedate the patient – before sledding them down to the
base and into the cage for the ski lift transfer up to the medical centre. While sedating a patient on the slopes is extremely
unusual, and Paul himself has never had that situation arise on
his watch, it has happened.

Once they get the patient into the clinic, they'll be resta-
bilised before evacuation to Melbourne in the ambulance. In
that rare case where a patient is critically injured, a trauma
retrieval team will fly out by helicopter from Melbourne.
There's always a police presence on the mountain ready to help
in any medical emergency. They'll organise traffic and clear
the carpark for a chopper to land. Even though really terrible
accidents are rare, everyone has to be prepared for them.

The collective team works very efficiently and smoothly;
they practise search and rescues and retrievals regularly, and
at the start of every snow season Paul helps his colleague Dr
Chris O'Brien deliver training sessions to the doctors and ski
patrollers from all the ski villages. For the patrols, the sessions
are about search and rescue and boning up on every conceiv-
able kind of first aid. For the doctors, it's all about trauma
response as people throw themselves down the mountain day
after day in the pursuit of the perfect run.

At the end of every day, the slopes are completely trashed. As evening approaches, the snow groomers prepare the slopes for the next day's skiing. Using snowploughs, they sweep down and smooth out any bumps and moguls, leaving the downhill runs patterned like corduroy, which stops them being too slick and icy after the overnight freeze.

Avalanche is always a consideration, too, but the ski patrols can usually tell if one's threatening and they'll close the slope. Worst-case scenario, they'll blast the slope to get it over and done with.

Of course, avalanche and frozen, slippery slopes are still risks for people skiing outside the resort area, as is getting lost or, worse yet, lost and hurt. Despite the orange ropes and signs designating the boundaries of the resort, someone will ski off one of the off-piste slopes just as they'll swim outside the flags at the beach. If they're badly smashed up, it can take a while to get to them.

There's a whole industry built around experienced skiers looking for that ever more exhilarating challenge and however good they are on skis, accidents will happen, and sometimes they're fatal. Any death in the snowfields is clearly tragic but, Paul says, 'The toughest thing is young people dying. We'll explain everything to a family, exactly what the injury is and precisely how it impacted, in just the same way any emergency room doctor does but it is always a little harder in the snowfields because everyone is there having fun; the accidents invariably happen when the person is having fun.' Because of that fun factor associated with skiing and the snowfields generally, hopefully there is a sliver of consolation for family and friends in knowing that their loved one died doing something that they enjoyed.

Unfortunately, there are also a number of car accidents on the mountain; usually someone in holiday mode driving too fast for the conditions on the alpine roads. If they're close to the top, the ambulance will bring anyone requiring treatment up to the medical centre.

While the doctors' work at the centre is heavily trauma based, about 50 per cent of their workload will be sick people – lots of kids with runny noses and high temperatures – and people who've forgotten to bring their medications. And then there are times when a seriously ill patient presents and things don't go according to plan, like the night when the ambulance broke down with the sick baby on board.

It transpired the fuel had frozen in the ambulance, which had come up to the resort earlier in the day and apparently hadn't been filled with alpine fuel, an anti-freeze mix of diesel and heating oil used in all the resort vehicles. When it conked out, the ambo had flagged down a passing motorist, who took him to the medical centre.

All these years later, Paul admits that he was a bit toey driving down the mountain that night. The mother was afraid the baby was going to die and, as the doctor, he knew they had to do what they had to do to get the baby to specialist help, but as the de facto ambulance driver in a private vehicle, he was being very cautious.

Any number of things could have gone wrong; fortunately, they didn't. Paul managed to get them safely down to Harrietville, where they met another ambulance that took the pair on to Wangaratta. Safely relieved of their precious cargo, he and the nurse trundled much more easily back up the mountain. About a year later, Paul was delighted to get a letter from the young mother, thanking him and enclosing a photo of her thriving toddler.

While back then he was up for doing whatever he needed to do to get the baby down the mountain, it would never happen now. These days, he says, they are compelled by the risk managers to use chains all the time to traverse the 35 kilometres from the top to the bottom.

Even with all the advances made in ski, car and medical technology to date, the human factor guarantees Paul a busy seven-day rotation at the Mount Hotham medical centre, although the weather has a role to play, too.

The 2016 winter was a bit of a fizzer, especially towards the end, because there wasn't a lot of snow, which would have been manageable had it been fine, but it was rainy and very messy. There've been some shockers, when numbers of skiers are right down which, Paul says, 'is very bad for the Mount Hotham economy. It's only about a four-month period anyway and some businesses up there rely totally on the visiting skiers for their income. There are very few off-season businesses in the high country, which is why it's so expensive to ski in Australia. That is changing but it's nothing like Europe yet.'

Even so, the medical centre must be open and staffed throughout the season and, for Paul, there's something a bit special about being there and being a fundamental part of the successful operations of the resort. He says he always looks forward to his turn at the Mount Hotham clinic, although he doesn't ski quite as much as he used to. He sticks to clear days and blue skies but enjoys being in the snowfields even if he isn't skiing.

Living 50 kilometres down the mountain in Bright for the rest of the year still works beautifully for him and while sports medicine – and particularly orthopaedics in the snow-fields – remains fairly high on his list of special interests, preventative care, computers in medicine and aged care are up there too now. Computers fascinate him and, along with his aptitude for maths, that makes him the geek in the practice. And he's evolved into aged care because all the 45-year-old patients he started with are now 70; he's been there long enough to have matured with them.

Along the way, he's seen a few changes to the medical service too. They used to offer obstetric services at the nine-bed Bright hospital until the mishandling of some deliveries at another rural hospital in Victoria prompted the state gov-ernment to restrict all birthings to specific locations. The Bright doctors now refer their maternity patients 80 kilome-tres away to the hospital in Wangaratta. Likewise, any surgery that can't be done in the medical centre is also referred there. Nevertheless, they offer a wide range of services that cater to the needs of their growing community.

As the town undergoes a bit of a tree change boom and tourism becomes even more integral to the economy of the area, more people are moving up from Melbourne to live. They come and see it and fall in love. Added to that, they know they can sell their Melbourne house and buy a comparable one in Bright for a fraction of the price and have a nest egg left over.

Consequently, as the population grows, so does the poten-tial for young professionals to move into the community.

Certainly it all keeps Bright Medical Centre buzzing and Paul enjoys working in a busy rural practice as much as ever. He has absolutely no interest in retiring until he's at least sixty-five or seventy, by which time, he hopes, another enthusiastic young doctor – just like he was – will have recognised the wonderful potential in being a rural doctor – just as he did.

Although Paul and Catherine return to Ireland every year to see their surviving mothers and remaining families, Paul no longer skis in Europe; he's content to swish down his local slopes when the snow beckons. He'd much rather travel around Australia and does as often as he can. In fact, because he can think of nothing worse than retirement, he'll travel until he's really old and can travel no more. After that, he chuckles with a dash of exaggerated brogue, 'I'm after us having one of those nice little houses up at the old people's home.' He reckons he'll book in there and see out his days reminiscing about the incredible opportunities in life thanks to chance . . .

Acknowledgements

Firstly, thanks to all the doctors who entrusted me with their stories. I appreciate your candour and your generosity, particularly when you're all so incredibly busy. I have to tell you, it was an absolute joy to write this book!

As always, lots of people helped get this collection of stories from idea to hard copy. Thanks to Andrea McNamara, my publisher at Penguin when I signed the contract, for supporting and encouraging my interest in the doctors who work in our rural and remote areas.

Subsequently, Cate Blake picked up the project and my sincere thanks for enabling me to get on with the task at hand. You've facilitated a smooth road to production and I am very excited about this resulting collection of stories. Thanks also to Fay Helfenbaum for keeping the various editorial strands in order along the way.

Special thanks yet again to RN extraordinaire Judy Treloar, for your first responses and for generously answering my many queries about 'all things medical' promptly and clearly. Special thanks also to my favourite daughter Chloe Miller for applying your prodigious reading experience to reviewing the first drafts, to Rosie Bryant for pitching in when I needed you, to Rosemary Young for your invaluable counsel, to Chris Belshaw for the geography lesson, and to Angus Stirton for explaining bench cuts. Accurate interpretation lies in the detail and having friends who know stuff!

Some of the doctors I obviously already knew, some I found on Twitter and some were referred to me by others. Thank you Karen Illingworth Emmott for sharing your excellent network, and Margareta Osborn for helping me find the one I was seeking.

Having rounded up the stories and written them, my grateful thanks go to Sonja Heijn for editing them with such skill; your endless warmth and good humour made the process so much fun even as you were nudging out my superfluous adjectives! And thank you Andrea Davison for proofreading; knowing you and Sonja had it in hand definitely took the pressure off.

First impressions are vital and thanks must go to Alex Ross and Louisa Maggio for producing this absolutely splendid cover. Likewise huge thanks to photographer Katrina Lehmann in Charleville (klehmannphotography.com) for your smashing photo of Dr Claire Schmidt, and to Claire for being the face of *Bush Doctors*. Clearly you were both perfect choices!

And last but never least, heart, hugs and warmest thanks to Ian and our immediate and extended family and friends who continue to support and encourage me.

BUSH NURSES

It takes something special to be a bush nurse working in rural and remote Australia. These remarkable women patch people up and keep them alive while waiting for the doctor to arrive. They drive the ambulances, operate the clinics and deliver the babies. They are on call around the clock and there are no days off. They often make do with whatever is at hand while working in some of the most isolated places on the planet.

Be they devastating family tragedies, close scrapes with bushfires or encounters with true larrikins of the outback, some stories will make your hair stand on end, others will make you laugh and some will make your cry. With tales from Birdsville to Bedourie, Oodnadatta to Uluru, you'll be amazed at the courage and resourcefulness of these nurses who have been the backbone of medical practice in remote Australia for more than a hundred years.

'Full of battle tales, with all their comedy, farce and sadness.'
WEEKEND AUSTRALIAN

NURSES OF THE
OUTBACK

The work of a nurse is challenging enough, but when you add a remote location, the stakes are so much higher. Meet fifteen courageous people who prove that the inland runs on nurse power.

There's Anna, who is on duty as the fury of Cyclone Yasi tears through inland Queensland; Maureen in outback New South Wales, who faces everything from a snakebite to a helicopter crash; Aggie, who overcomes her demons to help young people in the Kimberley; and Catherine, newly graduated and determined to make a difference in the Gulf Country she and her rodeo-riding husband call home.

From some of the most remote places on the earth, these stories bring the outback to life – we witness the harshness and isolation as well as the camaraderie of life in small towns in the middle of nowhere. These intrepid nurses tend to life-threatening emergencies, manage everyday health care and even patch up the local pets. From Bidyadanga to Broken Hill, Mount Isa to Marree, these tales are by turns moving and inspiring, full of gutsy feats and classic outback spirit.

'Incredible stories of incredible people.'
BLUE'S COUNTRY MAGAZINE

OUR VIETNAM NURSES

From the bestselling author of *Bush Nurses* and *Nurses of the Outback comes* this collection of compelling and moving stories of our heroic nurses in the Vietnam War.

Being a nurse always requires a cool head, a steady hand and an open heart. But if you're working in a war zone, the challenges are much harder. When Australia joined the Vietnam War, civilian and military nurses were there to save lives and comfort the wounded. With spirit and good humour, they worked hard and held strong, even though most of them were completely unprepared for the war before they landed in the middle of it.

Working incredibly long hours and surrounded by chaos and turmoil, these brave nurses and medics were integral to our war effort. These fifteen stories show a side to the Vietnam War that has received little recognition but played an important part in shaping Australia's presence in the war. From flying with critically wounded Australian soldiers out of turbulent war zones, to being held at gunpoint, the compassion, courage and grace under fire in *Our Vietnam Nurses* will inspire and astound.

'It is a remarkable tribute – confronting,
touching and gently amusing in equal measure.'
READER'S DIGEST